JUSTIN **JORDAN**   RAÚL **TREVIÑO**   JUAN **USECHE**

SOMBRA ™

ROSS RICHIE CEO & Founder
MATT GAGNON Editor-in-Chief
FILIP SABLIK President of Publishing & Marketing
STEPHEN CHRISTY President of Development
LANCE KREITER VP of Licensing & Merchandising
PHIL BARBARO VP of Finance
ARUNE SINGH VP of Marketing
BRYCE CARLSON Managing Editor
MEL CAYLO Marketing Manager
SCOTT NEWMAN Production Design Manager
KATE HENNING Operations Manager
SIERRA HAHN Senior Editor
DAFNA PLEBAN Editor, Talent Development
SHANNON WATTERS Editor
ERIC HARBURN Editor
WHITNEY LEOPARD Editor
JASMINE AMIRI Editor
CHRIS ROSA Associate Editor
ALEX GALER Associate Editor
CAMERON CHITTOCK Associate Editor
MATTHEW LEVINE Assistant Editor
SOPHIE PHILIPS-ROBERTS Assistant Editor
KELSEY DIETERICH Designer
JILLIAN CRAB Production Designer
MICHELLE ANKLEY Production Designer
GRACE PARK Production Design Assistant
ELIZABETH LOUGHRIDGE Accounting Coordinator
STEPHANIE HOCUTT Social Media Coordinator
JOSÉ MEZA Event Coordinator
JAMES ARRIOLA Mailroom Assistant
HOLLY AITCHISON Operations Assistant
AMBER PARKER Administrative Assistant

SOMBRA, July 2017. Published by BOOM! Studios, a division of Boom Entertainment, Inc. Sombra is ™ & © 2017 Justin Jordan and Raúl Treviño. Originally published in single magazine form as SOMBRA No. 1-4, ™ & © 2016 Justin Jordan and Raúl Treviño. All Rights Reserved. BOOM! Studios™ and the BOOM! Studios logo are trademarks of Boom Entertainment, Inc., registered in various countries and categories. All characters, events, and institutions depicted herein are fictional. Any similarity between any of the names, characters, persons, events, and/or institutions in this publication to actual names, characters, and persons, whether living or dead, events, and/or institutions is unintended and purely coincidental. BOOM! Studios does not read or accept unsolicited submissions of ideas, stories, or artwork.

BOOM! Studios, 5670 Wilshire Boulevard, Suite 450, Los Angeles, CA 90036-5679. Printed in China. First Printing.

ISBN: 978-1-60886-988-6, eISBN: 978-1-61398-659-2

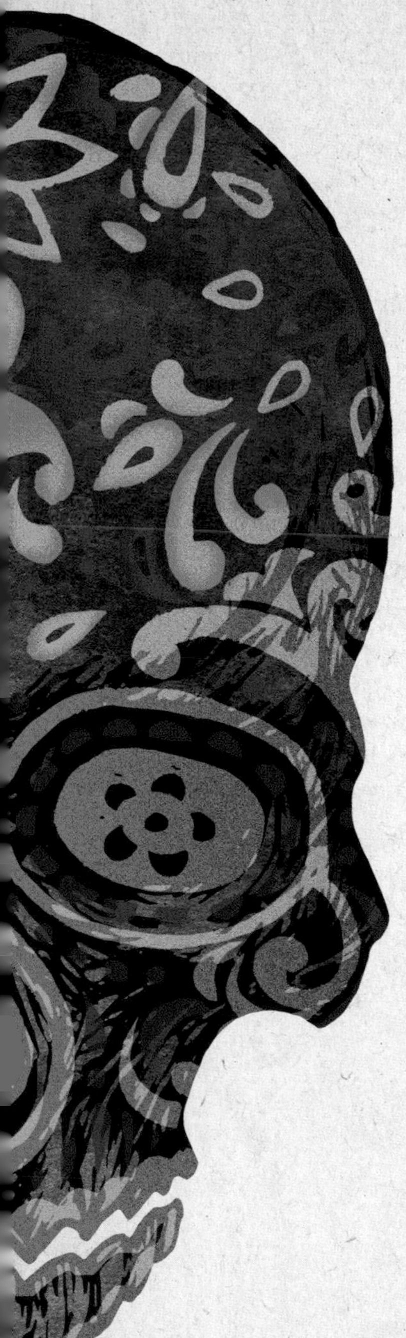

SOMBRA™

CREATED BY
JUSTIN **JORDAN** & RAÚL **TREVIÑO**

WRITTEN BY
JUSTIN **JORDAN**

ILLUSTRATED BY
RAÚL **TREVIÑO**

COLORED BY
JUAN **USECHE**

LETTERED BY
JIM **CAMPBELL**

COVER BY
JILIPOLLO

DESIGNER
SCOTT **NEWMAN**

ASSOCIATE EDITOR
CAMERON **CHITTOCK**

EDITOR
ERIC **HARBURN**

DARKER HEARTS
FOREWORD

I've been fascinated by Joseph Conrad's *Heart of Darkness* since I was in high school. If you haven't read it, the short novel is the story of an expedition downriver in Africa to retrieve a once great man who's gone mad. Of course, he was never great.

The point of *Heart of Darkness* was exploitation, and the lies we tell ourselves to justify that. In the book, it was the European exploitation of Africa. In *Apocalypse Now*, probably the most famous adaptation of the book, it was America in Vietnam, wrecking another country to achieve our goals.

Sombra is another version of that story. And it still applies, more than a hundred years after the original. The places and players change, but the story does not. I was struck, reading about the Mexican Cartels and the cost our War on Drugs has placed on the Mexican people, how we keep on repeating the same mistakes.

There's horror going on, just across the border. A country where thousands of people die each year and more still live in fear because of American policy. This isn't new. We've been doing that since the time *Heart of Darkness* was written. Before that. And yet we generally move on, thinking of ourselves as righteous while turning a blind eye.

I got very lucky, doing this book. I knew I needed a Mexican co-creator, because this is not really my story to tell. I was lucky that we got Raul, who I already admired and wanted to work with. And he elevated this story so far beyond what I could have hoped.

I'm not arrogant enough to expect to have written a classic, but I do hope we make you think and feel about this. I hope, in some small part, we make a difference.

JUSTIN JORDAN
Pennsylvania, U.S.A.

CORAZONES MÁS OSCUROS
PREFACIO

He estado fascinado por *El corazón de las tinieblas*, de Joseph Conrad, desde que estaba en la preparatoria. Si no lo han leído aún, la novela corta relata la historia de una expedición río abajo en África, con el objetivo de traer de vuelta a un gran hombre que se ha sumido en la locura; pero claro, el hombre nunca fue grande.

El tema de *El corazón de las tinieblas* es la explotación y las mentiras que nos decimos para justificarla. En el libro se relata la explotación europea en África, y en *Apocalypse Now*, tal vez la adaptación más famosa del libro, sobre Estados Unidos en Vietnam, trata acerca de la destrucción de otro país a favor de nuestros intereses.

Sombra es otra versión de esa historia, una que aún es válida el día de hoy, a más de cien años del original. Los lugares y protagonistas cambian, pero la historia no. Produjo un gran impacto sobre mí leer acerca de los cárteles mexicanos y el peso que nuestra guerra contra las drogas pone sobre el pueblo mexicano, y darme cuenta de cómo seguimos repitiendo los mismos errores.

El horror está ahí, cruzando la frontera, en un país donde miles de personas mueren cada año y aún más viven con miedo, todo a causa de las políticas estadounidenses. Esto no es nuevo, y lo hemos estado haciendo desde la época en la que *El corazón de las tinieblas* fue escrito, incluso antes. Y, sin embargo, seguimos adelante, ignorándolo y pensando que nosotros somos los justos.

Soy afortunado de poder escribir este libro. Sabía que necesitaría a un cocreador mexicano, ya que esta no es realmente mi historia. Tuve mucha suerte de que consiguiéramos a Raúl, a quien ya admiraba y con quien quería trabajar, y cuya labor elevó esta historia aún más de lo que hubiera esperado.

No soy lo suficientemente arrogante para creer que he escrito un clásico, pero espero hacerlos pensar y sentir con esto. Quisiera saber que hicimos la diferencia, aunque sea un poco.

JUSTIN JORDAN
Pennsylvania, E.U.A.

CHAPTER

ONE

CAPÍTULO UNO

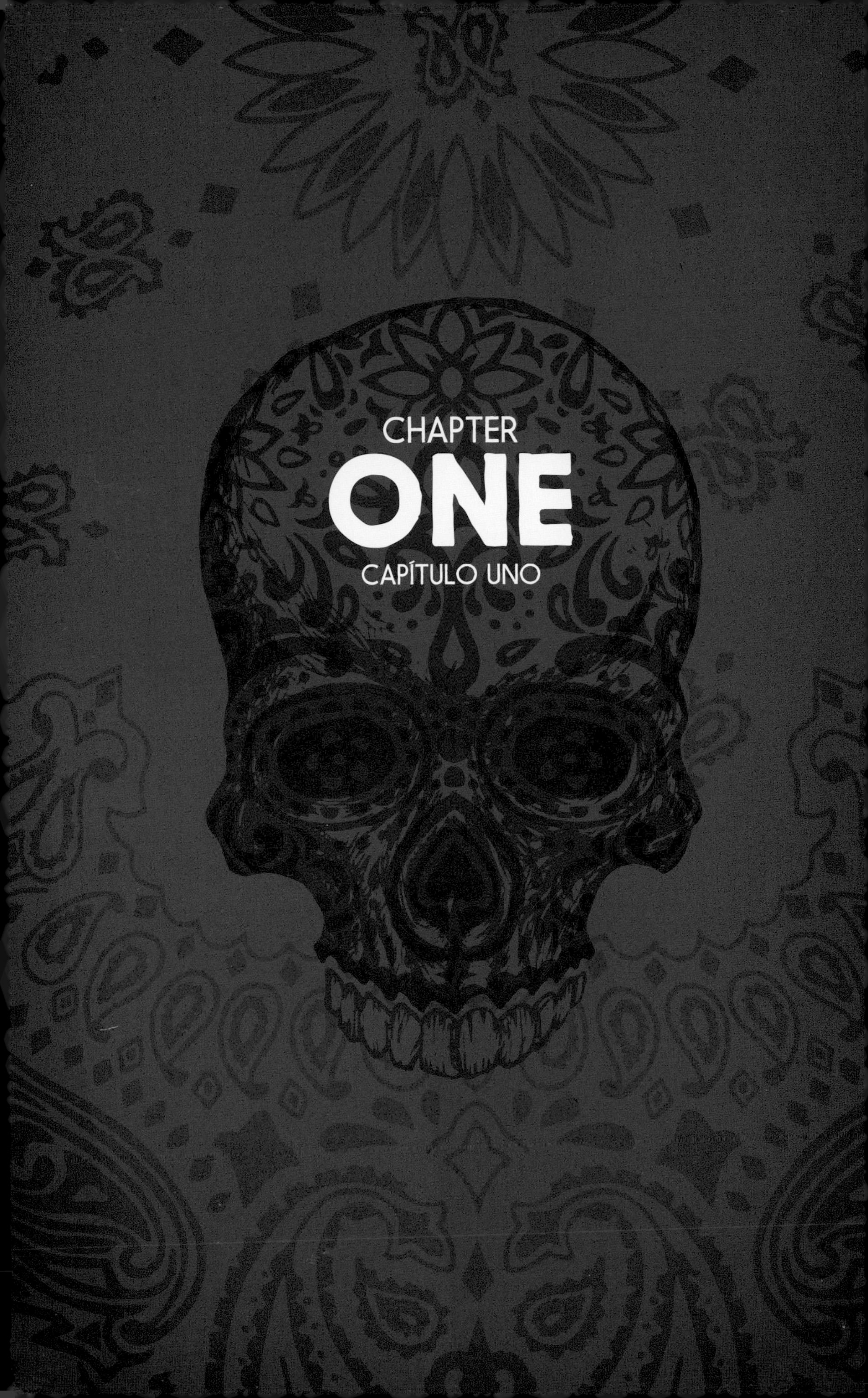

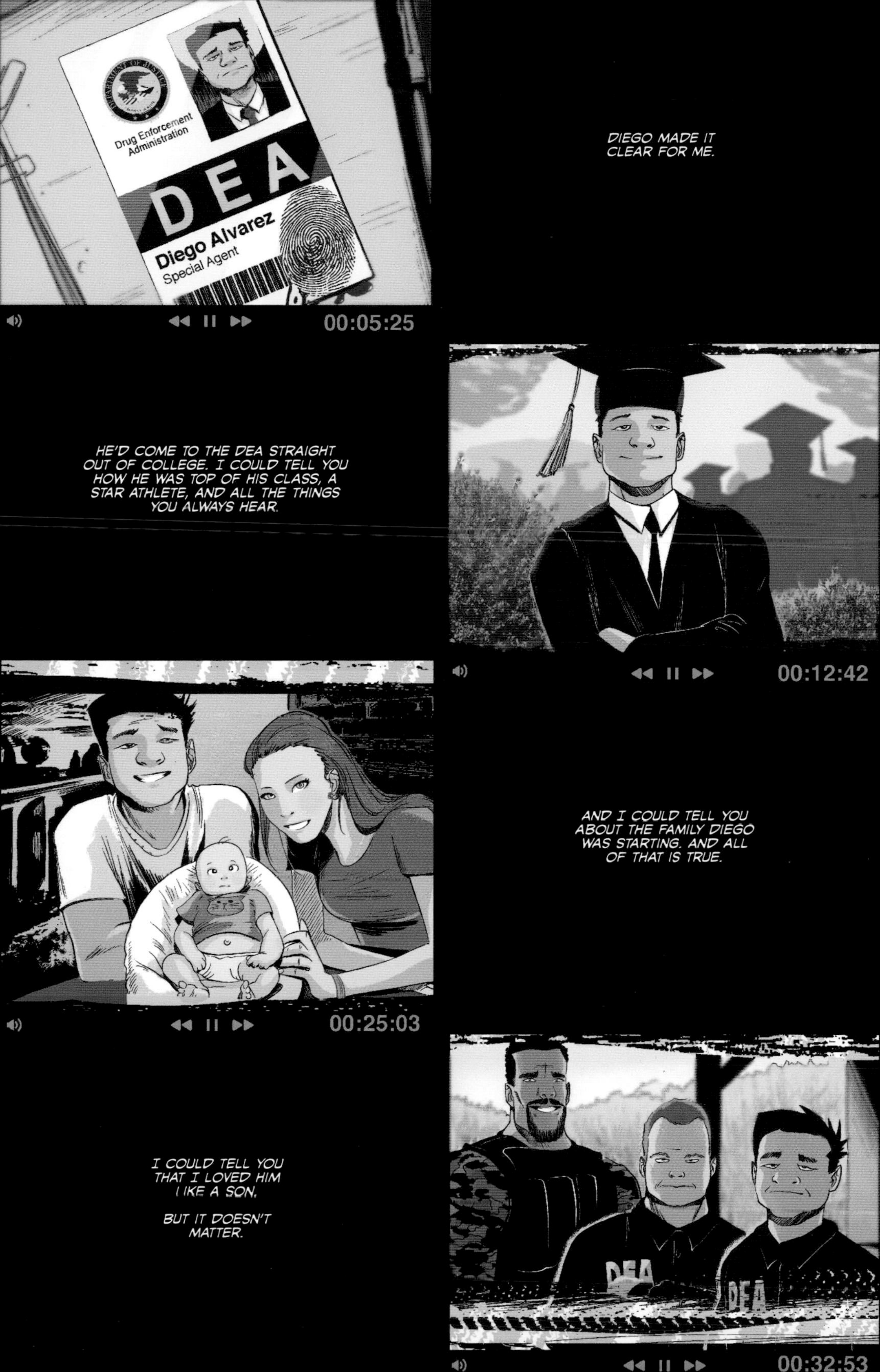
Drug Enforcement Administration
DEA
Diego Alvarez
Special Agent
00:05:25
DIEGO MADE IT CLEAR FOR ME.
HE'D COME TO THE DEA STRAIGHT OUT OF COLLEGE. I COULD TELL YOU HOW HE WAS TOP OF HIS CLASS, A STAR ATHLETE, AND ALL THE THINGS YOU ALWAYS HEAR.
00:12:42
00:25:03
AND I COULD TELL YOU ABOUT THE FAMILY DIEGO WAS STARTING. AND ALL OF THAT IS TRUE.
I COULD TELL YOU THAT I LOVED HIM LIKE A SON.
BUT IT DOESN'T MATTER.
DEA
DEA
00:32:53

POR FAVOR...
00:38:13

POR FAVOR...
00:40:34

NECESITAS SONREÍR A LA CÁMARA.
00:41:18

NECESITO QUE LES DIGAS ALGO DE MI PARTE.
00:41:33

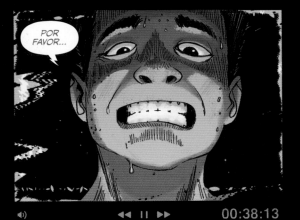

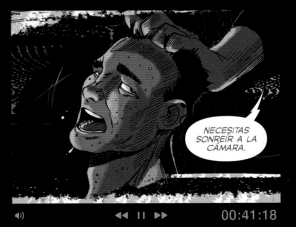

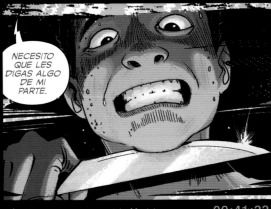

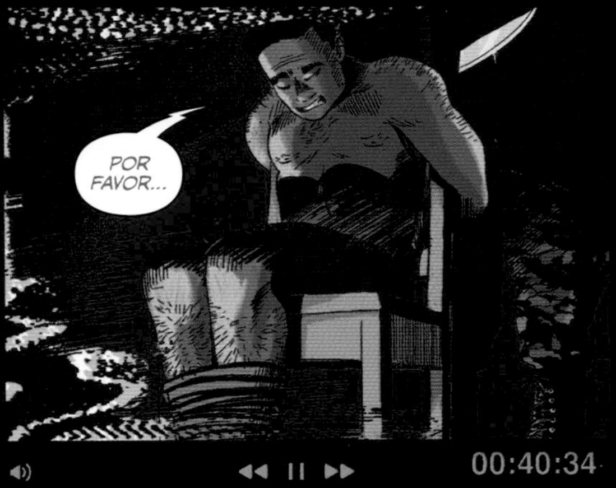

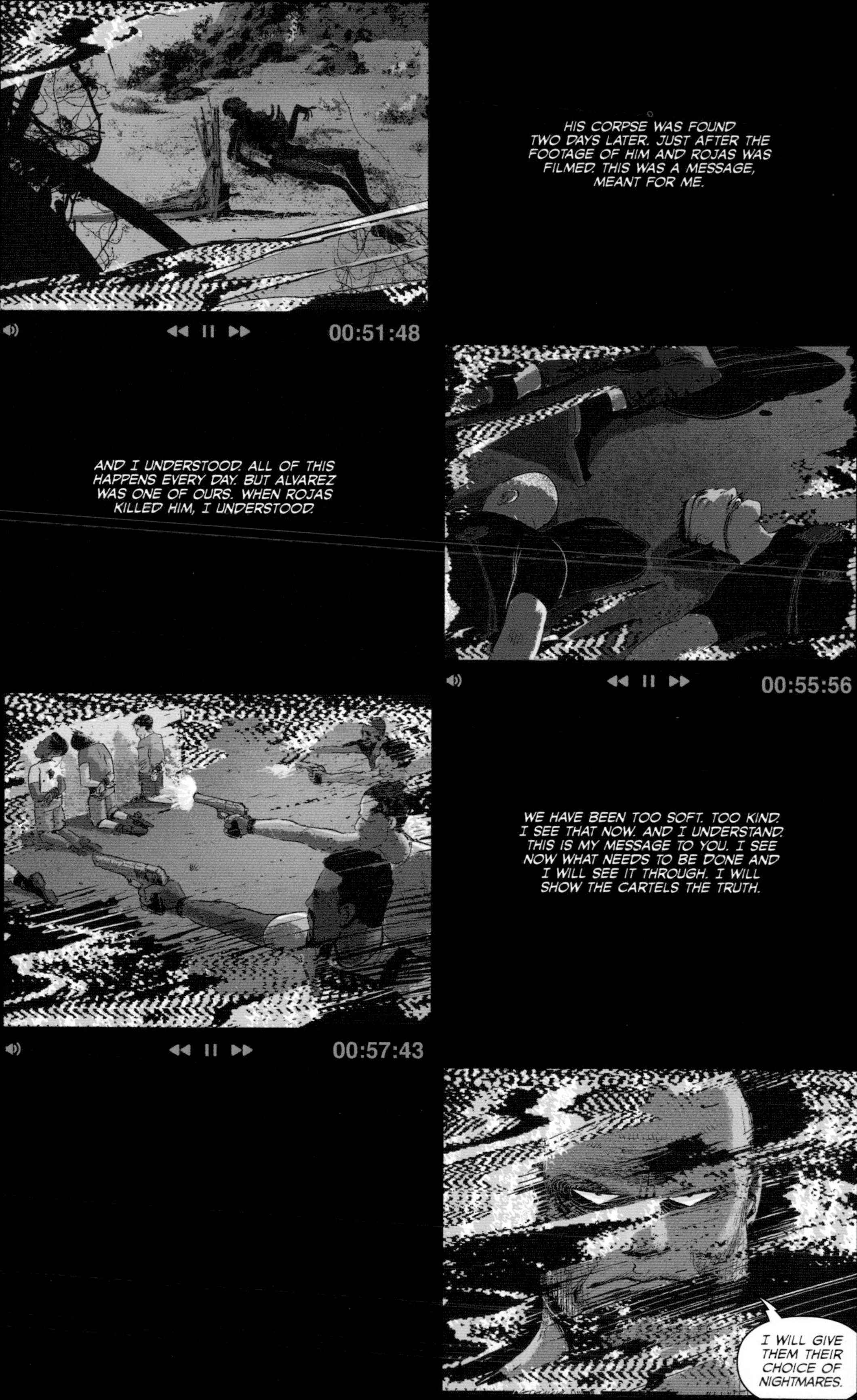
HIS CORPSE WAS FOUND TWO DAYS LATER. JUST AFTER THE FOOTAGE OF HIM AND ROJAS WAS FILMED. THIS WAS A MESSAGE, MEANT FOR ME.
00:51:48
AND I UNDERSTOOD. ALL OF THIS HAPPENS EVERY DAY. BUT ALVAREZ WAS ONE OF OURS. WHEN ROJAS KILLED HIM, I UNDERSTOOD.
00:55:56
00:57:43
WE HAVE BEEN TOO SOFT. TOO KIND. I SEE THAT NOW. AND I UNDERSTAND. THIS IS MY MESSAGE TO YOU. I SEE NOW WHAT NEEDS TO BE DONE AND I WILL SEE IT THROUGH. I WILL SHOW THE CARTELS THE TRUTH.
I WILL GIVE THEM THEIR CHOICE OF NIGHTMARES.

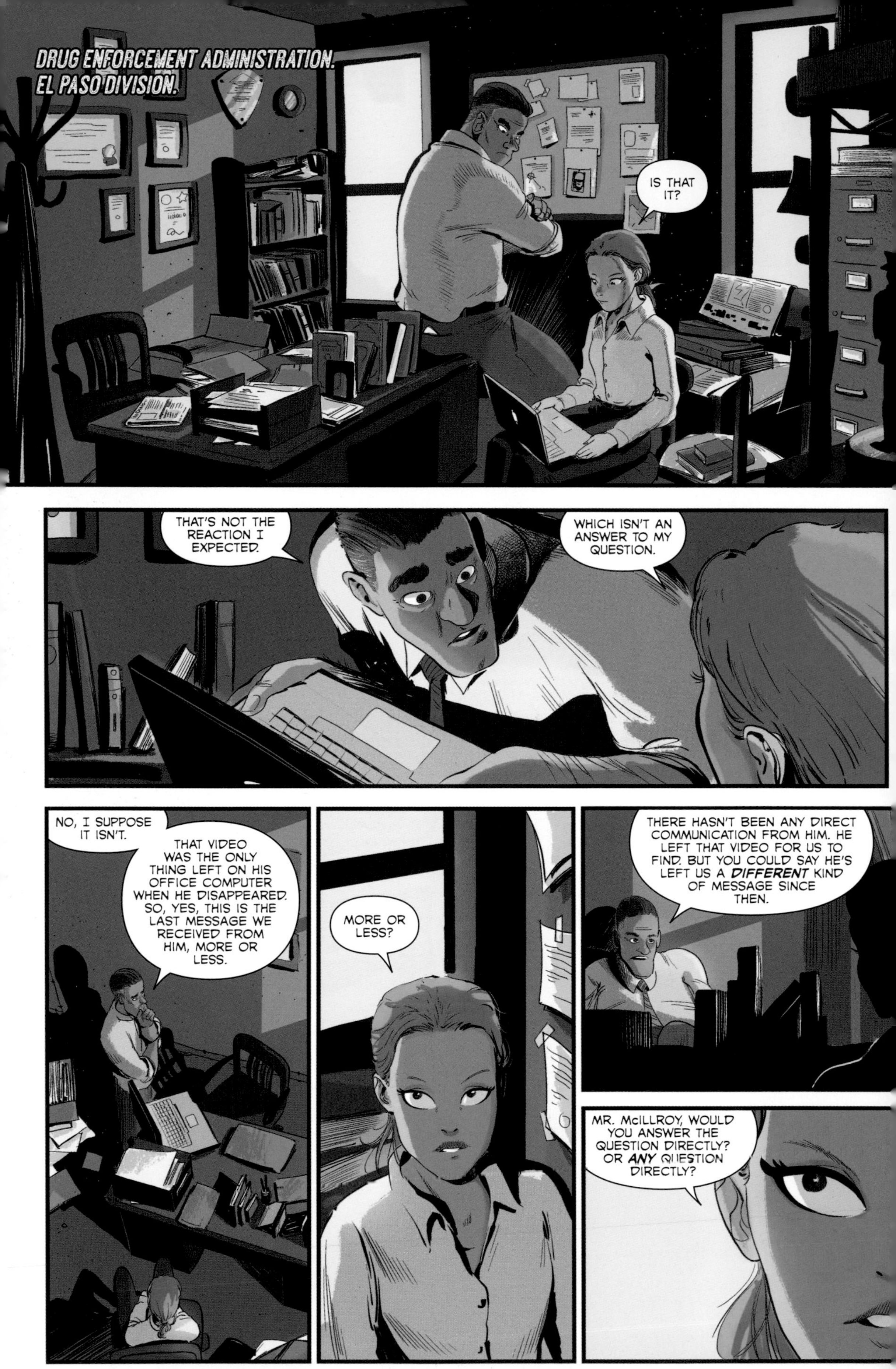
DRUG ENFORCEMENT ADMINISTRATION. EL PASO DIVISION.
IS THAT IT?
THAT'S NOT THE REACTION I EXPECTED.
WHICH ISN'T AN ANSWER TO MY QUESTION.
NO, I SUPPOSE IT ISN'T.
THAT VIDEO WAS THE ONLY THING LEFT ON HIS OFFICE COMPUTER WHEN HE DISAPPEARED. SO, YES, THIS IS THE LAST MESSAGE WE RECEIVED FROM HIM, MORE OR LESS.
MORE OR LESS?
THERE HASN'T BEEN ANY DIRECT COMMUNICATION FROM HIM. HE LEFT THAT VIDEO FOR US TO FIND. BUT YOU COULD SAY HE'S LEFT US A *DIFFERENT* KIND OF MESSAGE SINCE THEN.
MR. McILLROY, WOULD YOU ANSWER THE QUESTION DIRECTLY? OR *ANY* QUESTION DIRECTLY?

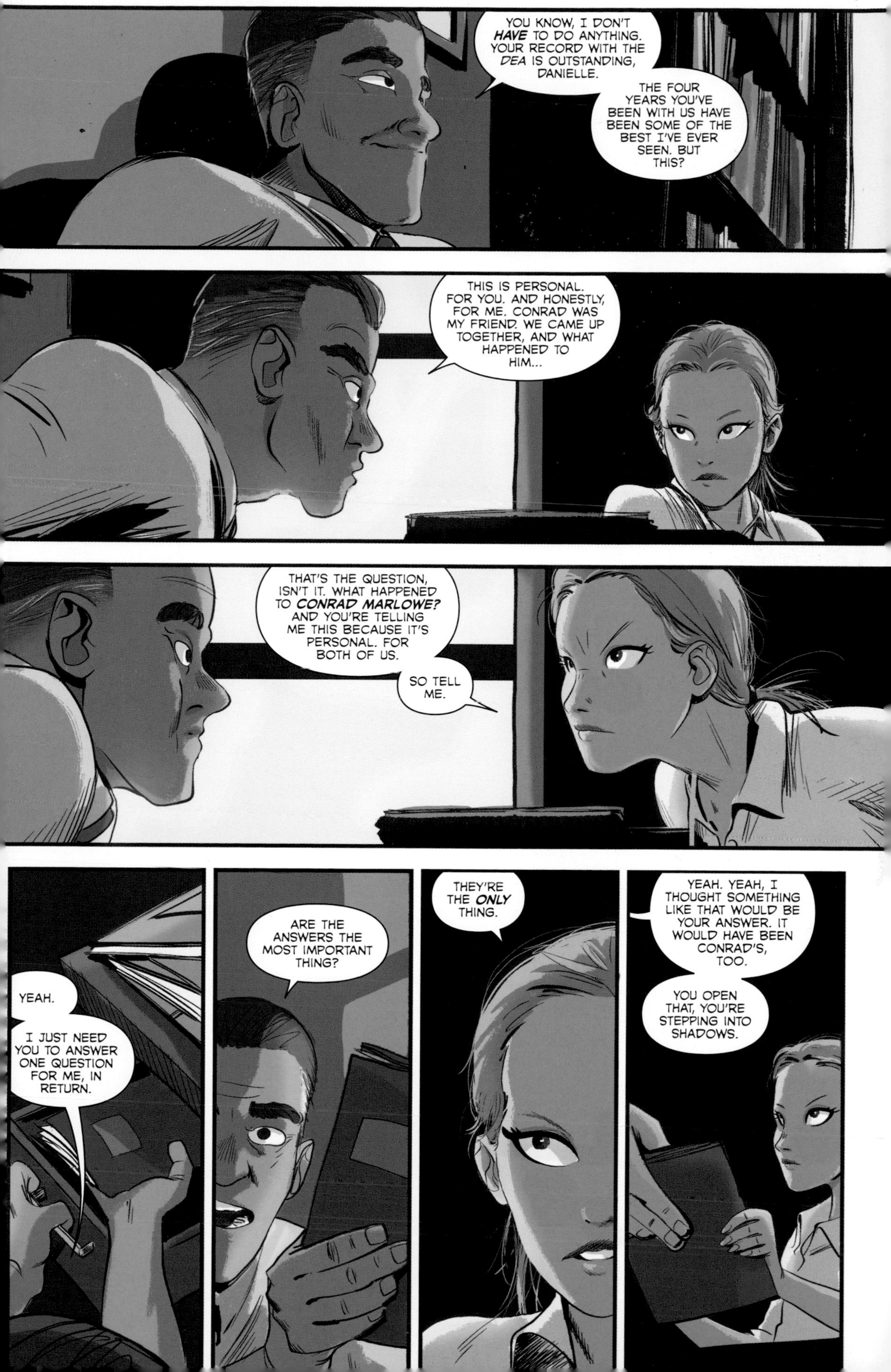
YOU KNOW, I DON'T **HAVE** TO DO ANYTHING. YOUR RECORD WITH THE *DEA* IS OUTSTANDING, DANIELLE.
THE FOUR YEARS YOU'VE BEEN WITH US HAVE BEEN SOME OF THE BEST I'VE EVER SEEN. BUT THIS?
THIS IS PERSONAL. FOR YOU. AND HONESTLY, FOR ME. CONRAD WAS MY FRIEND. WE CAME UP TOGETHER, AND WHAT HAPPENED TO HIM...
THAT'S THE QUESTION, ISN'T IT. WHAT HAPPENED TO **CONRAD MARLOWE?** AND YOU'RE TELLING ME THIS BECAUSE IT'S PERSONAL. FOR BOTH OF US.
SO TELL ME.
YEAH.
I JUST NEED YOU TO ANSWER ONE QUESTION FOR ME, IN RETURN.
ARE THE ANSWERS THE MOST IMPORTANT THING?
THEY'RE THE **ONLY** THING.
YEAH. YEAH, I THOUGHT SOMETHING LIKE THAT WOULD BE YOUR ANSWER. IT WOULD HAVE BEEN CONRAD'S, TOO.
YOU OPEN THAT, YOU'RE STEPPING INTO SHADOWS.

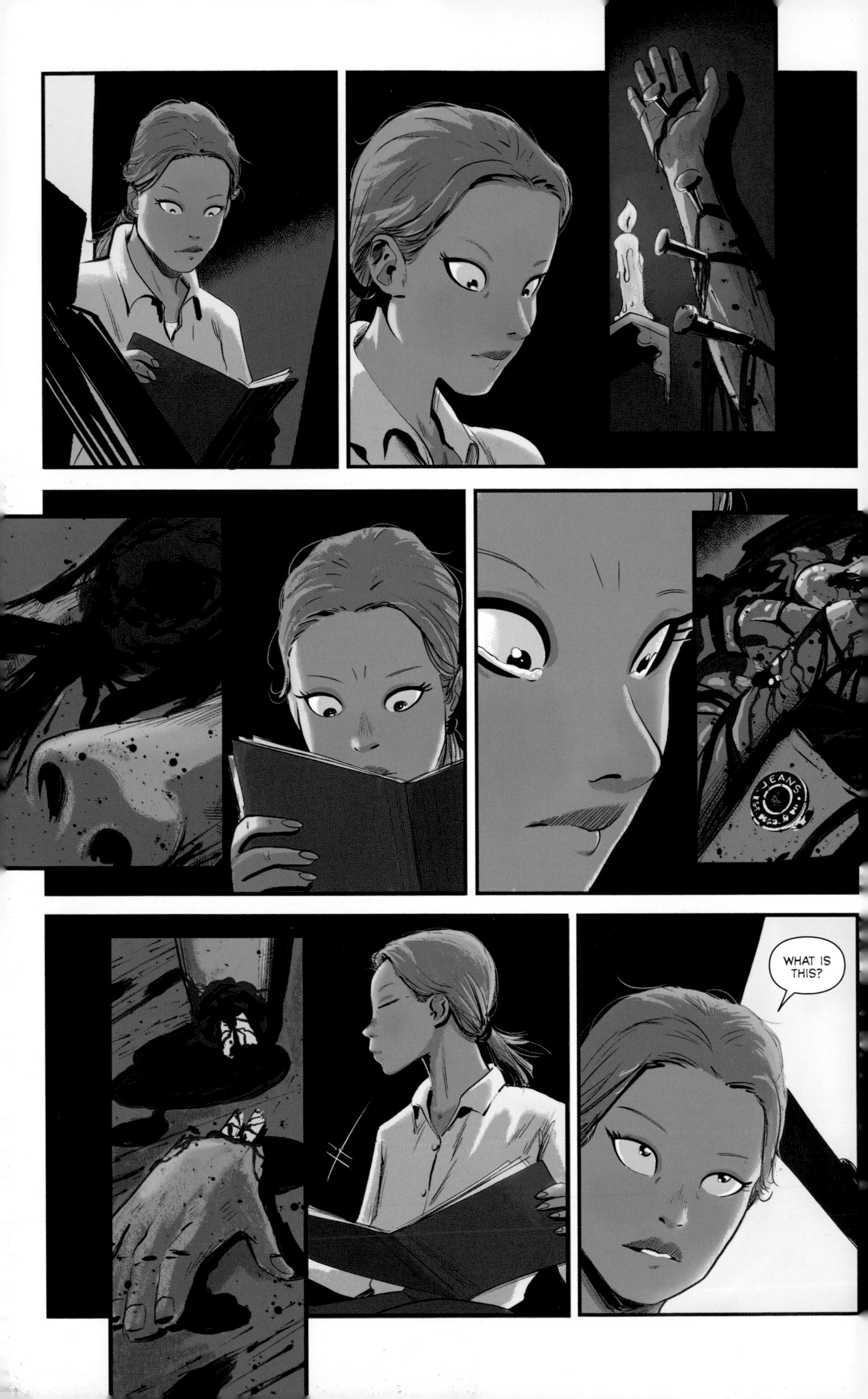
JEANS
WHAT IS THIS?

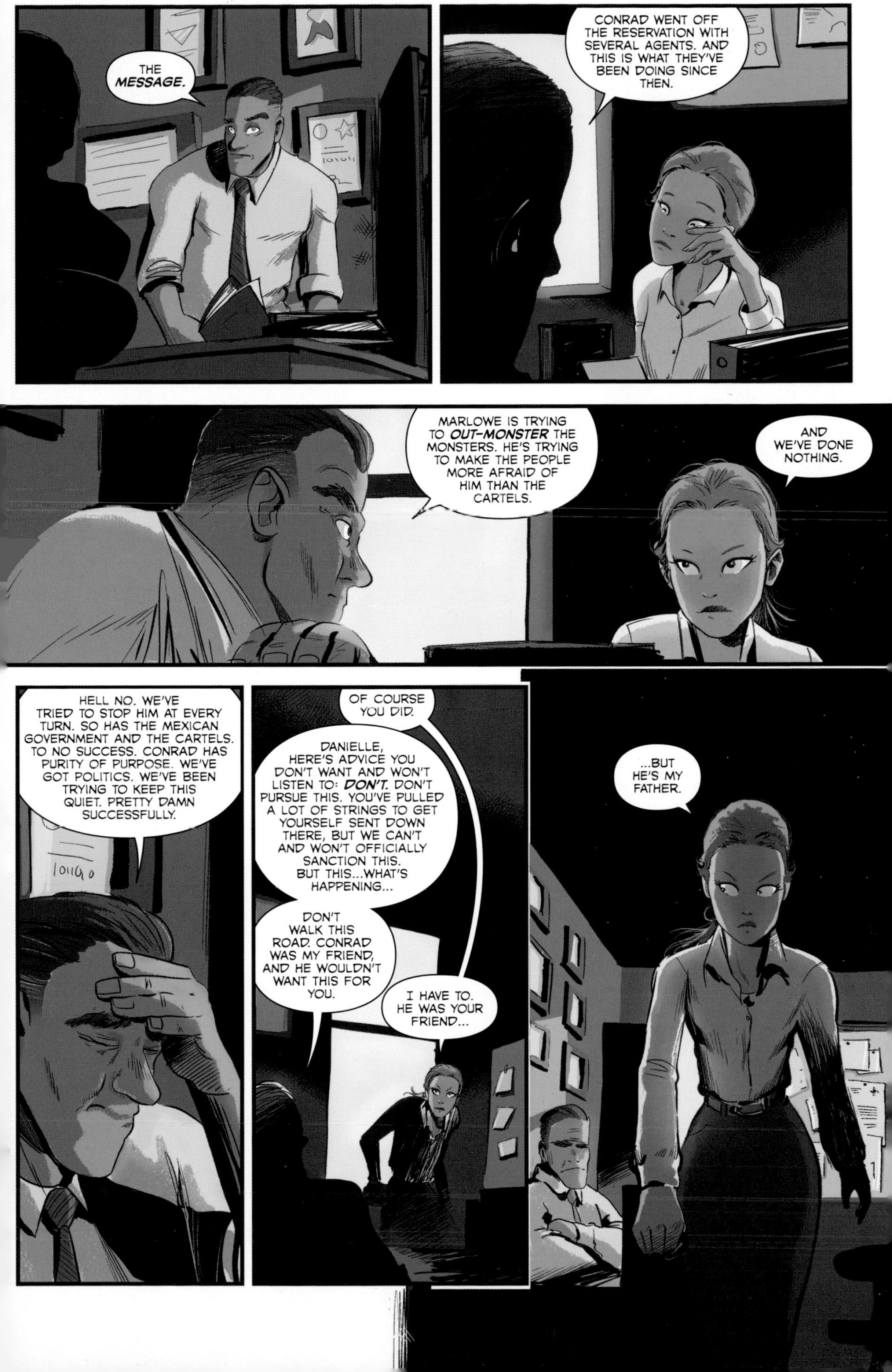
THE MESSAGE.
CONRAD WENT OFF THE RESERVATION WITH SEVERAL AGENTS. AND THIS IS WHAT THEY'VE BEEN DOING SINCE THEN.
MARLOWE IS TRYING TO OUT-MONSTER THE MONSTERS. HE'S TRYING TO MAKE THE PEOPLE MORE AFRAID OF HIM THAN THE CARTELS.
AND WE'VE DONE NOTHING.
HELL NO. WE'VE TRIED TO STOP HIM AT EVERY TURN. SO HAS THE MEXICAN GOVERNMENT AND THE CARTELS. TO NO SUCCESS. CONRAD HAS PURITY OF PURPOSE. WE'VE GOT POLITICS. WE'VE BEEN TRYING TO KEEP THIS QUIET. PRETTY DAMN SUCCESSFULLY.
OF COURSE YOU DID.
DANIELLE, HERE'S ADVICE YOU DON'T WANT AND WON'T LISTEN TO: DON'T. DON'T PURSUE THIS. YOU'VE PULLED A LOT OF STRINGS TO GET YOURSELF SENT DOWN THERE, BUT WE CAN'T AND WON'T OFFICIALLY SANCTION THIS. BUT THIS...WHAT'S HAPPENING...
DON'T WALK THIS ROAD. CONRAD WAS MY FRIEND, AND HE WOULDN'T WANT THIS FOR YOU.
I HAVE TO. HE WAS YOUR FRIEND...
...BUT HE'S MY FATHER.

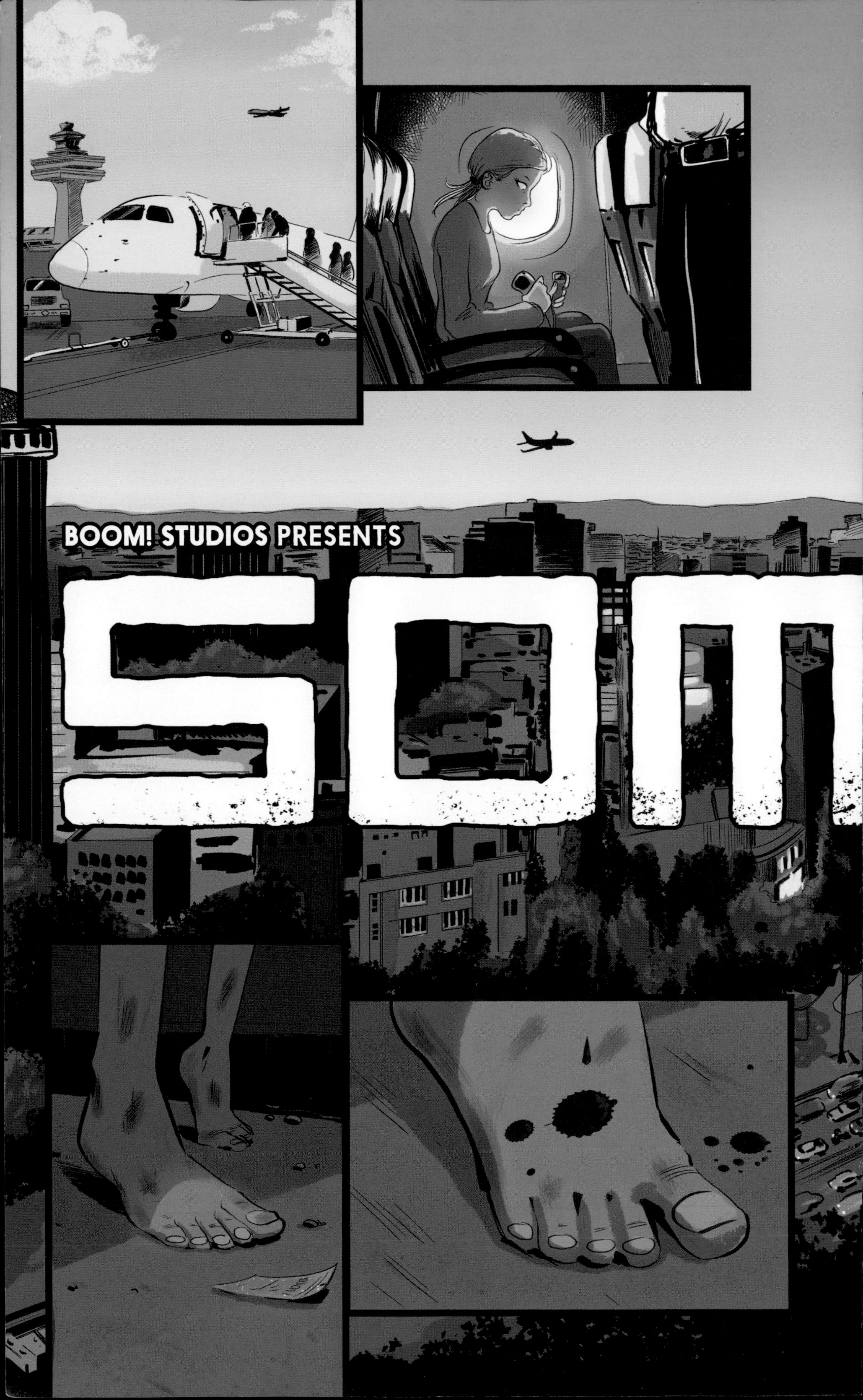
BOOM! STUDIOS PRESENTS
SOM

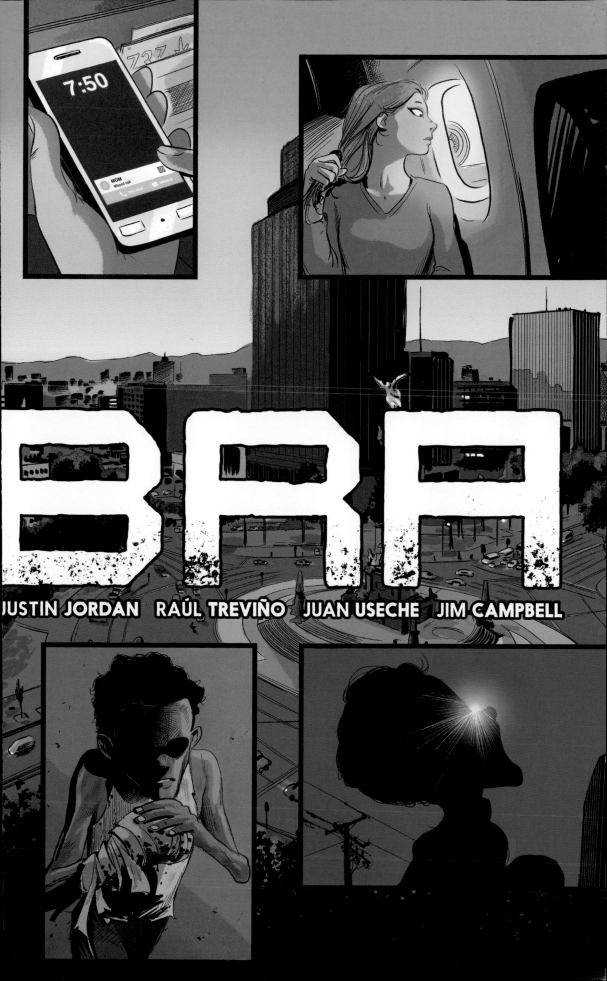

BRA

JUSTIN JORDAN   RAÚL TREVIÑO   JUAN USECHE   JIM CAMPBELL

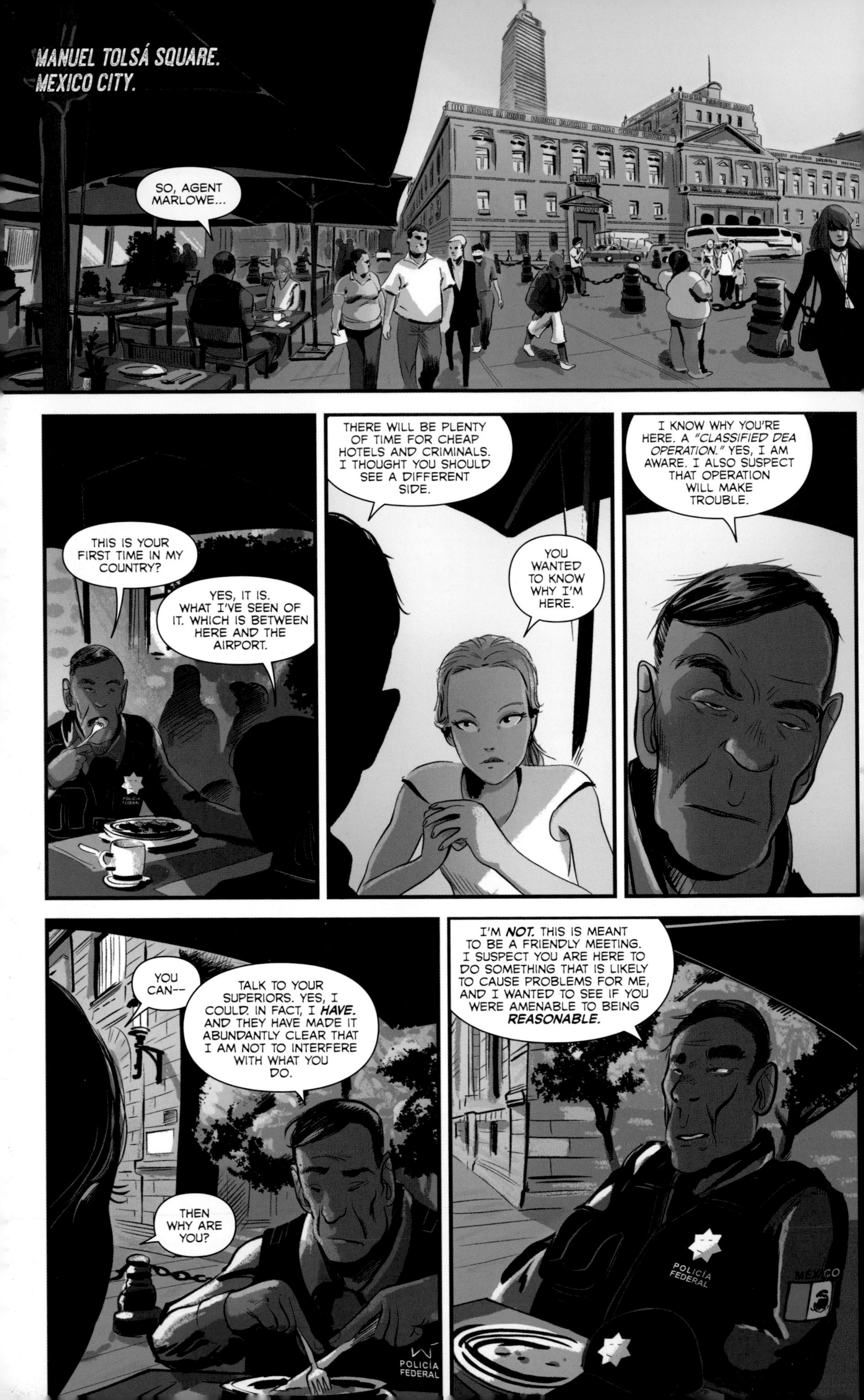
MANUEL TOLSÁ SQUARE.
MEXICO CITY.
SO, AGENT MARLOWE...
THIS IS YOUR FIRST TIME IN MY COUNTRY?
YES, IT IS. WHAT I'VE SEEN OF IT. WHICH IS BETWEEN HERE AND THE AIRPORT.
THERE WILL BE PLENTY OF TIME FOR CHEAP HOTELS AND CRIMINALS. I THOUGHT YOU SHOULD SEE A DIFFERENT SIDE.
YOU WANTED TO KNOW WHY I'M HERE.
I KNOW WHY YOU'RE HERE. A "CLASSIFIED DEA OPERATION." YES, I AM AWARE. I ALSO SUSPECT THAT OPERATION WILL MAKE TROUBLE.
YOU CAN--
TALK TO YOUR SUPERIORS. YES, I COULD. IN FACT, I HAVE. AND THEY HAVE MADE IT ABUNDANTLY CLEAR THAT I AM NOT TO INTERFERE WITH WHAT YOU DO.
THEN WHY ARE YOU?
I'M NOT. THIS IS MEANT TO BE A FRIENDLY MEETING. I SUSPECT YOU ARE HERE TO DO SOMETHING THAT IS LIKELY TO CAUSE PROBLEMS FOR ME, AND I WANTED TO SEE IF YOU WERE AMENABLE TO BEING REASONABLE.
POLICÍA FEDERAL
MÉXICO

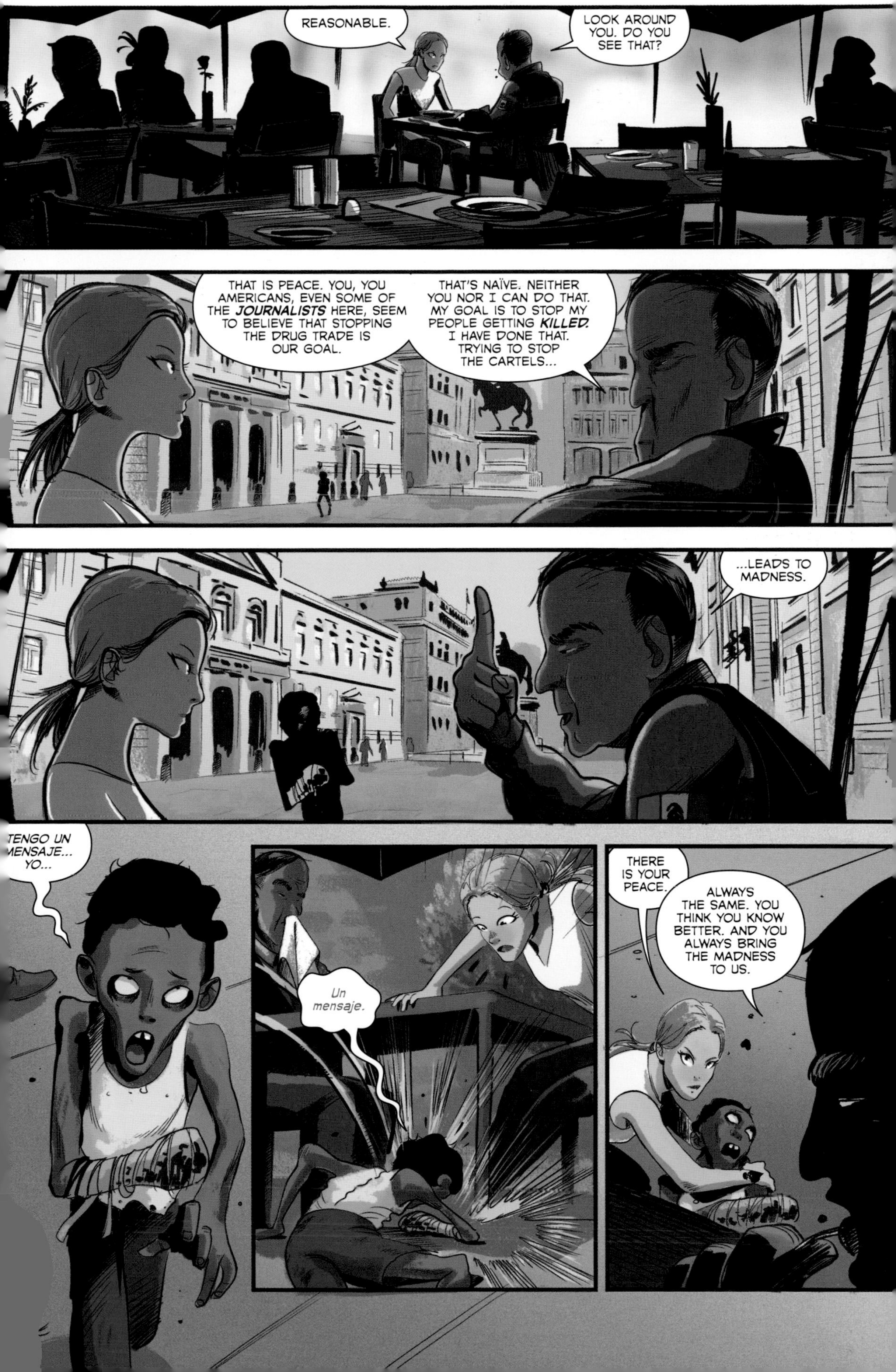
REASONABLE.
LOOK AROUND YOU. DO YOU SEE THAT?
THAT IS PEACE. YOU, YOU AMERICANS, EVEN SOME OF THE JOURNALISTS HERE, SEEM TO BELIEVE THAT STOPPING THE DRUG TRADE IS OUR GOAL.
THAT'S NAÏVE. NEITHER YOU NOR I CAN DO THAT. MY GOAL IS TO STOP MY PEOPLE GETTING KILLED. I HAVE DONE THAT. TRYING TO STOP THE CARTELS...
...LEADS TO MADNESS.
TENGO UN MENSAJE... YO...
Un mensaje.
THERE IS YOUR PEACE.
ALWAYS THE SAME. YOU THINK YOU KNOW BETTER. AND YOU ALWAYS BRING THE MADNESS TO US.

FEDERICO GÓMEZ
CHILDREN'S HOSPITAL.

⟨YOU SAID YOU HAD A MESSAGE.⟩

⟨I DID GOOD. HE WILL SEE. HE ALWAYS SEES. TOLVA TELLS OUR STORY.⟩

⟨YOU DON'T HAVE TO GO BACK. YOU'RE SAFE NOW. WHO IS HE? THIS **TOLVA**?⟩

⟨TOLVA TELLS OUR STORY.⟩

⟨WHOSE STORY? WHO DID THIS TO YOU? I CAN'T STOP THEM UNLESS YOU TELL ME WHO.⟩

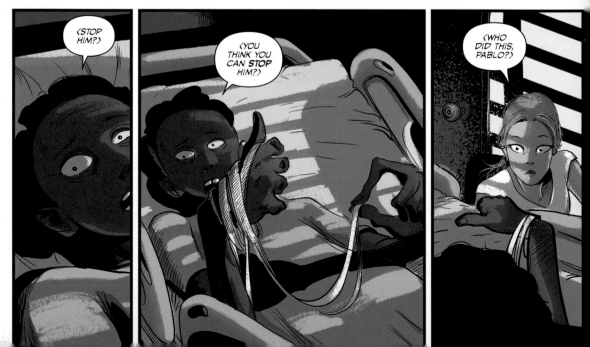

⟨STOP HIM?⟩

⟨YOU THINK YOU CAN **STOP** HIM?⟩

⟨WHO DID THIS, PABLO?⟩

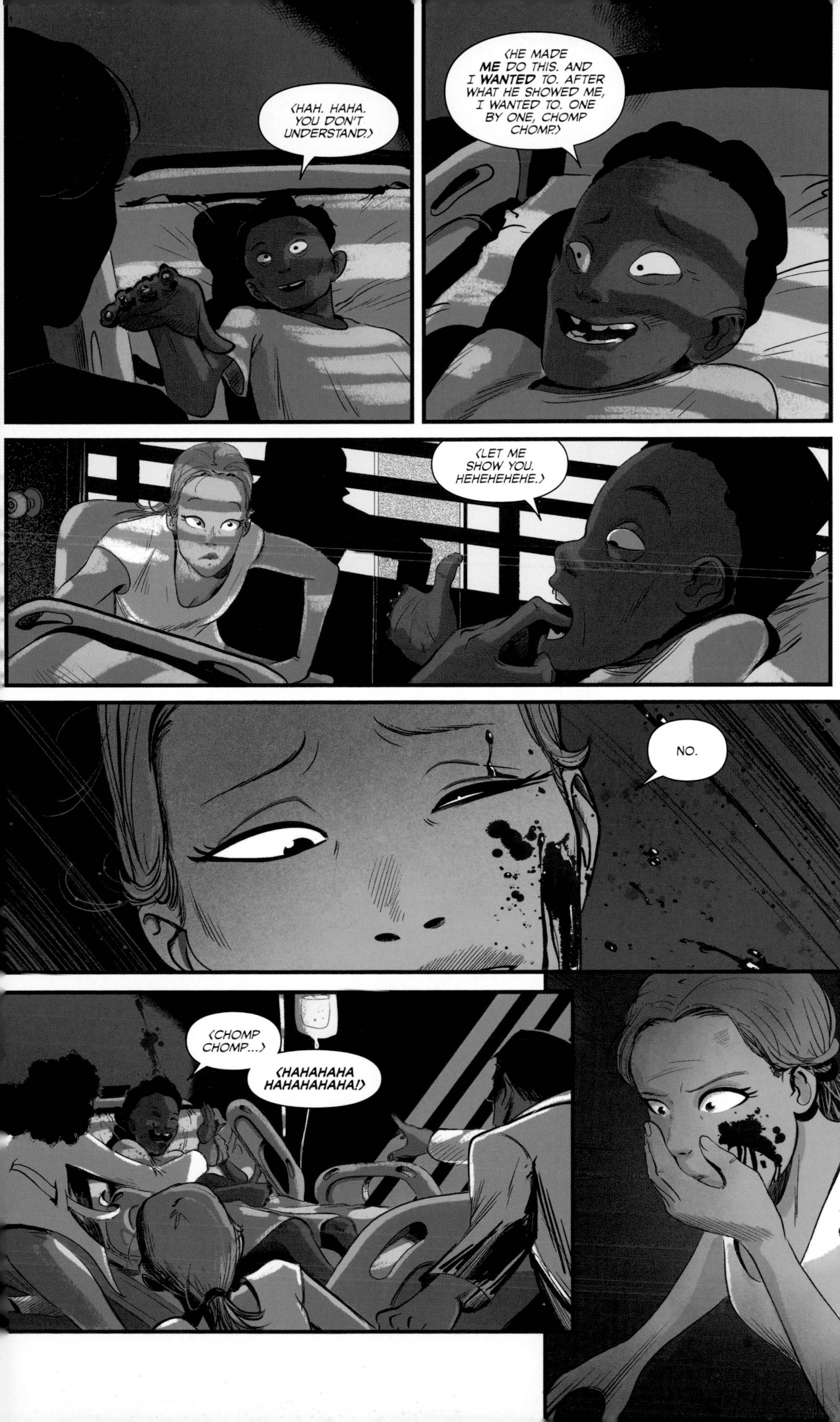

‹HAH. HAHA. YOU DON'T UNDERSTAND.›
‹HE MADE ME DO THIS. AND I WANTED TO. AFTER WHAT HE SHOWED ME, I WANTED TO. ONE BY ONE, CHOMP CHOMP.›
‹LET ME SHOW YOU. HEHEHEHEHE.›
NO.
‹CHOMP CHOMP...›
‹HAHAHAHA HAHAHAHAHA!›

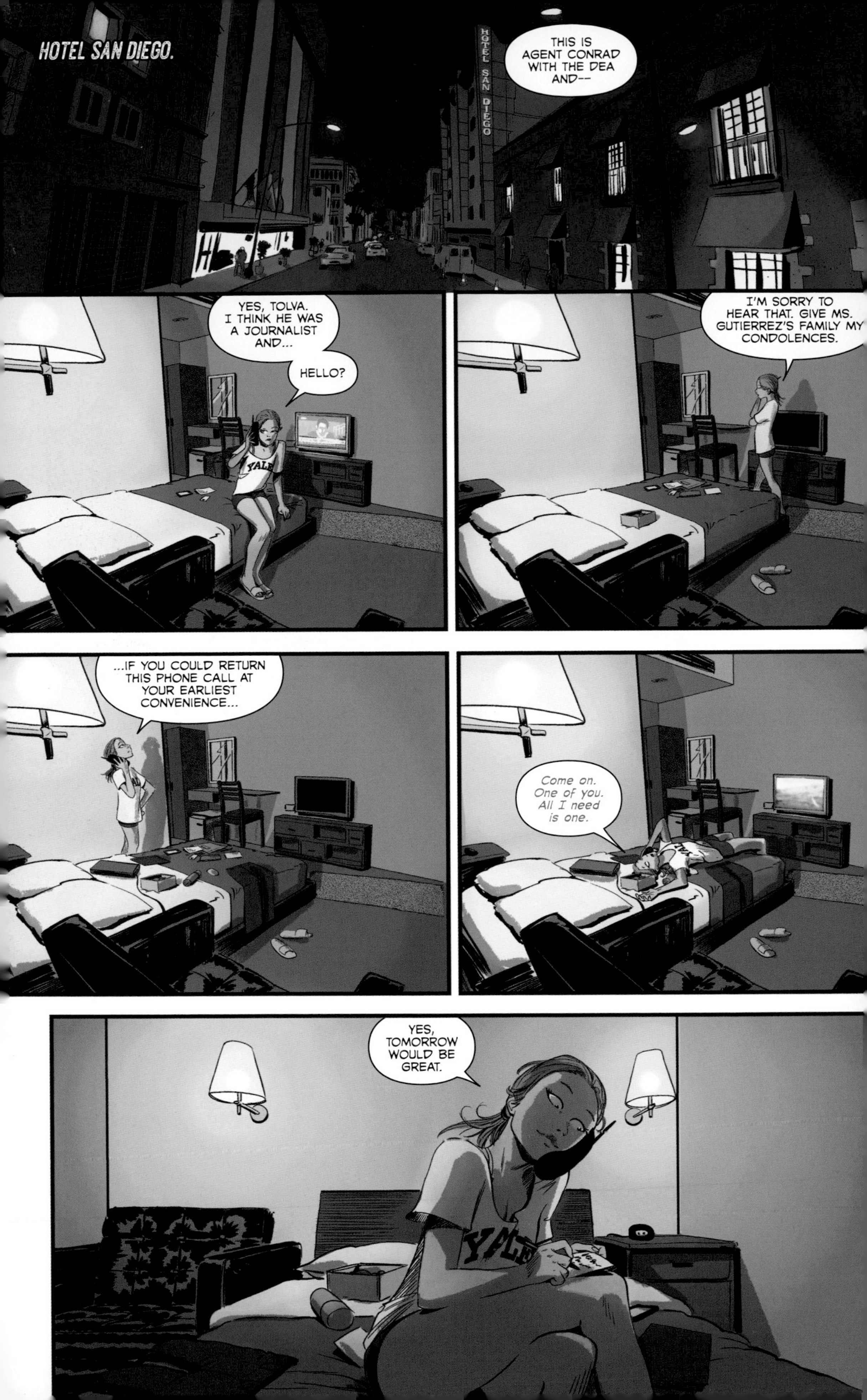
HOTEL SAN DIEGO.
HOTEL SAN DIEGO
THIS IS AGENT CONRAD WITH THE DEA AND--
YES, TOLVA. I THINK HE WAS A JOURNALIST AND...
HELLO?
I'M SORRY TO HEAR THAT. GIVE MS. GUTIERREZ'S FAMILY MY CONDOLENCES.
...IF YOU COULD RETURN THIS PHONE CALL AT YOUR EARLIEST CONVENIENCE...
Come on. One of you. All I need is one.
YES, TOMORROW WOULD BE GREAT.

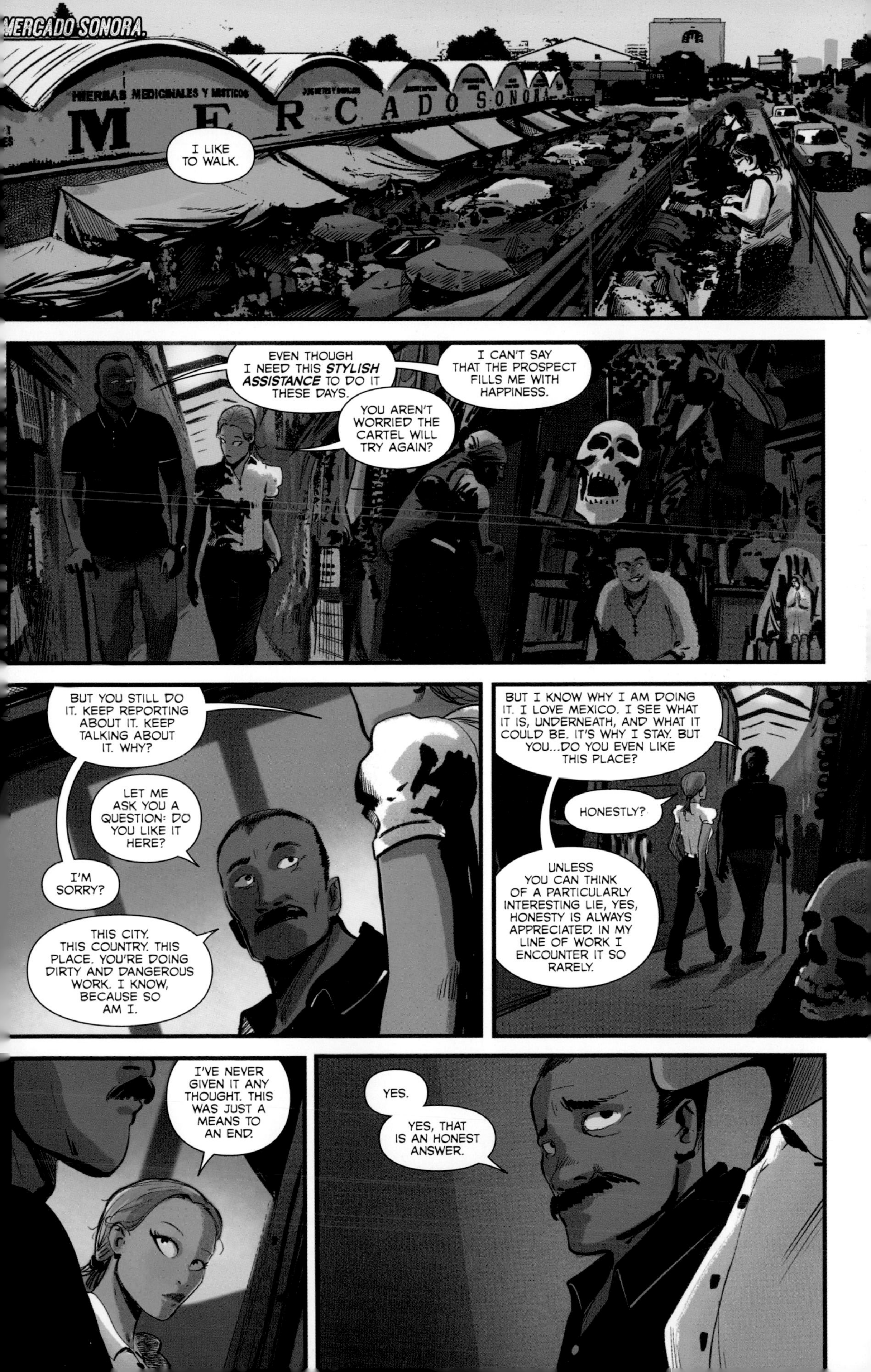
MERCADO SONORA.
MERCADO SONORA
I LIKE TO WALK.
EVEN THOUGH I NEED THIS *STYLISH ASSISTANCE* TO DO IT THESE DAYS.
YOU AREN'T WORRIED THE CARTEL WILL TRY AGAIN?
I CAN'T SAY THAT THE PROSPECT FILLS ME WITH HAPPINESS.
BUT YOU STILL DO IT. KEEP REPORTING ABOUT IT. KEEP TALKING ABOUT IT. WHY?
LET ME ASK YOU A QUESTION: DO YOU LIKE IT HERE?
I'M SORRY?
THIS CITY. THIS COUNTRY. THIS PLACE. YOU'RE DOING DIRTY AND DANGEROUS WORK. I KNOW, BECAUSE SO AM I.
BUT I KNOW WHY I AM DOING IT. I LOVE MEXICO. I SEE WHAT IT IS, UNDERNEATH, AND WHAT IT COULD BE. IT'S WHY I STAY. BUT YOU...DO YOU EVEN LIKE THIS PLACE?
HONESTLY?
UNLESS YOU CAN THINK OF A PARTICULARLY INTERESTING LIE, YES, HONESTY IS ALWAYS APPRECIATED. IN MY LINE OF WORK I ENCOUNTER IT SO RARELY.
I'VE NEVER GIVEN IT ANY THOUGHT. THIS WAS JUST A MEANS TO AN END.
YES.
YES, THAT IS AN HONEST ANSWER.

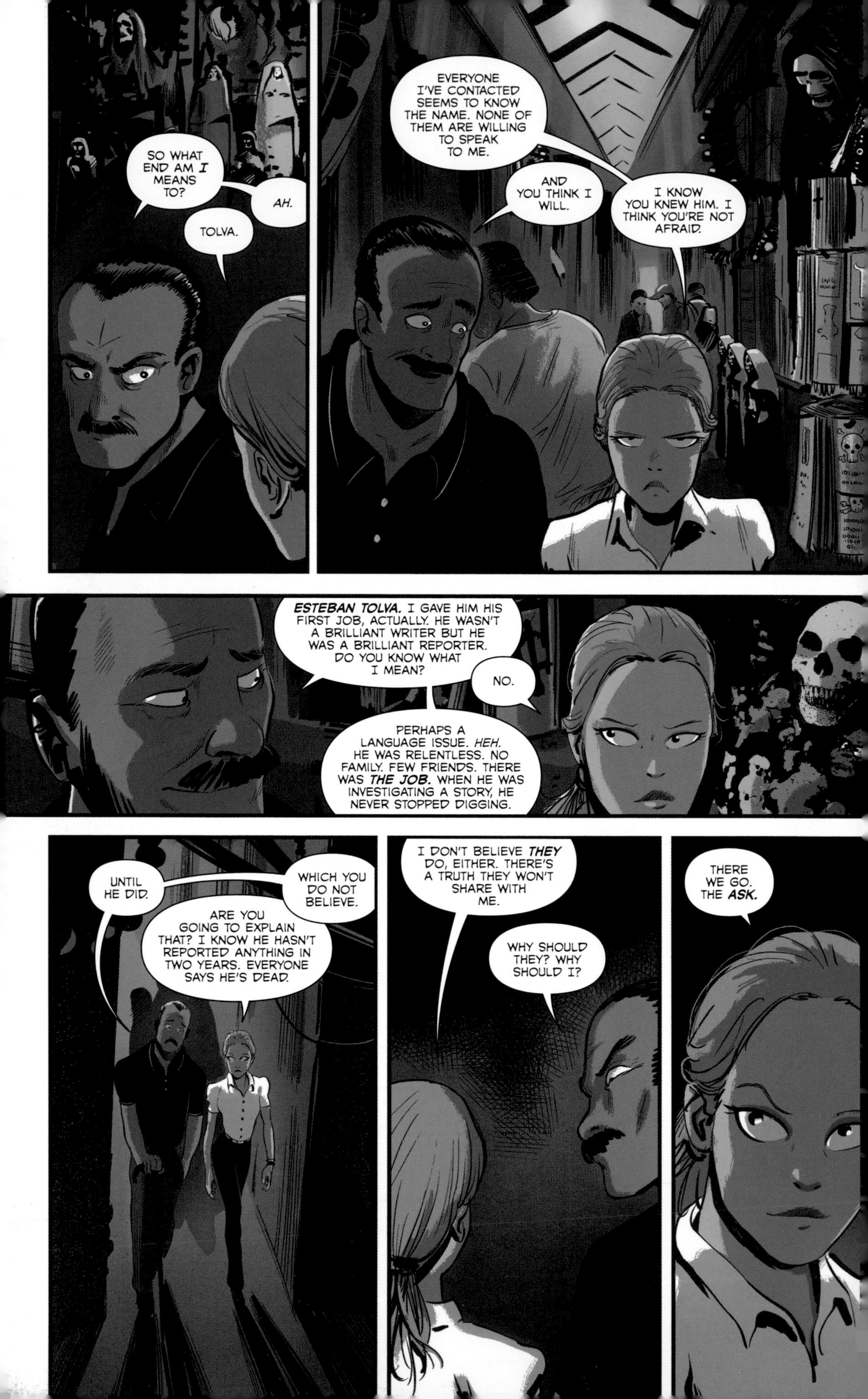
SO WHAT END AM *I* MEANS TO?
AH.
TOLVA.
EVERYONE I'VE CONTACTED SEEMS TO KNOW THE NAME. NONE OF THEM ARE WILLING TO SPEAK TO ME.
AND YOU THINK I WILL.
I KNOW YOU KNEW HIM. I THINK YOU'RE NOT AFRAID.
ESTEBAN TOLVA. I GAVE HIM HIS FIRST JOB, ACTUALLY. HE WASN'T A BRILLIANT WRITER BUT HE WAS A BRILLIANT REPORTER. DO YOU KNOW WHAT I MEAN?
NO.
PERHAPS A LANGUAGE ISSUE. *HEH.* HE WAS RELENTLESS. NO FAMILY. FEW FRIENDS. THERE WAS ***THE JOB.*** WHEN HE WAS INVESTIGATING A STORY, HE NEVER STOPPED DIGGING.
UNTIL HE DID.
WHICH YOU DO NOT BELIEVE.
ARE YOU GOING TO EXPLAIN THAT? I KNOW HE HASN'T REPORTED ANYTHING IN TWO YEARS. EVERYONE SAYS HE'S DEAD.
I DON'T BELIEVE ***THEY*** DO, EITHER. THERE'S A TRUTH THEY WON'T SHARE WITH ME.
WHY SHOULD THEY? WHY SHOULD I?
THERE WE GO. THE ***ASK.***

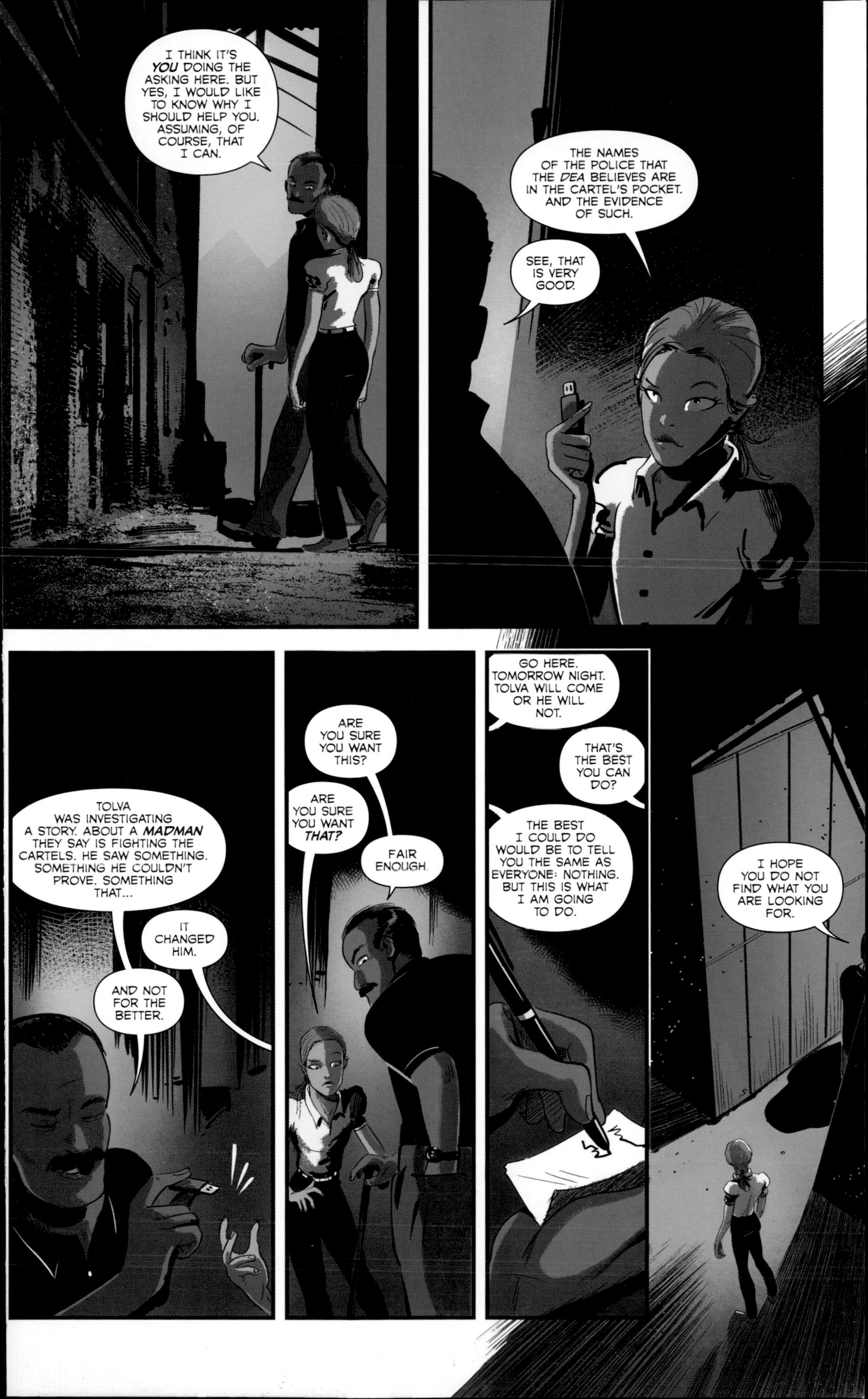
I THINK IT'S *YOU* DOING THE ASKING HERE. BUT YES, I WOULD LIKE TO KNOW WHY I SHOULD HELP YOU. ASSUMING, OF COURSE, THAT I CAN.
THE NAMES OF THE POLICE THAT THE *DEA* BELIEVES ARE IN THE CARTEL'S POCKET. AND THE EVIDENCE OF SUCH.
SEE, THAT IS VERY GOOD.
TOLVA WAS INVESTIGATING A STORY. ABOUT A *MADMAN* THEY SAY IS FIGHTING THE CARTELS. HE SAW SOMETHING. SOMETHING HE COULDN'T PROVE. SOMETHING THAT...
IT CHANGED HIM.
AND NOT FOR THE BETTER.
ARE YOU SURE YOU WANT THIS?
ARE YOU SURE YOU WANT *THAT?*
FAIR ENOUGH.
GO HERE. TOMORROW NIGHT. TOLVA WILL COME OR HE WILL NOT.
THAT'S THE BEST YOU CAN DO?
THE BEST I COULD DO WOULD BE TO TELL YOU THE SAME AS EVERYONE: NOTHING. BUT THIS IS WHAT I AM GOING TO DO.
I HOPE YOU DO NOT FIND WHAT YOU ARE LOOKING FOR.

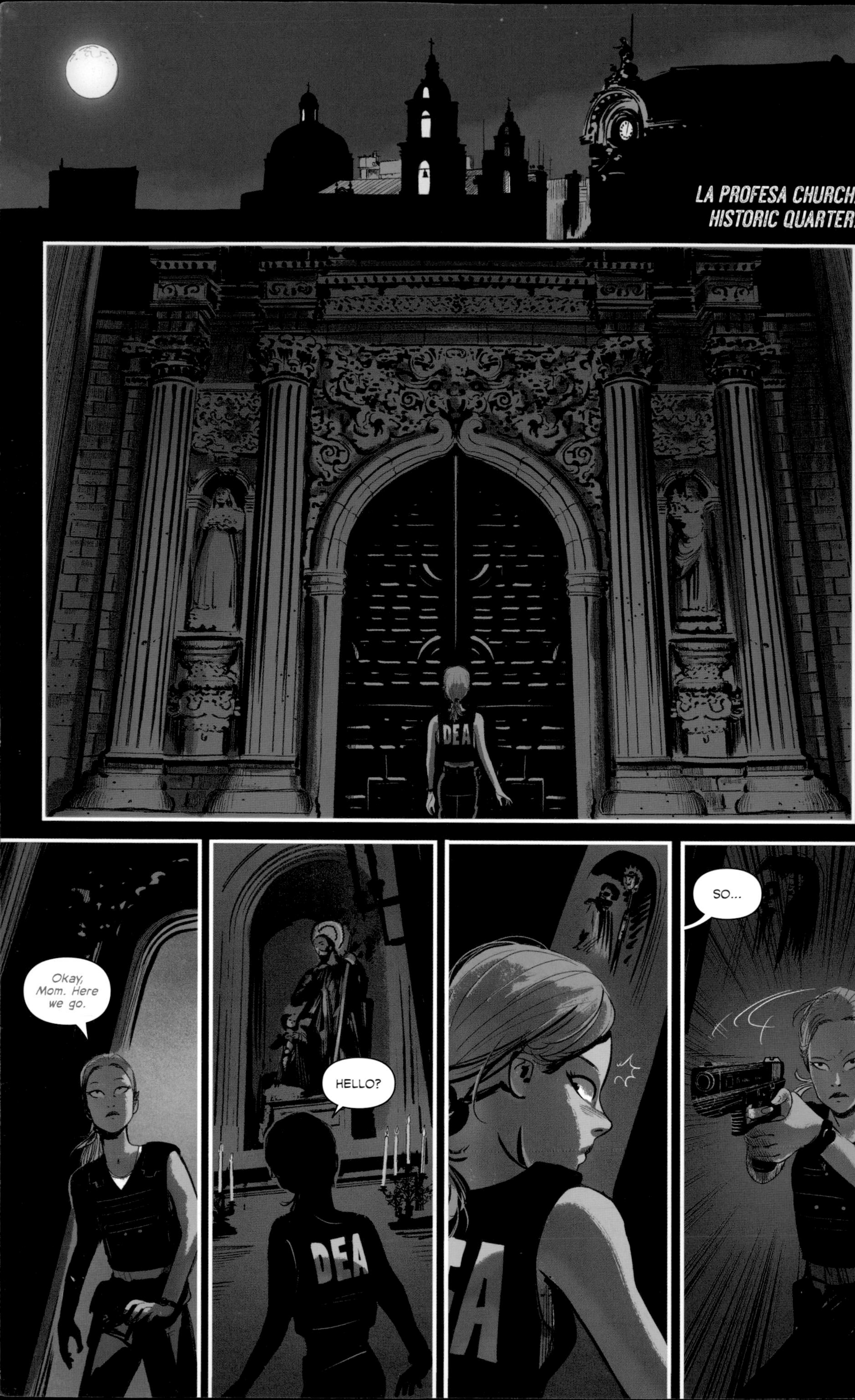
LA PROFESA CHURCH
HISTORIC QUARTER
DEA
Okay, Mom. Here we go.
HELLO?
DEA
SO...

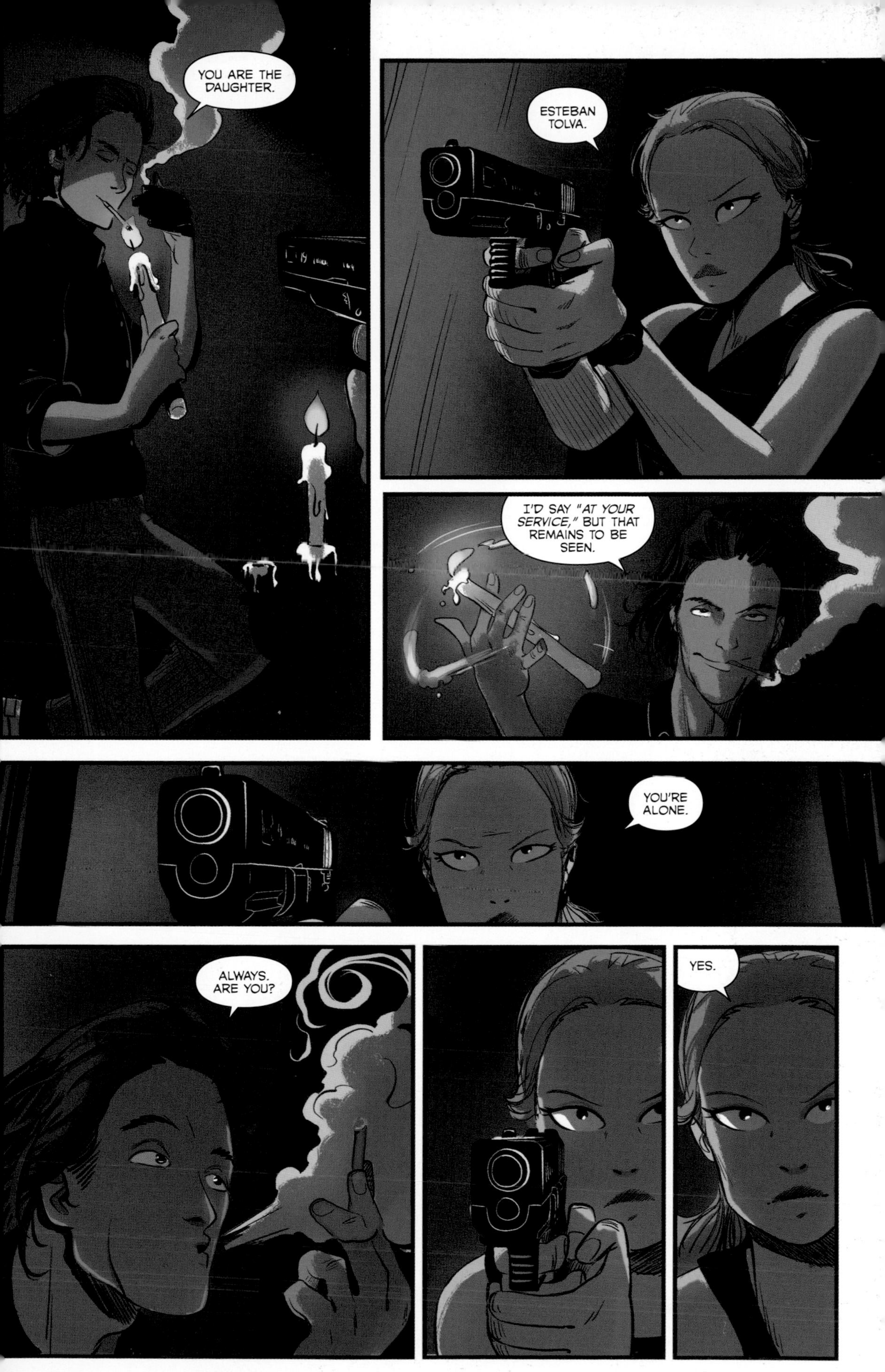
YOU ARE THE DAUGHTER.
ESTEBAN TOLVA.
I'D SAY *"AT YOUR SERVICE,"* BUT THAT REMAINS TO BE SEEN.
YOU'RE ALONE.
ALWAYS. ARE YOU?
YES.

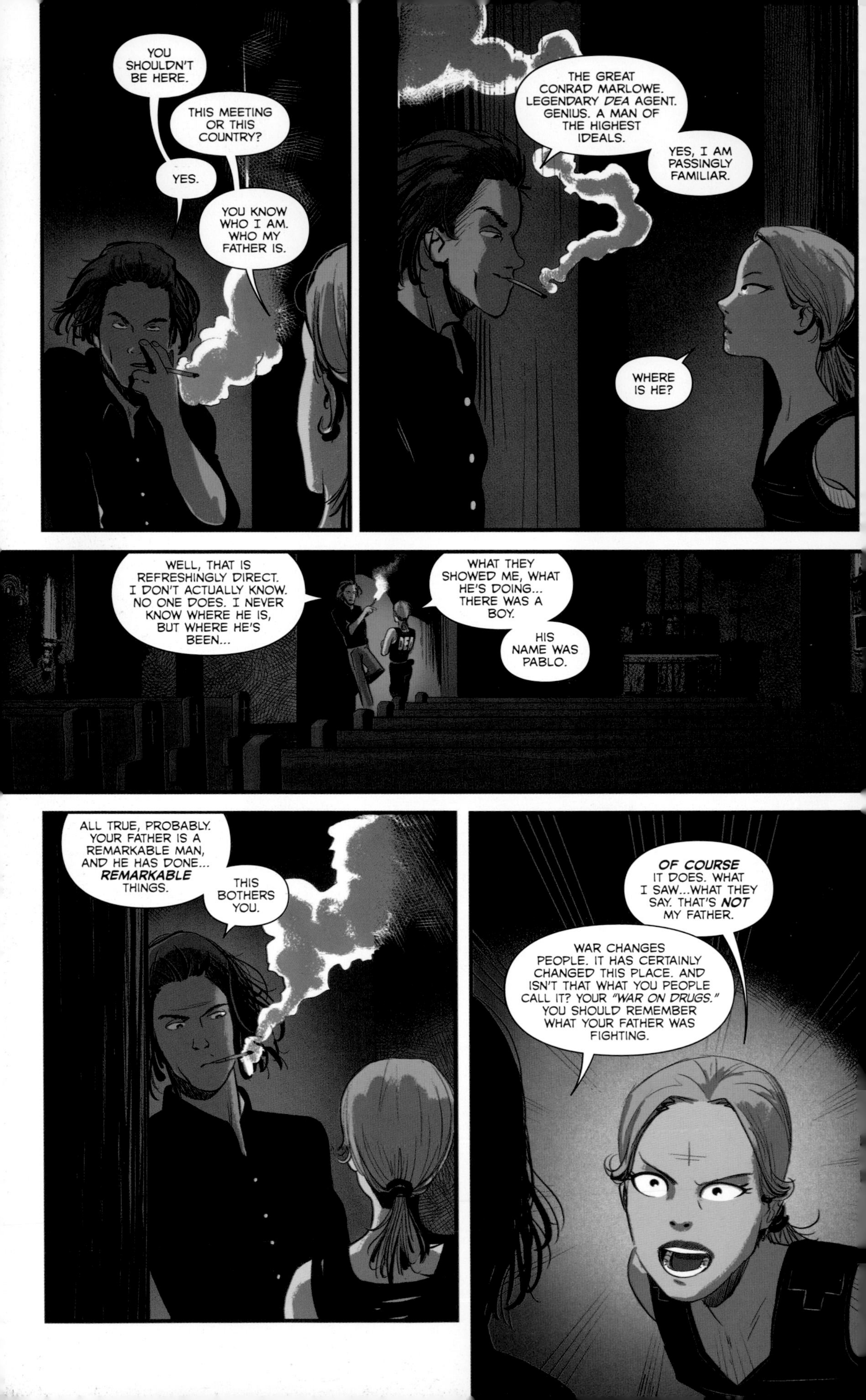
YOU SHOULDN'T BE HERE.
THIS MEETING OR THIS COUNTRY?
YES.
YOU KNOW WHO I AM. WHO MY FATHER IS.
THE GREAT CONRAD MARLOWE. LEGENDARY DEA AGENT. GENIUS. A MAN OF THE HIGHEST IDEALS.
YES, I AM PASSINGLY FAMILIAR.
WHERE IS HE?
WELL, THAT IS REFRESHINGLY DIRECT. I DON'T ACTUALLY KNOW. NO ONE DOES. I NEVER KNOW WHERE HE IS, BUT WHERE HE'S BEEN...
WHAT THEY SHOWED ME, WHAT HE'S DOING... THERE WAS A BOY.
HIS NAME WAS PABLO.
ALL TRUE, PROBABLY. YOUR FATHER IS A REMARKABLE MAN, AND HE HAS DONE... REMARKABLE THINGS.
THIS BOTHERS YOU.
OF COURSE IT DOES. WHAT I SAW...WHAT THEY SAY. THAT'S NOT MY FATHER.
WAR CHANGES PEOPLE. IT HAS CERTAINLY CHANGED THIS PLACE. AND ISN'T THAT WHAT YOU PEOPLE CALL IT? YOUR "WAR ON DRUGS." YOU SHOULD REMEMBER WHAT YOUR FATHER WAS FIGHTING.

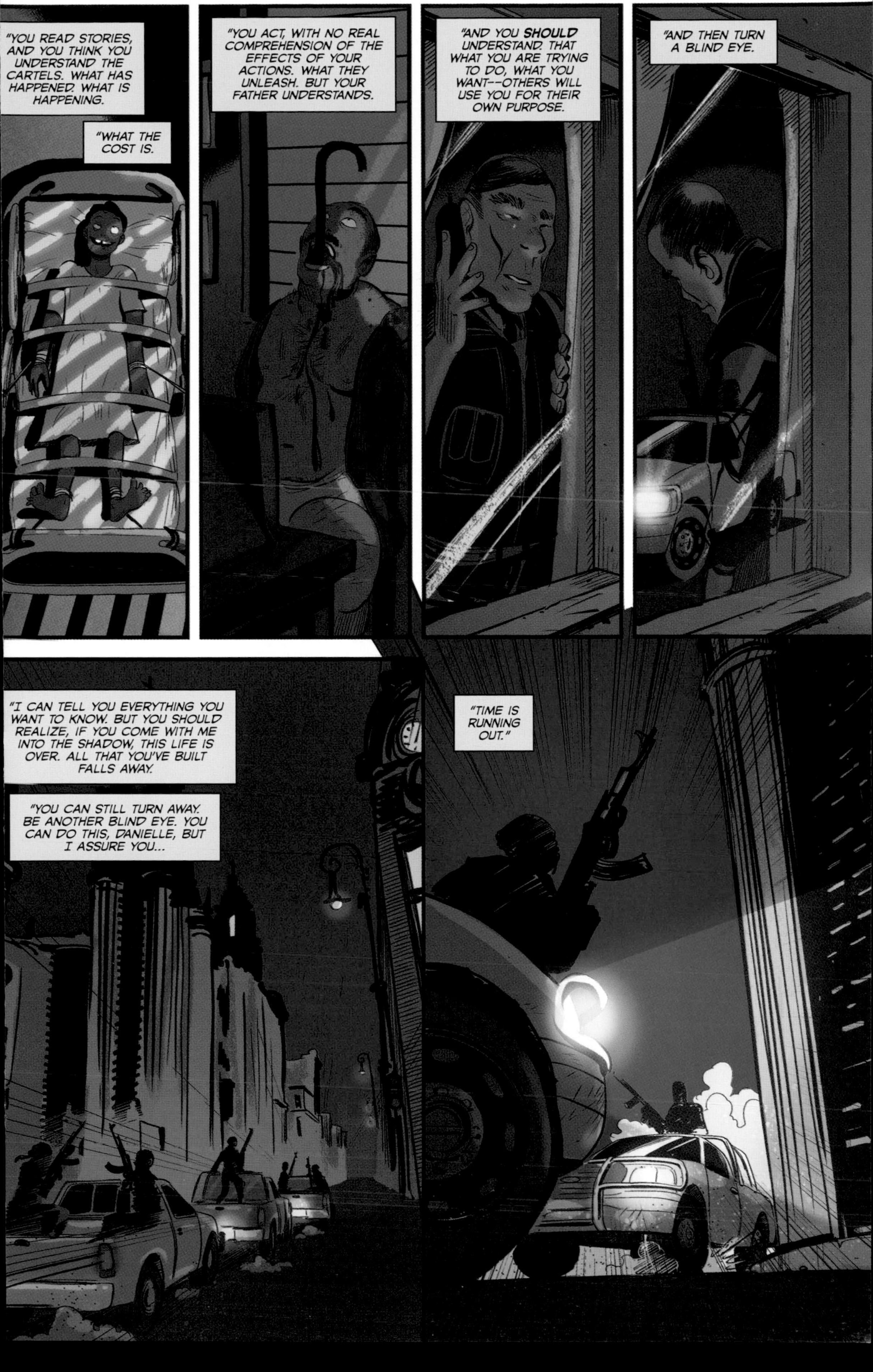
"YOU READ STORIES, AND YOU THINK YOU UNDERSTAND THE CARTELS. WHAT HAS HAPPENED. WHAT IS HAPPENING.
"WHAT THE COST IS.
"YOU ACT, WITH NO REAL COMPREHENSION OF THE EFFECTS OF YOUR ACTIONS. WHAT THEY UNLEASH. BUT YOUR FATHER UNDERSTANDS.
"AND YOU SHOULD UNDERSTAND. THAT WHAT YOU ARE TRYING TO DO, WHAT YOU WANT--OTHERS WILL USE YOU FOR THEIR OWN PURPOSE.
"AND THEN TURN A BLIND EYE.
"I CAN TELL YOU EVERYTHING YOU WANT TO KNOW. BUT YOU SHOULD REALIZE, IF YOU COME WITH ME INTO THE SHADOW, THIS LIFE IS OVER. ALL THAT YOU'VE BUILT FALLS AWAY.
"YOU CAN STILL TURN AWAY. BE ANOTHER BLIND EYE. YOU CAN DO THIS, DANIELLE, BUT I ASSURE YOU...
"TIME IS RUNNING OUT."

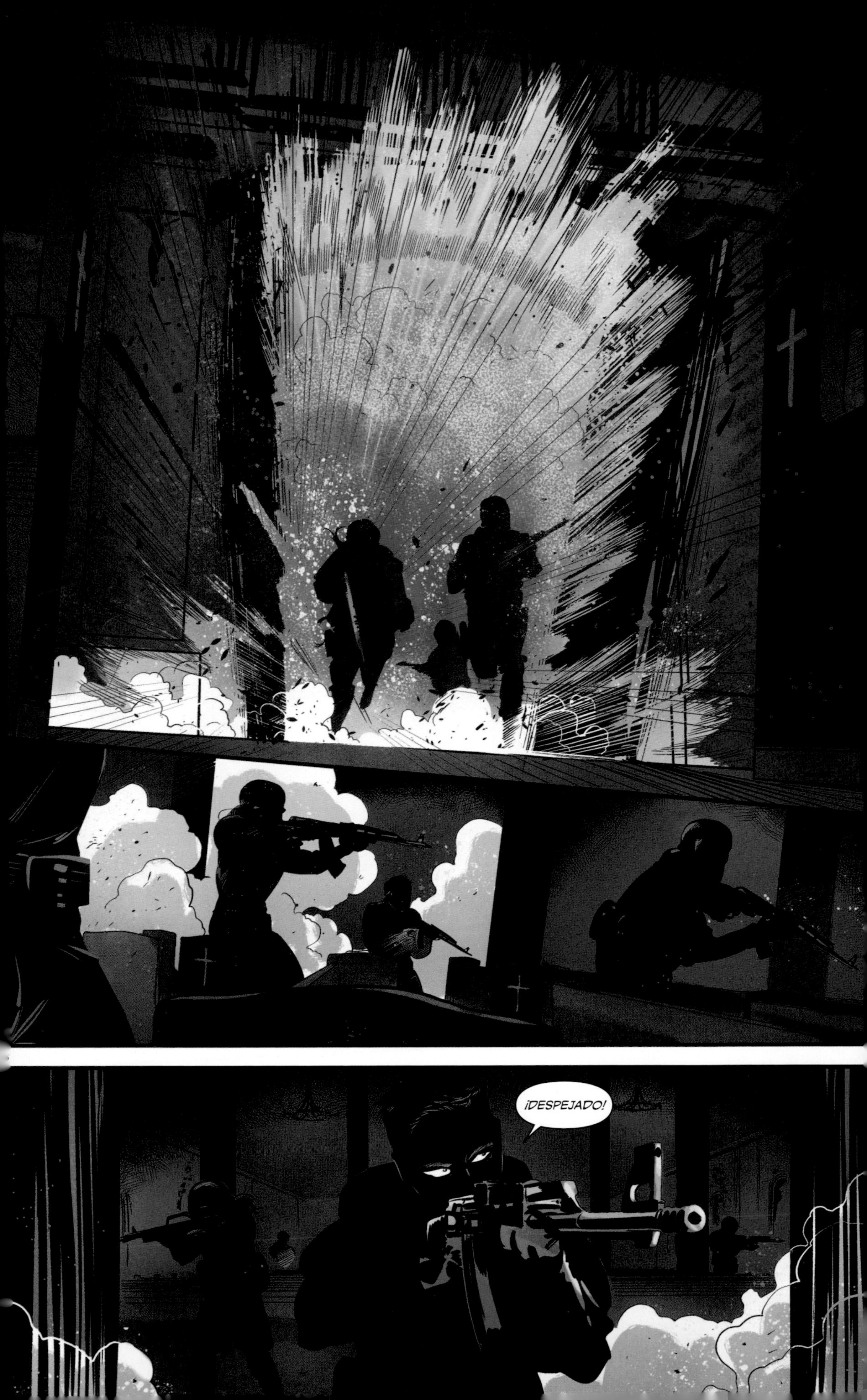
¡DESPEJADO!

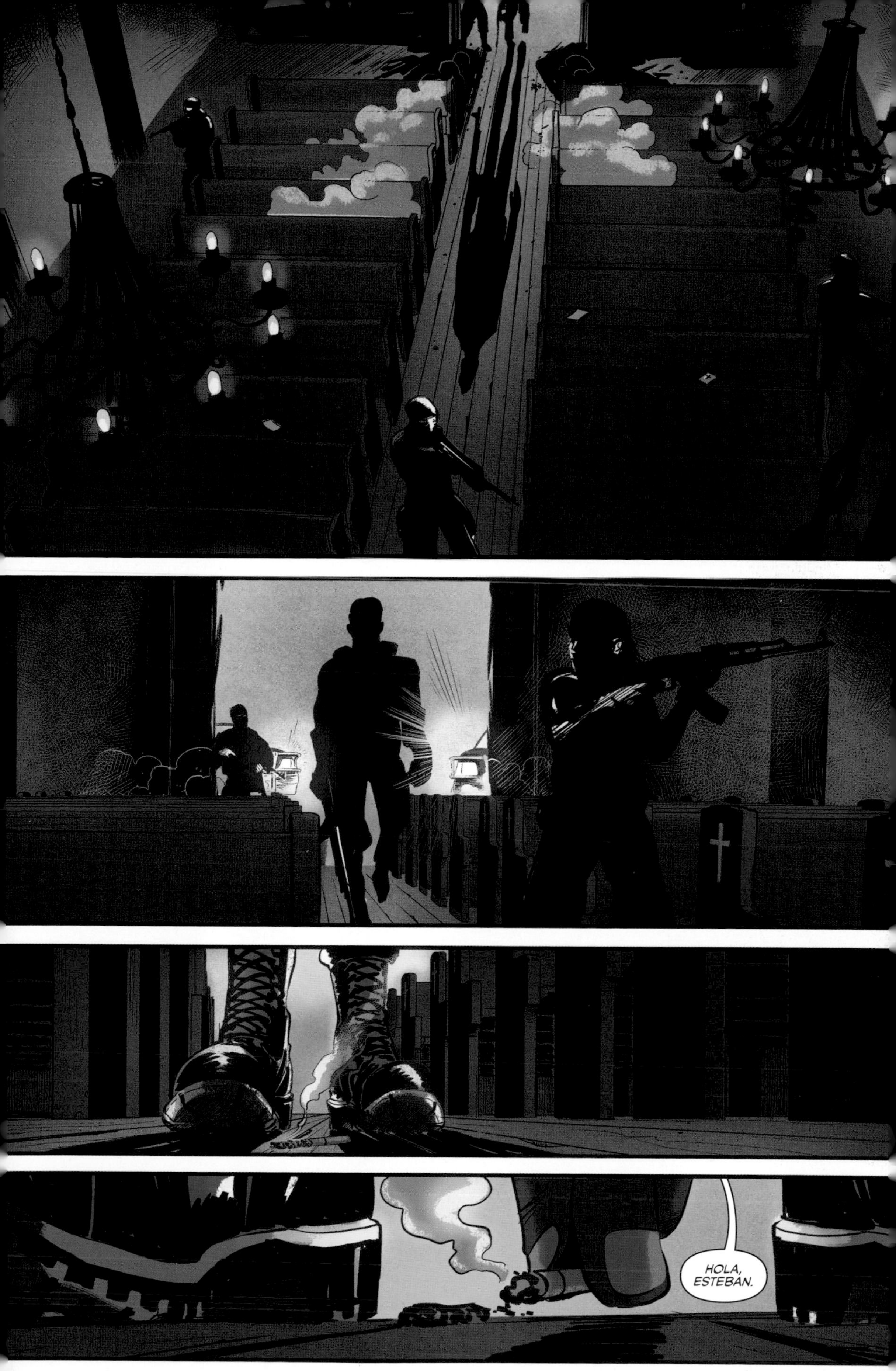
HOLA, ESTEBAN.

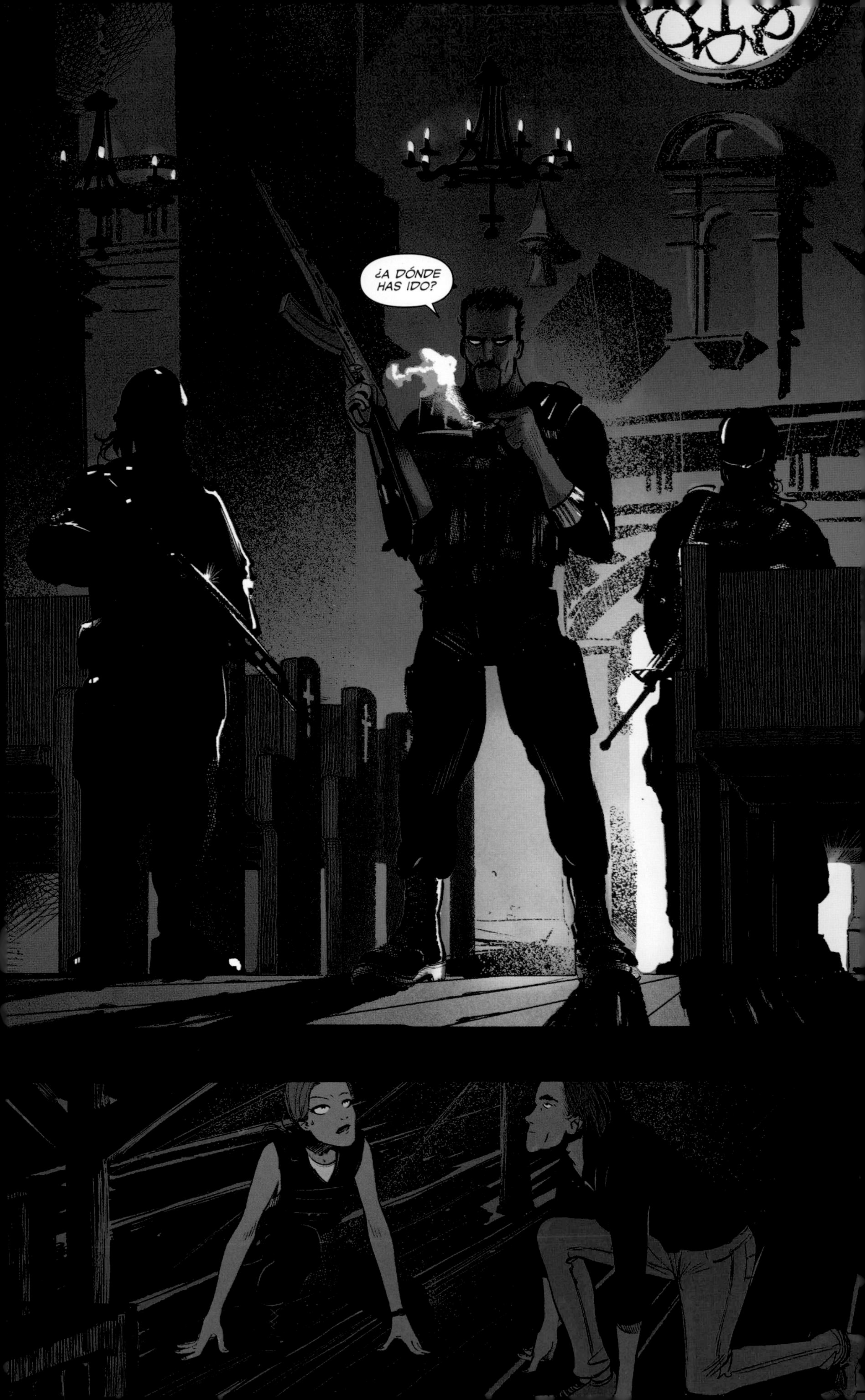
¿A DÓNDE HAS IDO?

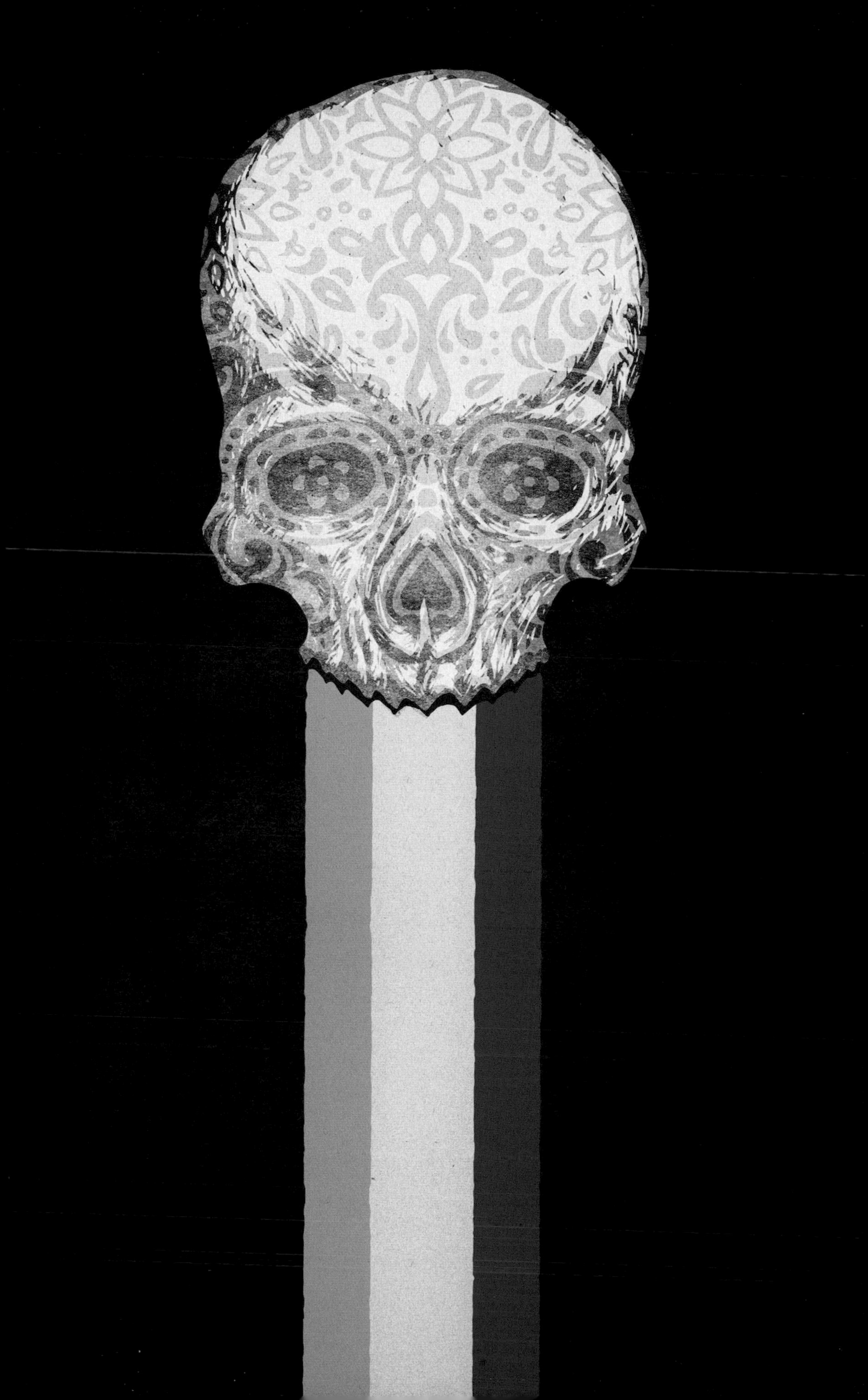

CHAPTER
TWO
CAPÍTULO DOS

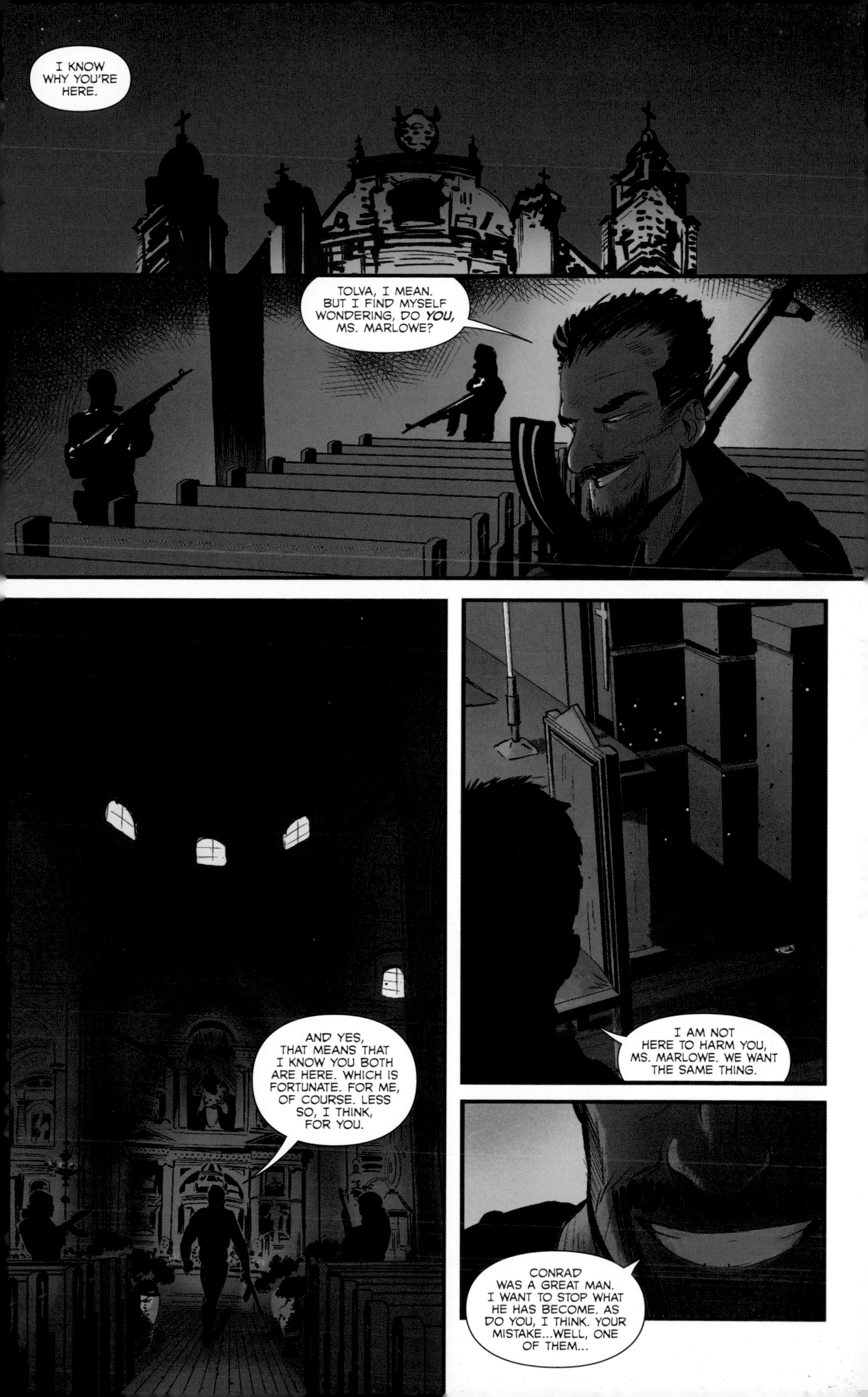
I KNOW WHY YOU'RE HERE.
TOLVA, I MEAN. BUT I FIND MYSELF WONDERING, DO *YOU,* MS. MARLOWE?
AND YES, THAT MEANS THAT I KNOW YOU BOTH ARE HERE. WHICH IS FORTUNATE. FOR ME, OF COURSE. LESS SO, I THINK, FOR YOU.
I AM NOT HERE TO HARM YOU, MS. MARLOWE. WE WANT THE SAME THING.
CONRAD WAS A GREAT MAN. I WANT TO STOP WHAT HE HAS BECOME. AS DO YOU, I THINK. YOUR MISTAKE...WELL, ONE OF THEM...

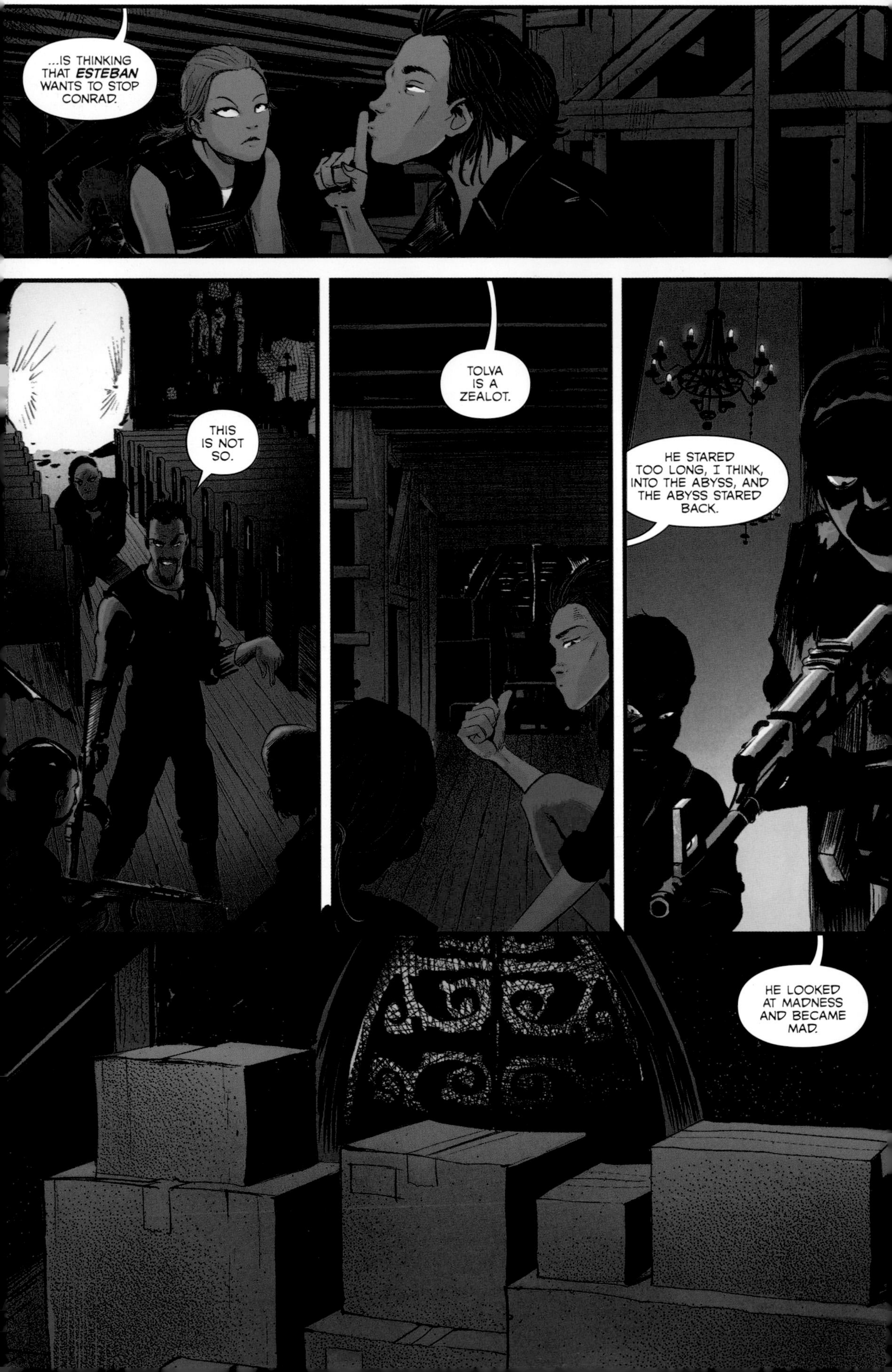
...IS THINKING THAT ESTEBAN WANTS TO STOP CONRAD.
THIS IS NOT SO.
TOLVA IS A ZEALOT.
HE STARED TOO LONG, I THINK, INTO THE ABYSS, AND THE ABYSS STARED BACK.
HE LOOKED AT MADNESS AND BECAME MAD.

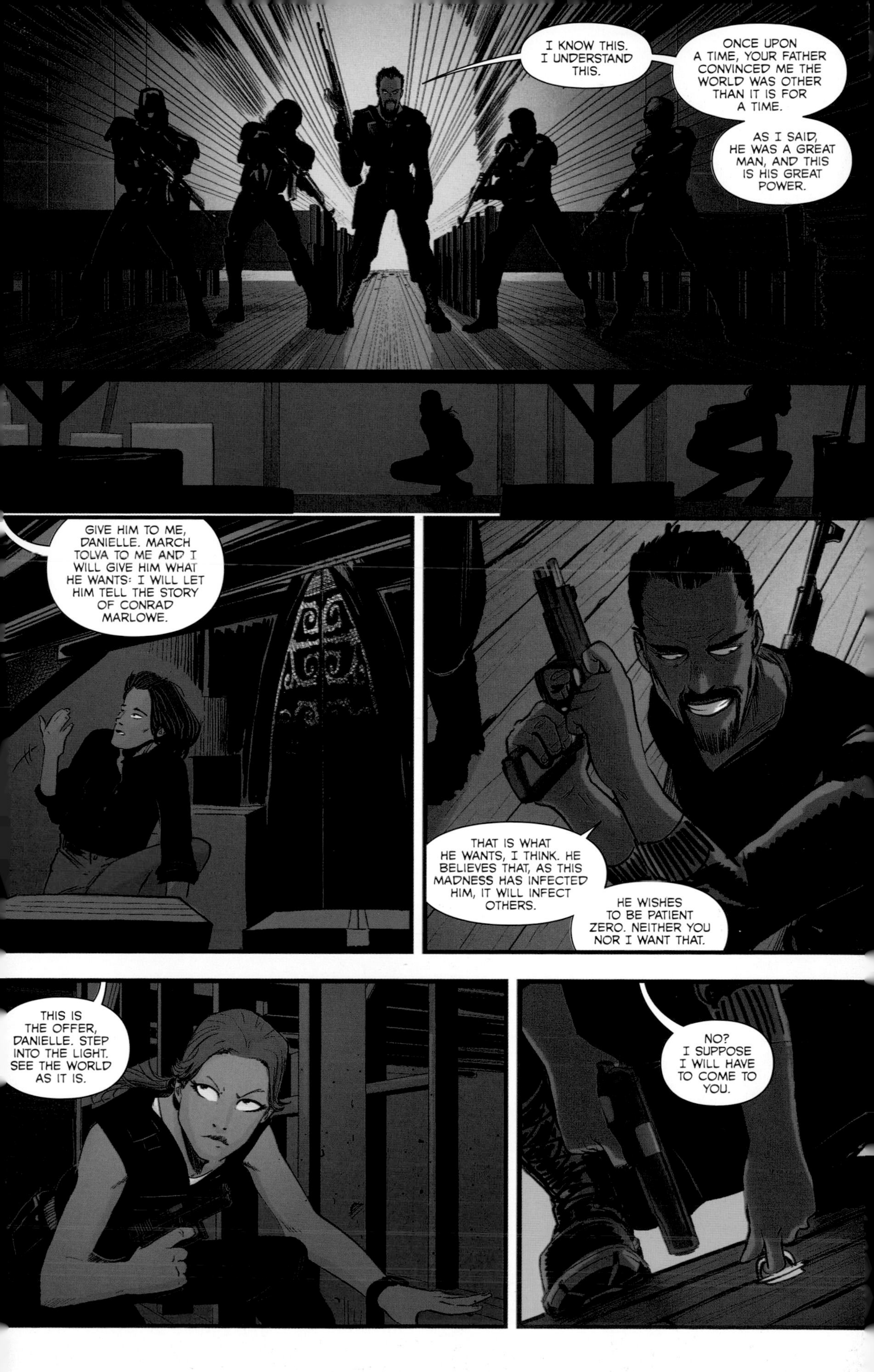
I KNOW THIS. I UNDERSTAND THIS.
ONCE UPON A TIME, YOUR FATHER CONVINCED ME THE WORLD WAS OTHER THAN IT IS FOR A TIME.
AS I SAID, HE WAS A GREAT MAN, AND THIS IS HIS GREAT POWER.
GIVE HIM TO ME, DANIELLE. MARCH TOLVA TO ME AND I WILL GIVE HIM WHAT HE WANTS: I WILL LET HIM TELL THE STORY OF CONRAD MARLOWE.
THAT IS WHAT HE WANTS, I THINK. HE BELIEVES THAT, AS THIS MADNESS HAS INFECTED HIM, IT WILL INFECT OTHERS.
HE WISHES TO BE PATIENT ZERO. NEITHER YOU NOR I WANT THAT.
THIS IS THE OFFER, DANIELLE. STEP INTO THE LIGHT. SEE THE WORLD AS IT IS.
NO? I SUPPOSE I WILL HAVE TO COME TO YOU.

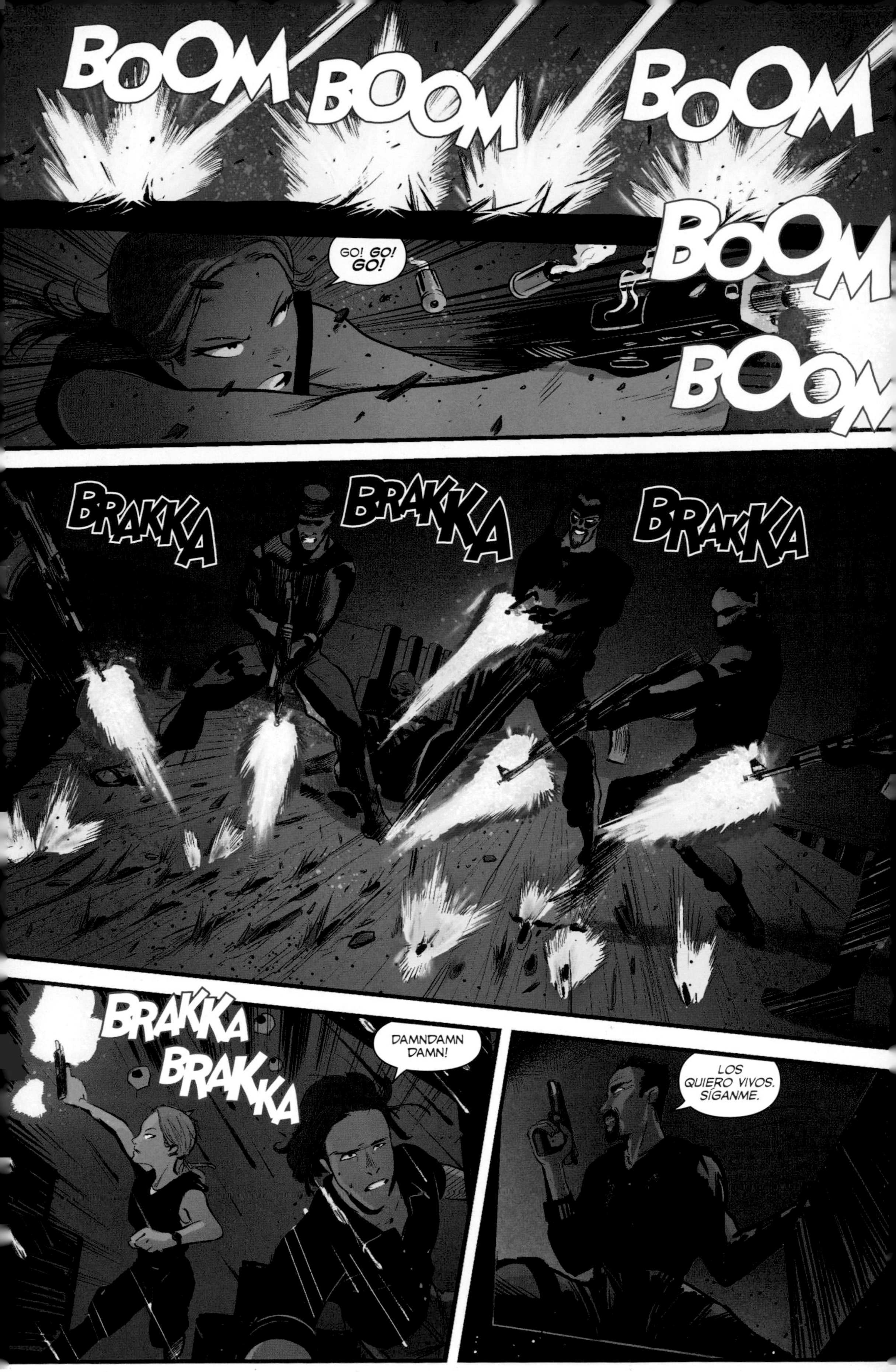
BOOM BOOM BOOM
GO! GO! GO!
BOOM
BOOM
BRAKKA
BRAKKA
BRAKKA
BRAKKA
BRAKKA
DAMNDAMN DAMN!
LOS QUIERO VIVOS. SÍGANME.

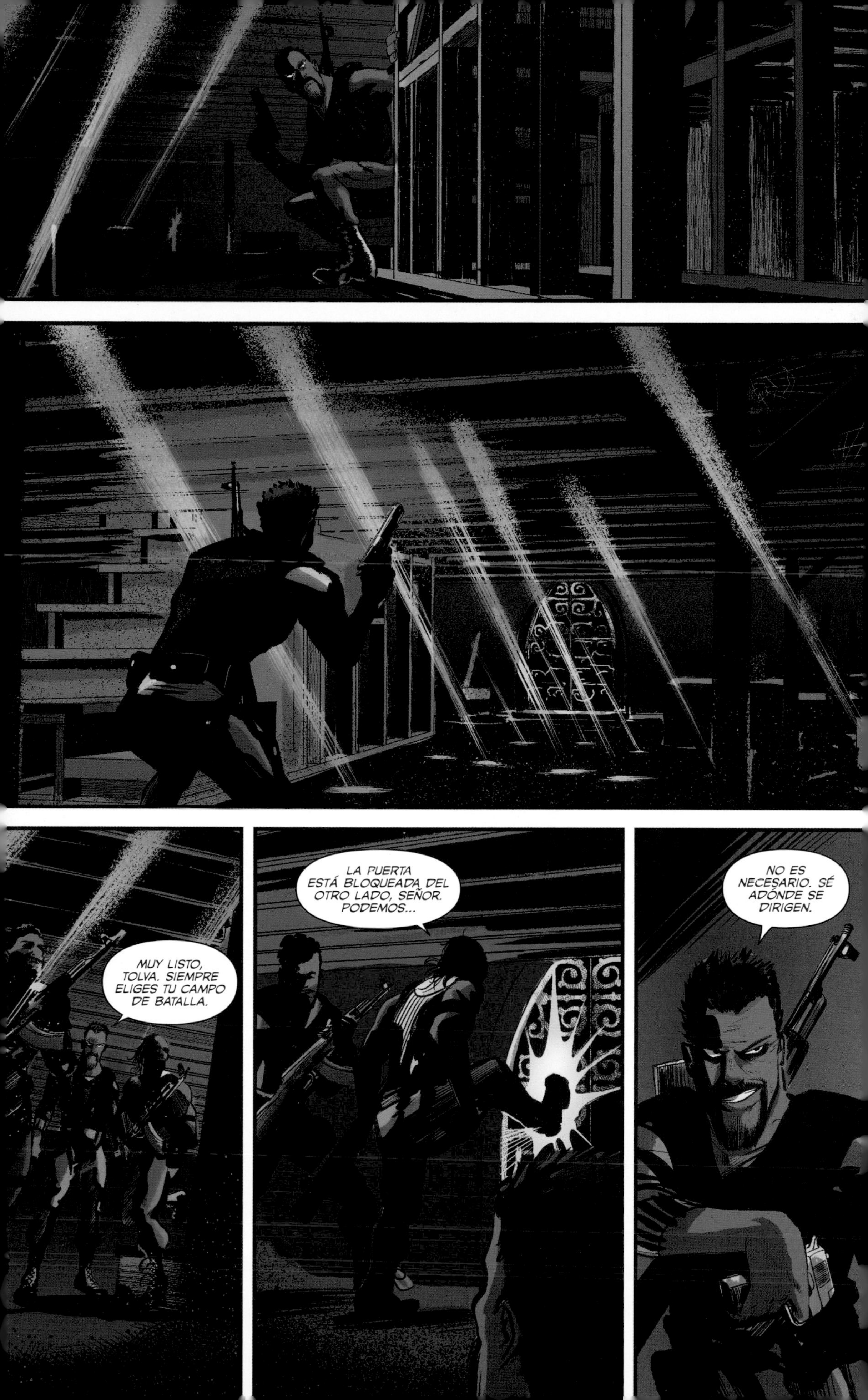
MUY LISTO, TOLVA. SIEMPRE ELIGES TU CAMPO DE BATALLA.
LA PUERTA ESTÁ BLOQUEADA DEL OTRO LADO, SEÑOR. PODEMOS...
NO ES NECESARIO. SÉ ADÓNDE SE DIRIGEN.

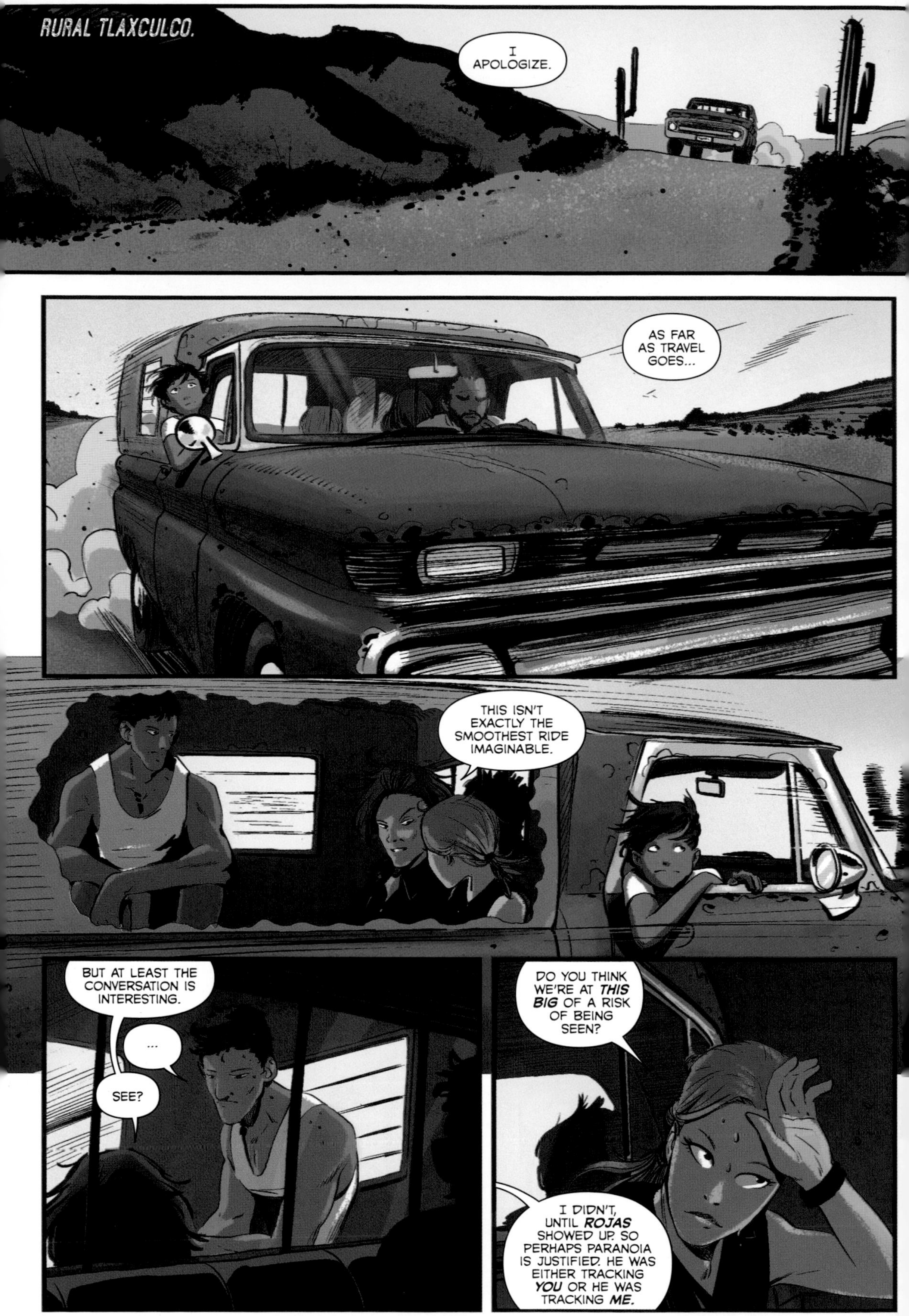
RURAL TLAXCULCO.
I APOLOGIZE.
AS FAR AS TRAVEL GOES...
THIS ISN'T EXACTLY THE SMOOTHEST RIDE IMAGINABLE.
BUT AT LEAST THE CONVERSATION IS INTERESTING.
...
SEE?
DO YOU THINK WE'RE AT THIS BIG OF A RISK OF BEING SEEN?
I DIDN'T, UNTIL ROJAS SHOWED UP. SO PERHAPS PARANOIA IS JUSTIFIED. HE WAS EITHER TRACKING YOU OR HE WAS TRACKING ME.

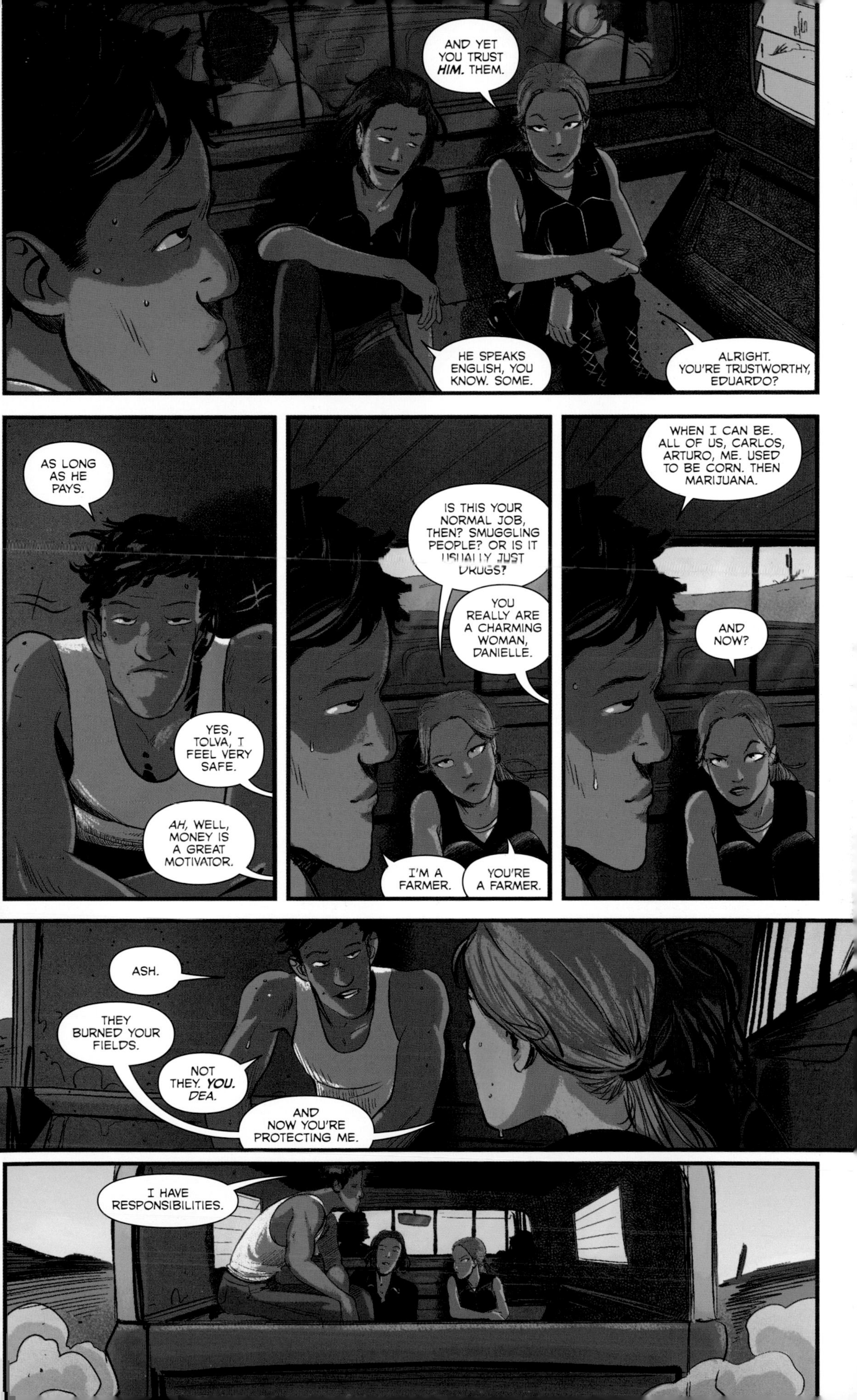

AND YET YOU TRUST *HIM.* THEM.
HE SPEAKS ENGLISH, YOU KNOW. SOME.
ALRIGHT. YOU'RE TRUSTWORTHY, EDUARDO?
AS LONG AS HE PAYS.
YES, TOLVA, I FEEL VERY SAFE.
AH, WELL, MONEY IS A GREAT MOTIVATOR.
IS THIS YOUR NORMAL JOB, THEN? SMUGGLING PEOPLE? OR IS IT USUALLY JUST DRUGS?
YOU REALLY ARE A CHARMING WOMAN, DANIELLE.
I'M A FARMER.
YOU'RE A FARMER.
WHEN I CAN BE. ALL OF US, CARLOS, ARTURO, ME. USED TO BE CORN. THEN MARIJUANA.
AND NOW?
ASH.
THEY BURNED YOUR FIELDS.
NOT THEY. ***YOU.*** *DEA.*
AND NOW YOU'RE PROTECTING ME.
I HAVE RESPONSIBILITIES.

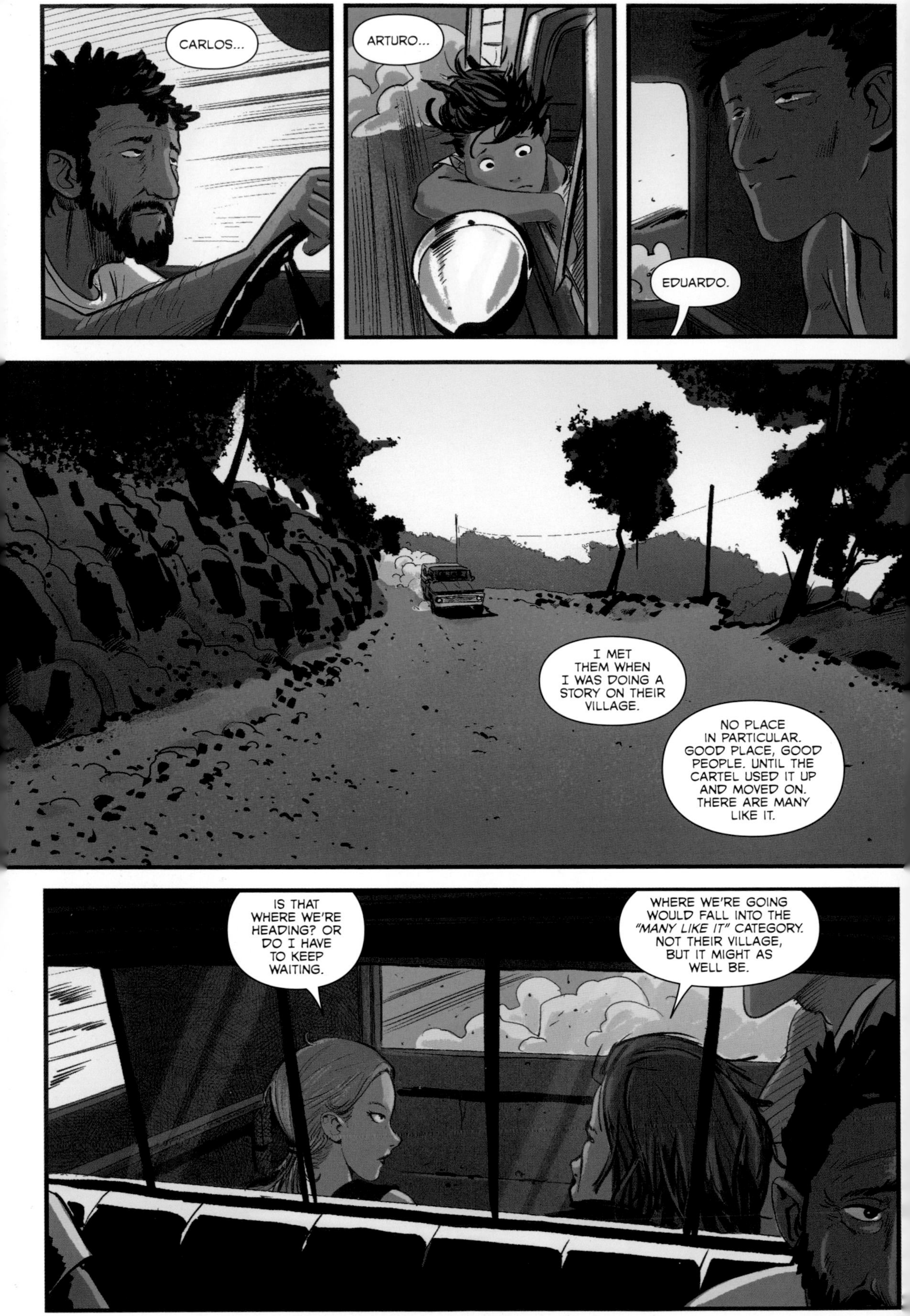
CARLOS...
ARTURO...
EDUARDO.
I MET THEM WHEN I WAS DOING A STORY ON THEIR VILLAGE.
NO PLACE IN PARTICULAR. GOOD PLACE, GOOD PEOPLE. UNTIL THE CARTEL USED IT UP AND MOVED ON. THERE ARE MANY LIKE IT.
IS THAT WHERE WE'RE HEADING? OR DO I HAVE TO KEEP WAITING.
WHERE WE'RE GOING WOULD FALL INTO THE *"MANY LIKE IT"* CATEGORY. NOT THEIR VILLAGE, BUT IT MIGHT AS WELL BE.

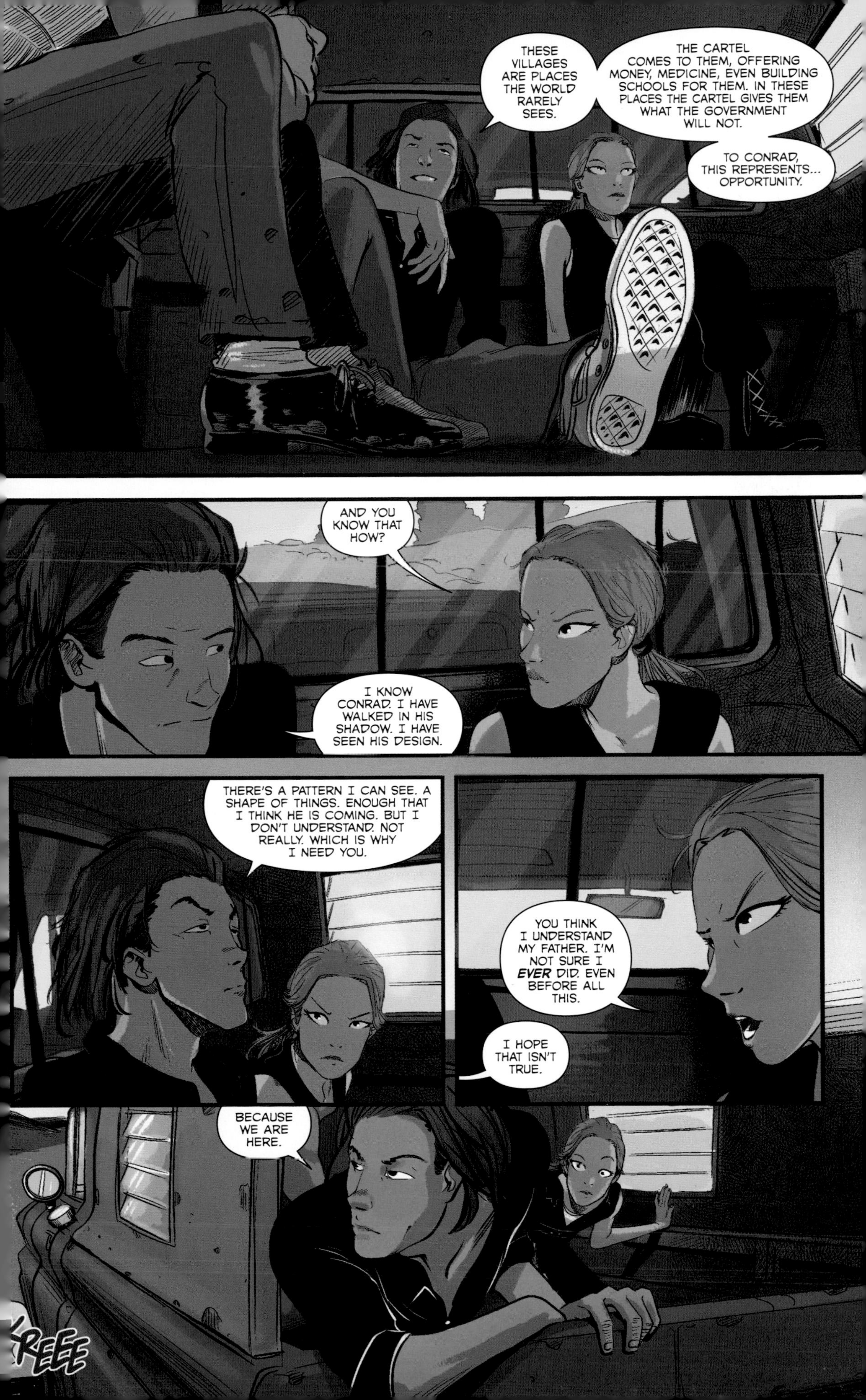
THESE VILLAGES ARE PLACES THE WORLD RARELY SEES.
THE CARTEL COMES TO THEM, OFFERING MONEY, MEDICINE, EVEN BUILDING SCHOOLS FOR THEM. IN THESE PLACES THE CARTEL GIVES THEM WHAT THE GOVERNMENT WILL NOT.
TO CONRAD, THIS REPRESENTS... OPPORTUNITY.
AND YOU KNOW THAT HOW?
I KNOW CONRAD. I HAVE WALKED IN HIS SHADOW. I HAVE SEEN HIS DESIGN.
THERE'S A PATTERN I CAN SEE. A SHAPE OF THINGS. ENOUGH THAT I THINK HE IS COMING. BUT I DON'T UNDERSTAND. NOT REALLY. WHICH IS WHY I NEED YOU.
YOU THINK I UNDERSTAND MY FATHER. I'M NOT SURE I *EVER* DID. EVEN BEFORE ALL THIS.
I HOPE THAT ISN'T TRUE.
BECAUSE WE ARE HERE.
REEE

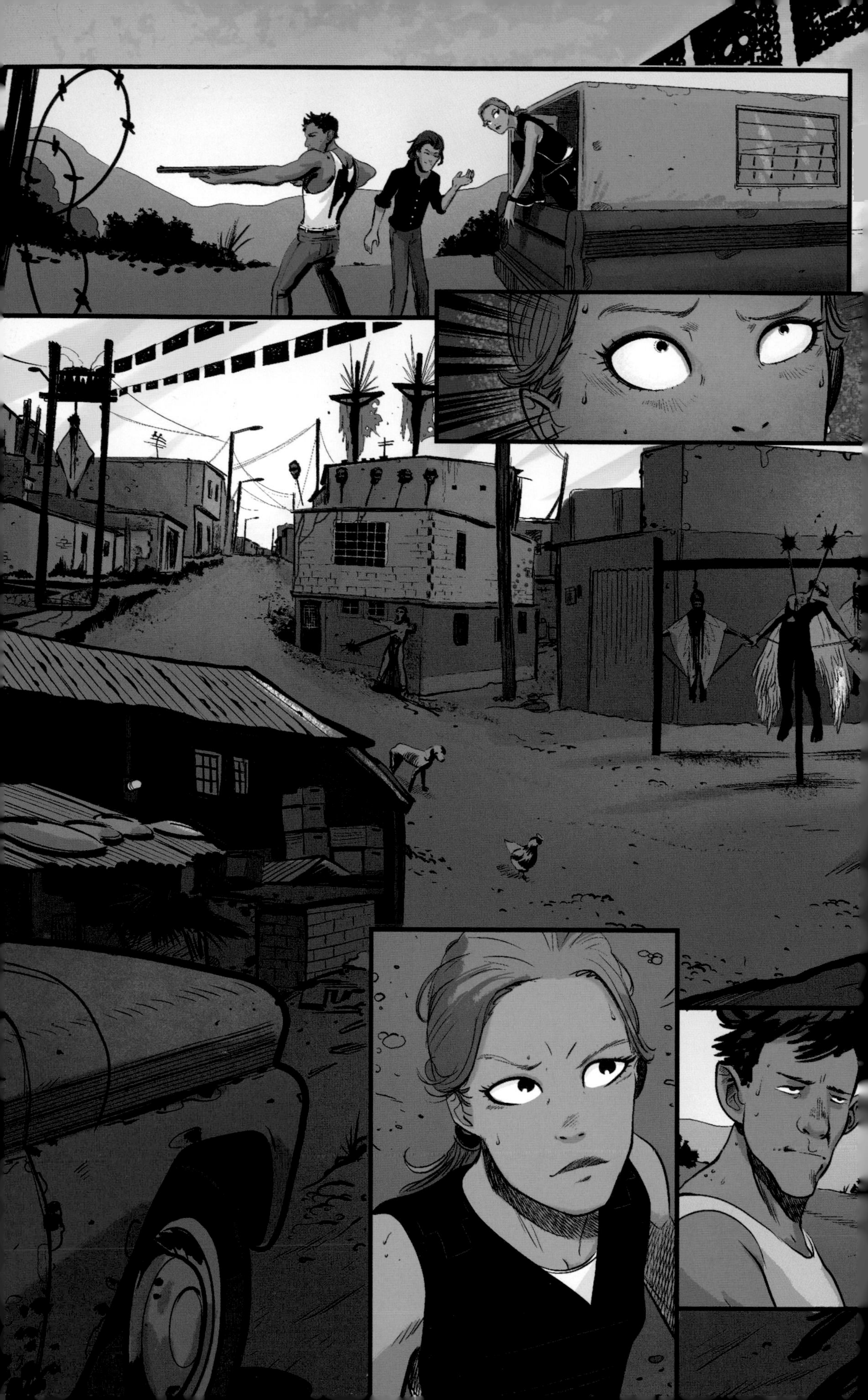

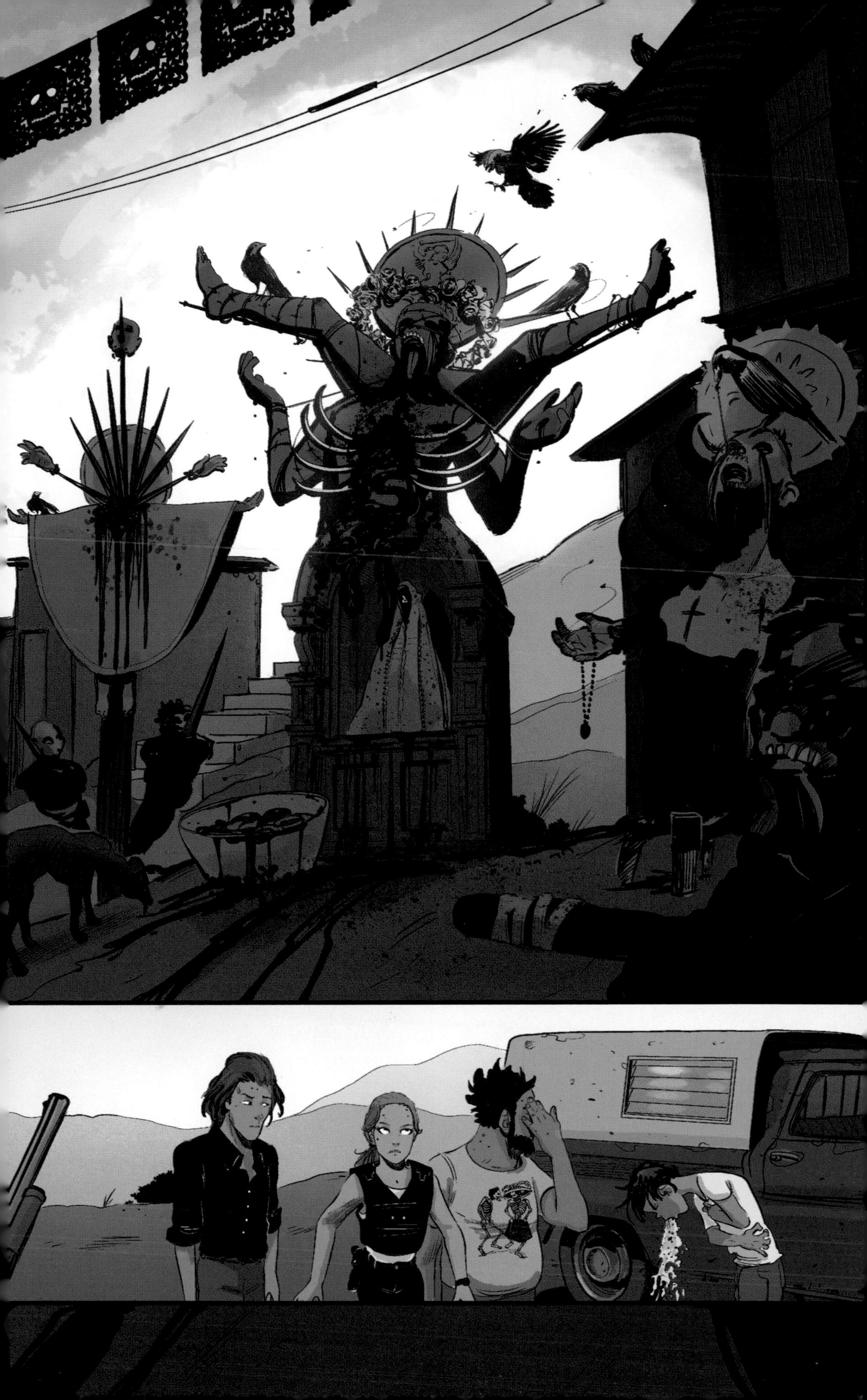

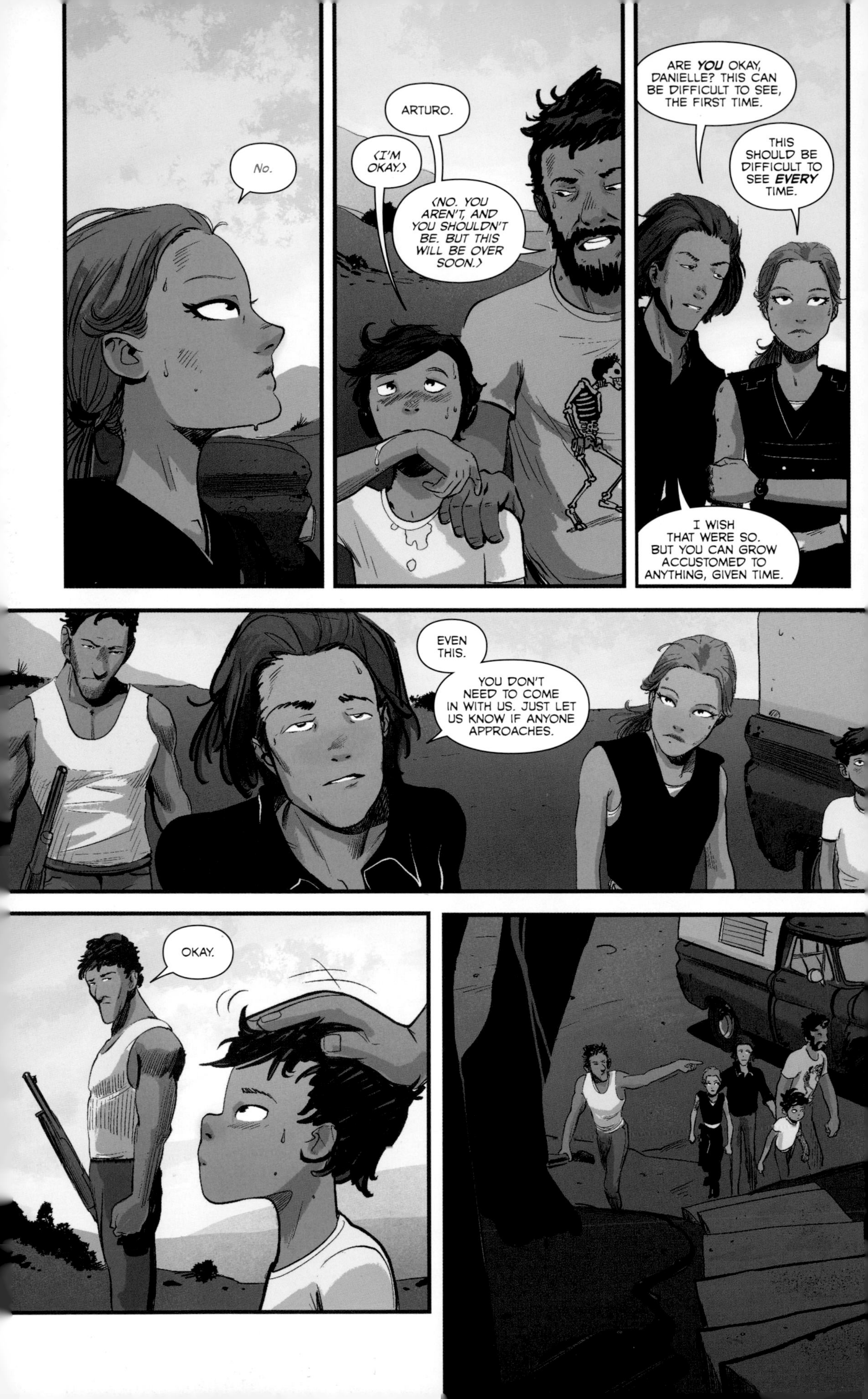
No.
ARTURO.
⟨I'M OKAY.⟩
⟨NO. YOU AREN'T, AND YOU SHOULDN'T BE. BUT THIS WILL BE OVER SOON.⟩
ARE YOU OKAY, DANIELLE? THIS CAN BE DIFFICULT TO SEE, THE FIRST TIME.
THIS SHOULD BE DIFFICULT TO SEE EVERY TIME.
I WISH THAT WERE SO. BUT YOU CAN GROW ACCUSTOMED TO ANYTHING, GIVEN TIME.
EVEN THIS.
YOU DON'T NEED TO COME IN WITH US. JUST LET US KNOW IF ANYONE APPROACHES.
OKAY.

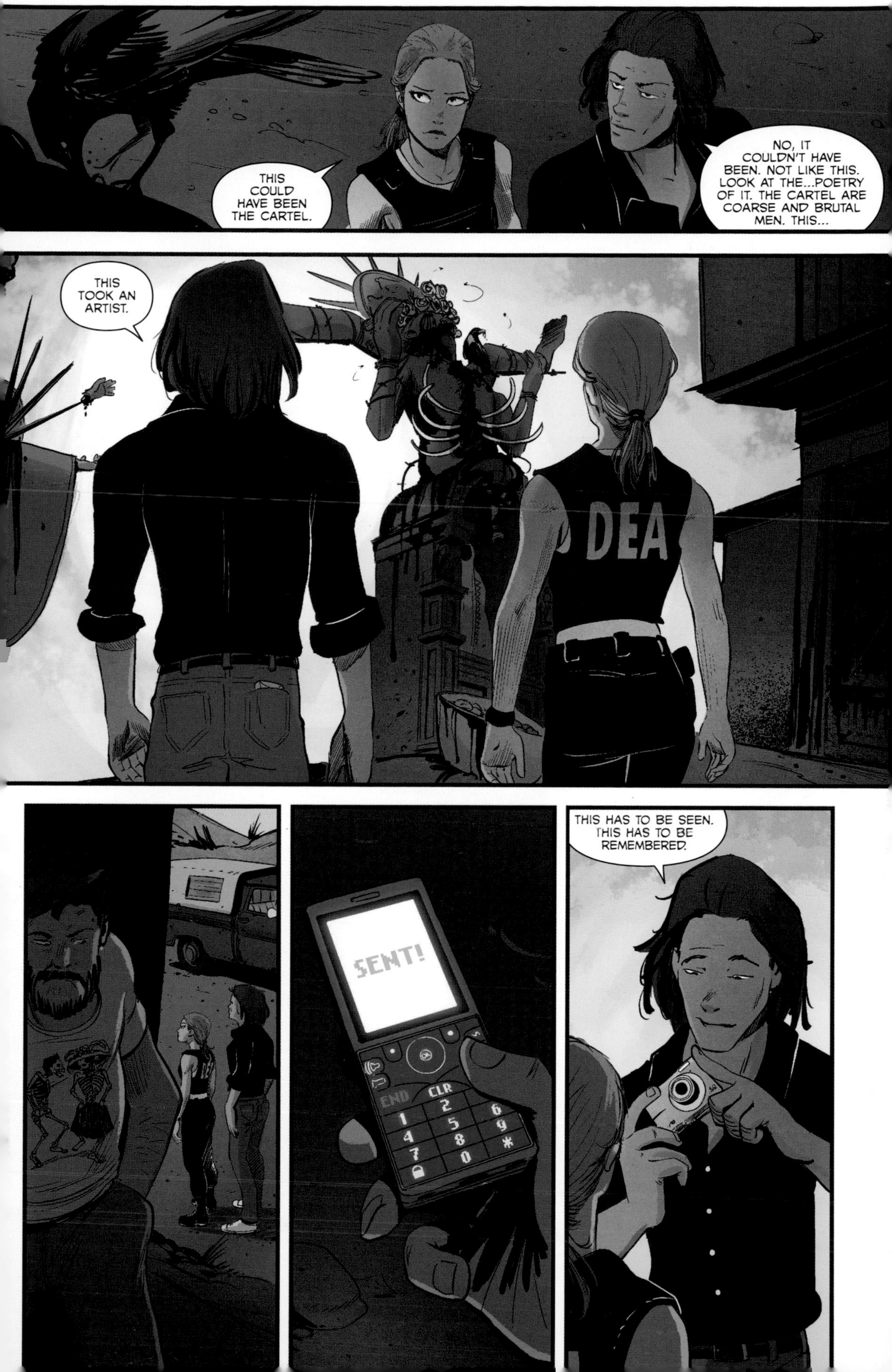
THIS COULD HAVE BEEN THE CARTEL.
NO, IT COULDN'T HAVE BEEN. NOT LIKE THIS. LOOK AT THE...POETRY OF IT. THE CARTEL ARE COARSE AND BRUTAL MEN. THIS...
THIS TOOK AN ARTIST.
DEA
SENT!
THIS HAS TO BE SEEN. THIS HAS TO BE REMEMBERED.

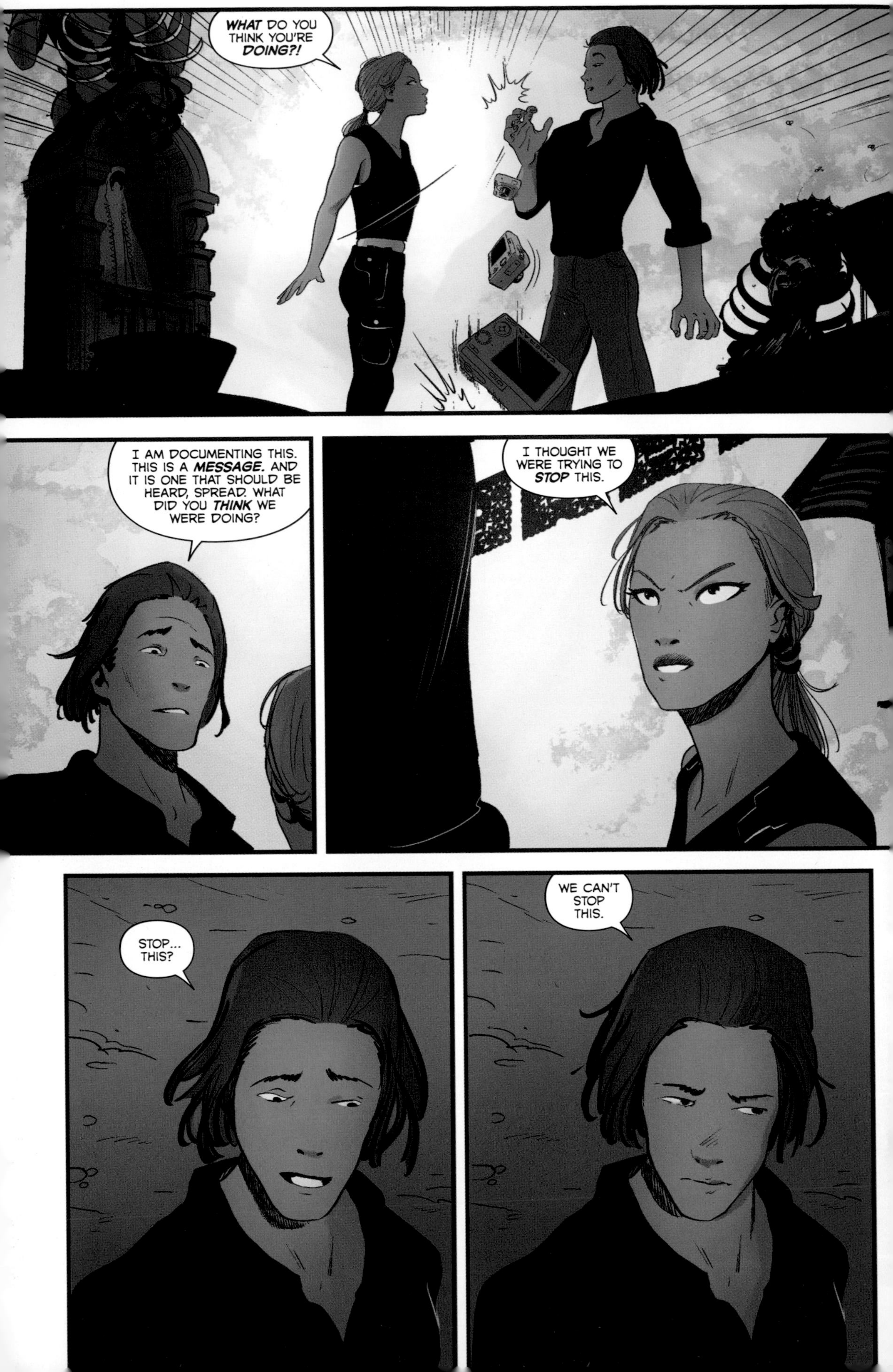
WHAT DO YOU THINK YOU'RE DOING?!
I AM DOCUMENTING THIS. THIS IS A MESSAGE. AND IT IS ONE THAT SHOULD BE HEARD, SPREAD. WHAT DID YOU THINK WE WERE DOING?
I THOUGHT WE WERE TRYING TO STOP THIS.
STOP... THIS?
WE CAN'T STOP THIS.

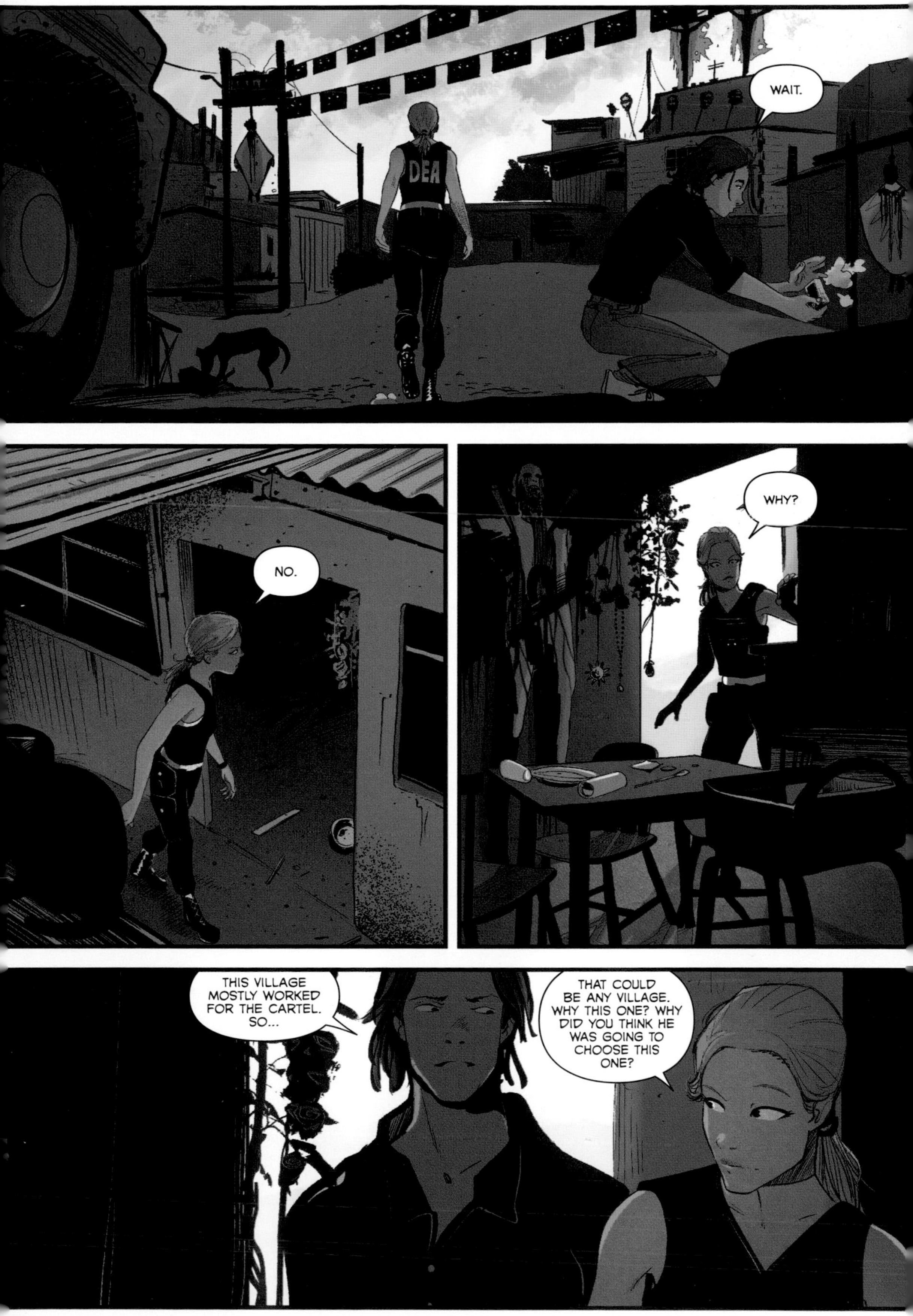
WAIT.
NO.
WHY?
THIS VILLAGE MOSTLY WORKED FOR THE CARTEL. SO...
THAT COULD BE ANY VILLAGE. WHY THIS ONE? WHY DID YOU THINK HE WAS GOING TO CHOOSE THIS ONE?
DEA

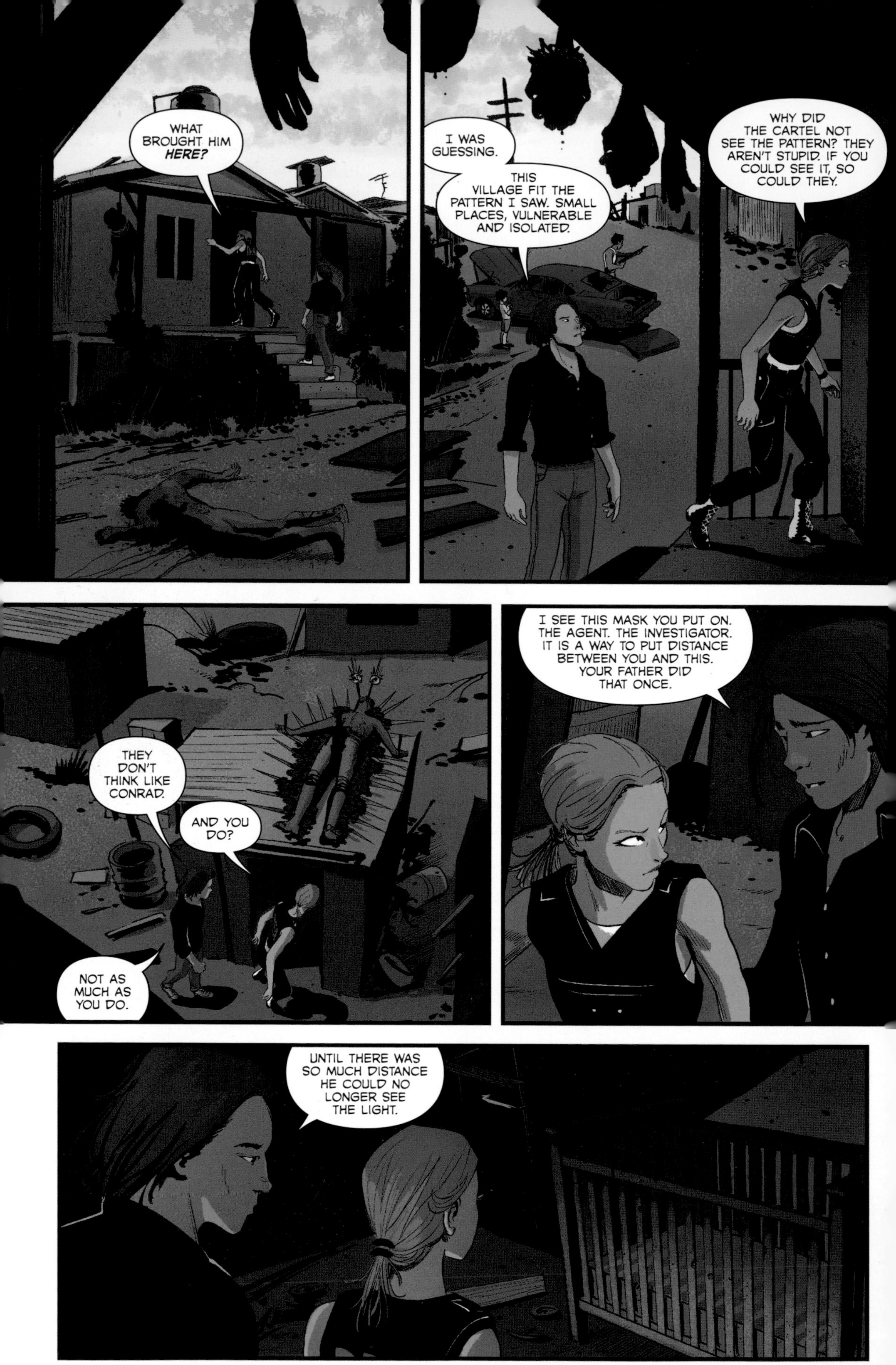
WHAT BROUGHT HIM *HERE?*
I WAS GUESSING.
THIS VILLAGE FIT THE PATTERN I SAW. SMALL PLACES, VULNERABLE AND ISOLATED.
WHY DID THE CARTEL NOT SEE THE PATTERN? THEY AREN'T STUPID. IF YOU COULD SEE IT, SO COULD THEY.
THEY DON'T THINK LIKE CONRAD.
AND YOU DO?
NOT AS MUCH AS YOU DO.
I SEE THIS MASK YOU PUT ON. THE AGENT. THE INVESTIGATOR. IT IS A WAY TO PUT DISTANCE BETWEEN YOU AND THIS. YOUR FATHER DID THAT ONCE.
UNTIL THERE WAS SO MUCH DISTANCE HE COULD NO LONGER SEE THE LIGHT.

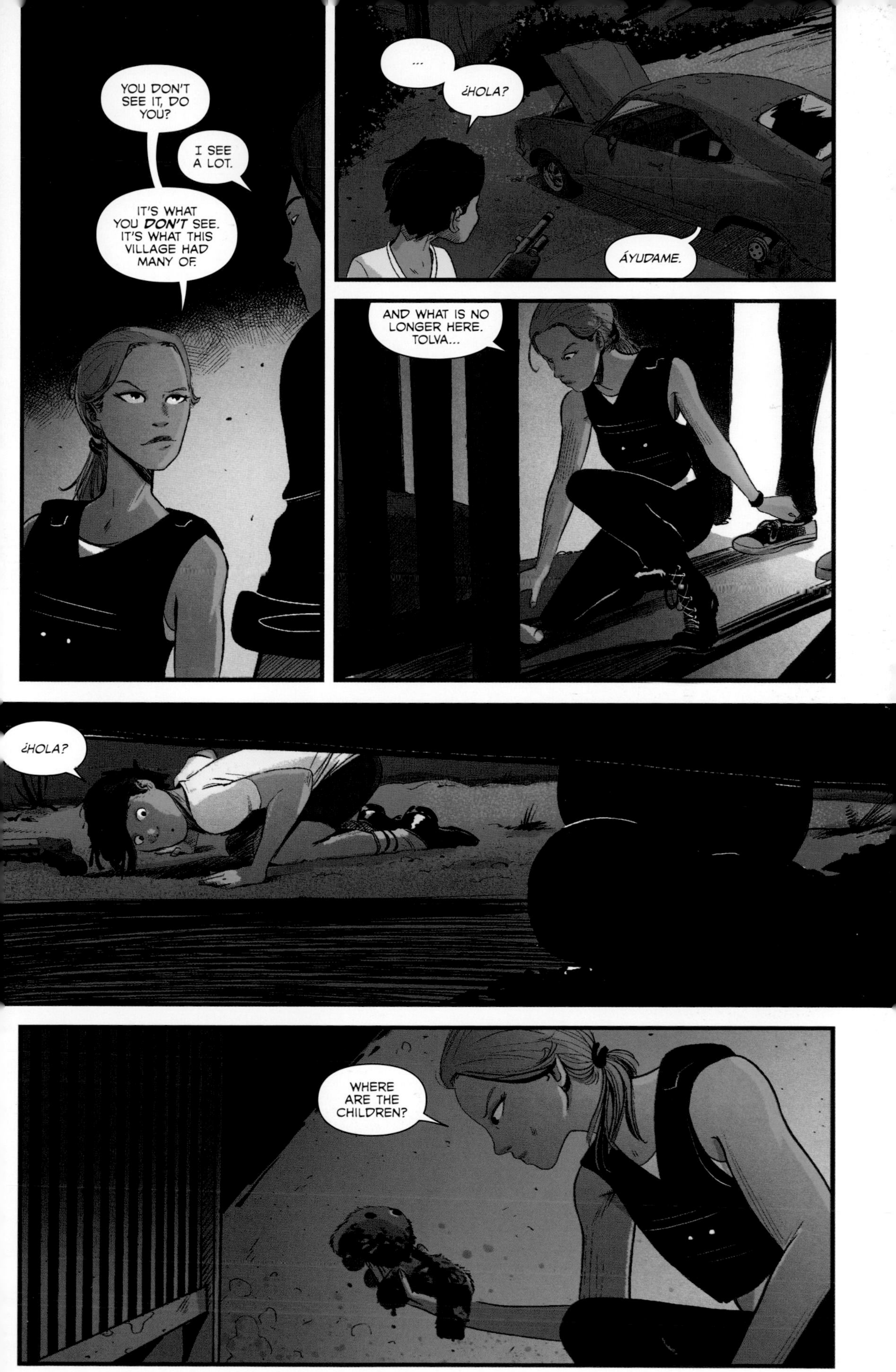
YOU DON'T SEE IT, DO YOU?
I SEE A LOT.
IT'S WHAT YOU DON'T SEE. IT'S WHAT THIS VILLAGE HAD MANY OF.
...
¿HOLA?
ÁYUDAME.
AND WHAT IS NO LONGER HERE. TOLVA...
¿HOLA?
WHERE ARE THE CHILDREN?

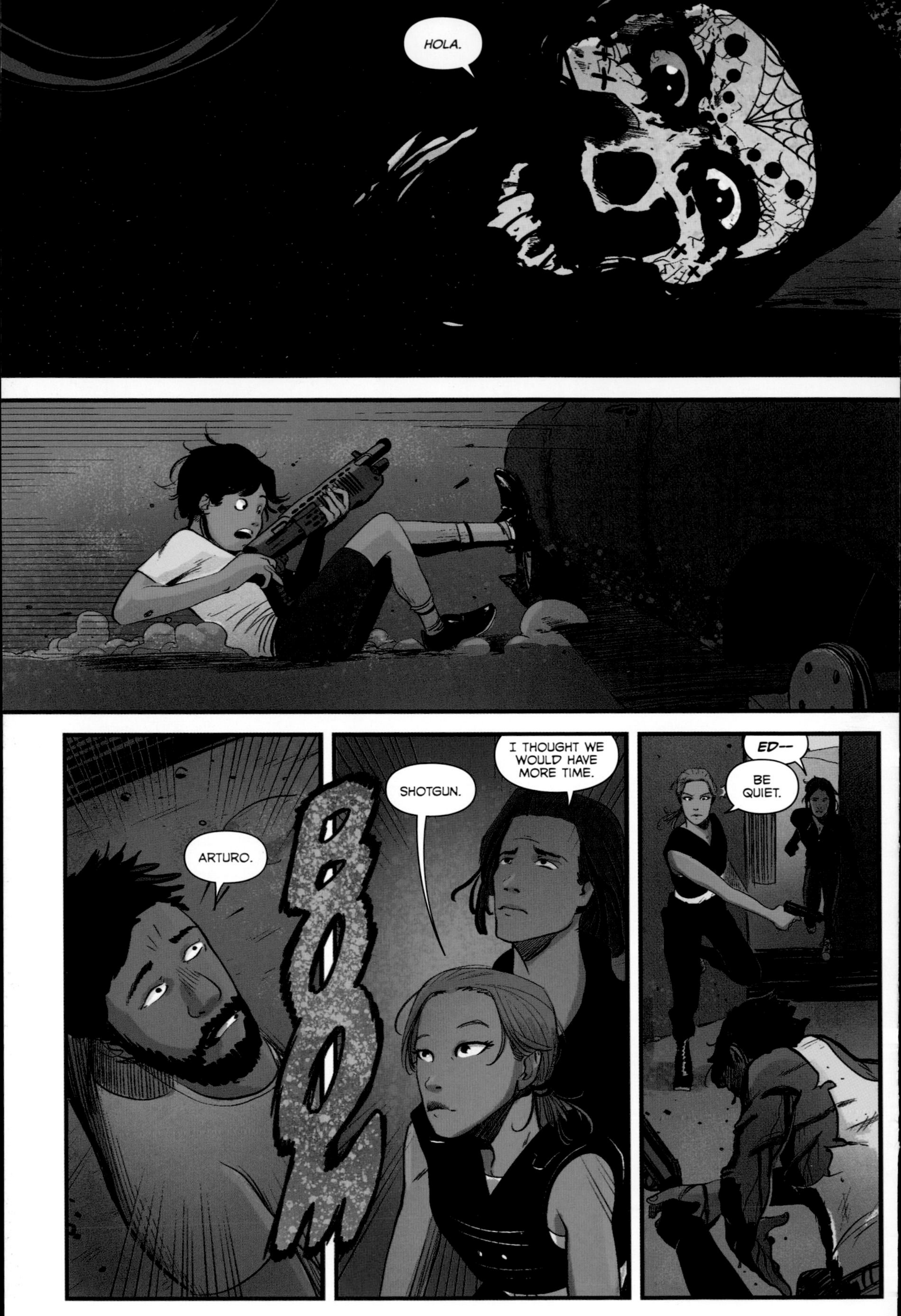
HOLA.
ARTURO.
BOOM
SHOTGUN.
I THOUGHT WE WOULD HAVE MORE TIME.
ED--
BE QUIET.

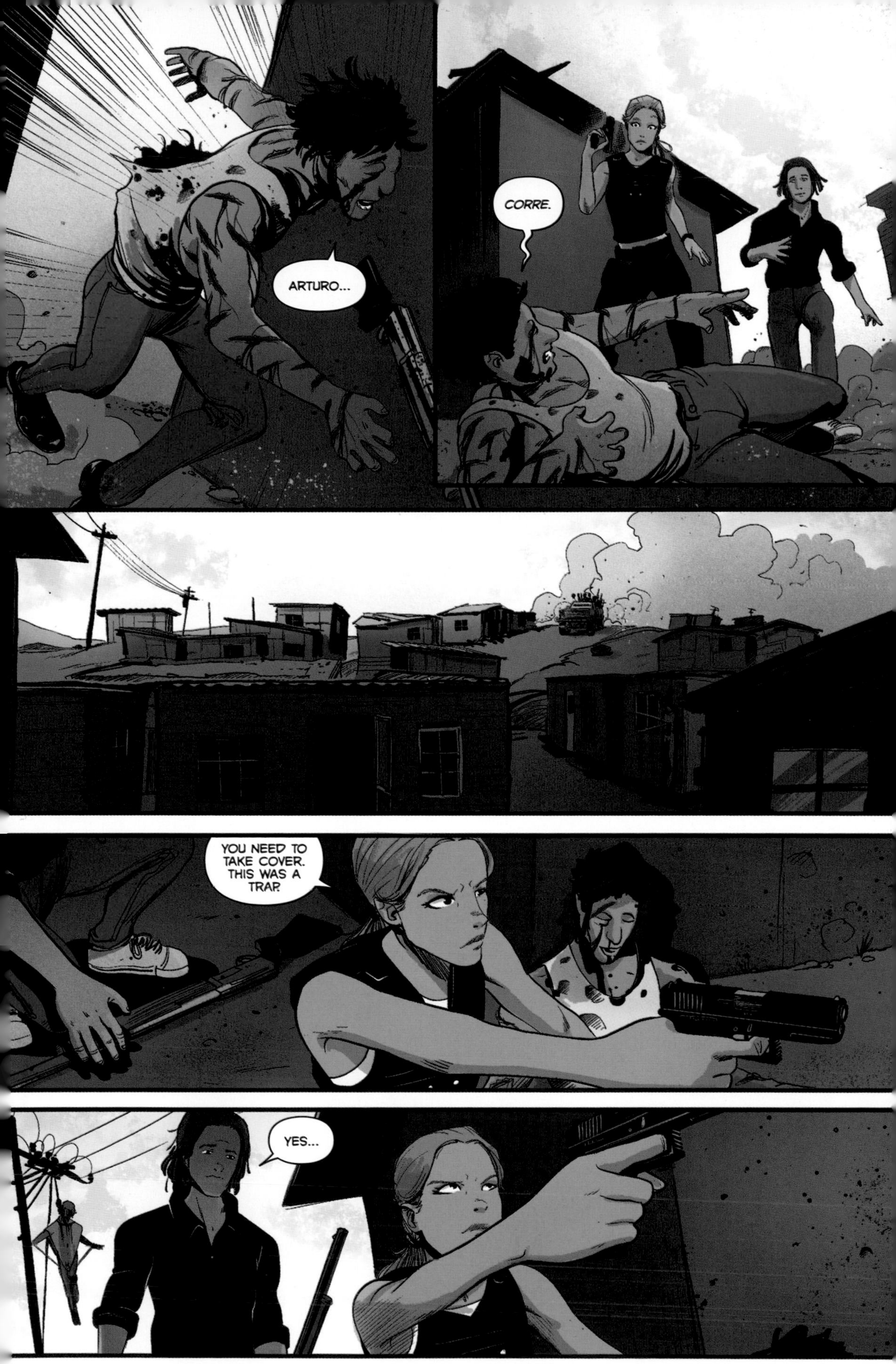
ARTURO...
CORRE.
YOU NEED TO TAKE COVER. THIS WAS A TRAP.
YES...

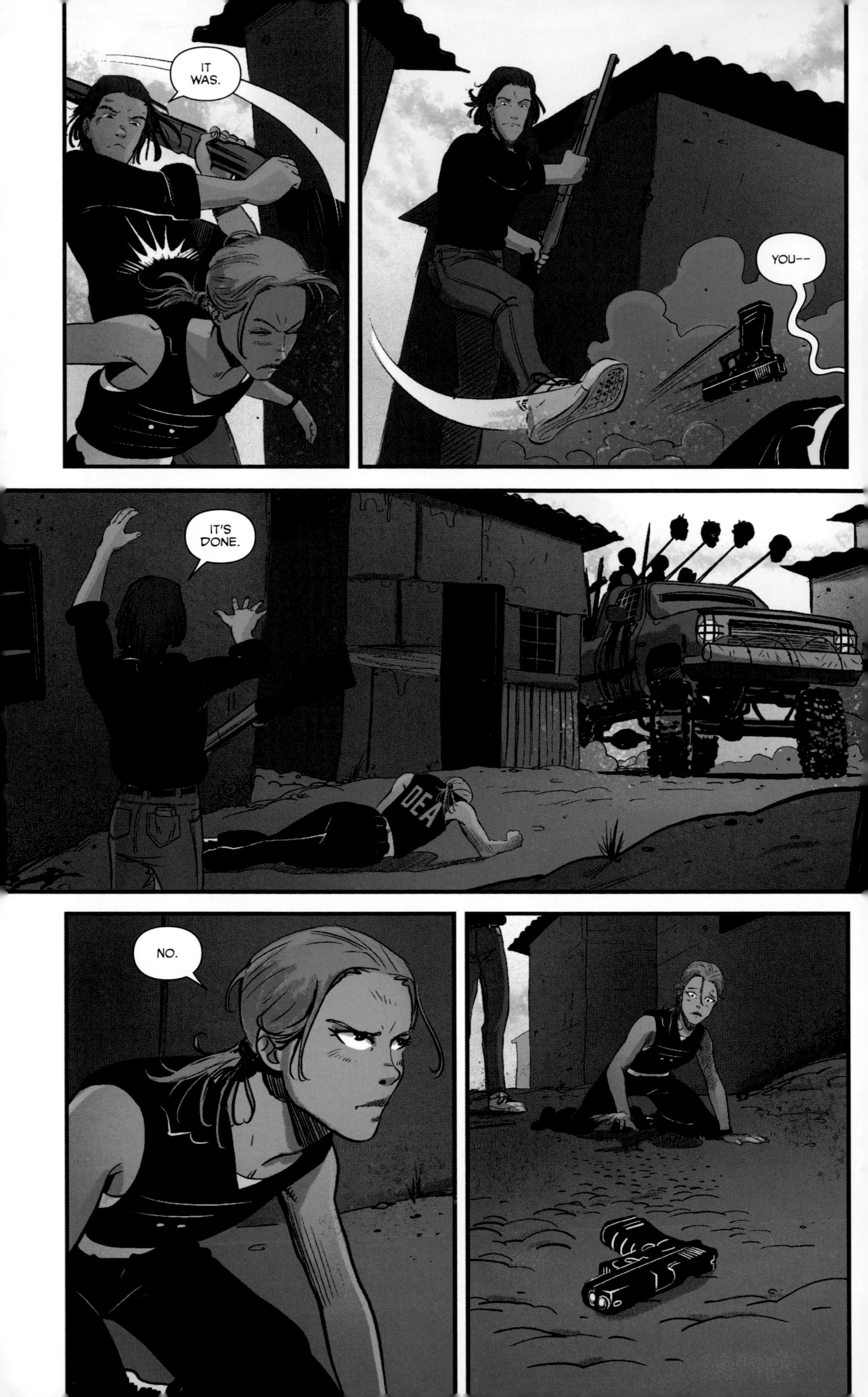
IT WAS.
YOU--
IT'S DONE.
DEA
NO.

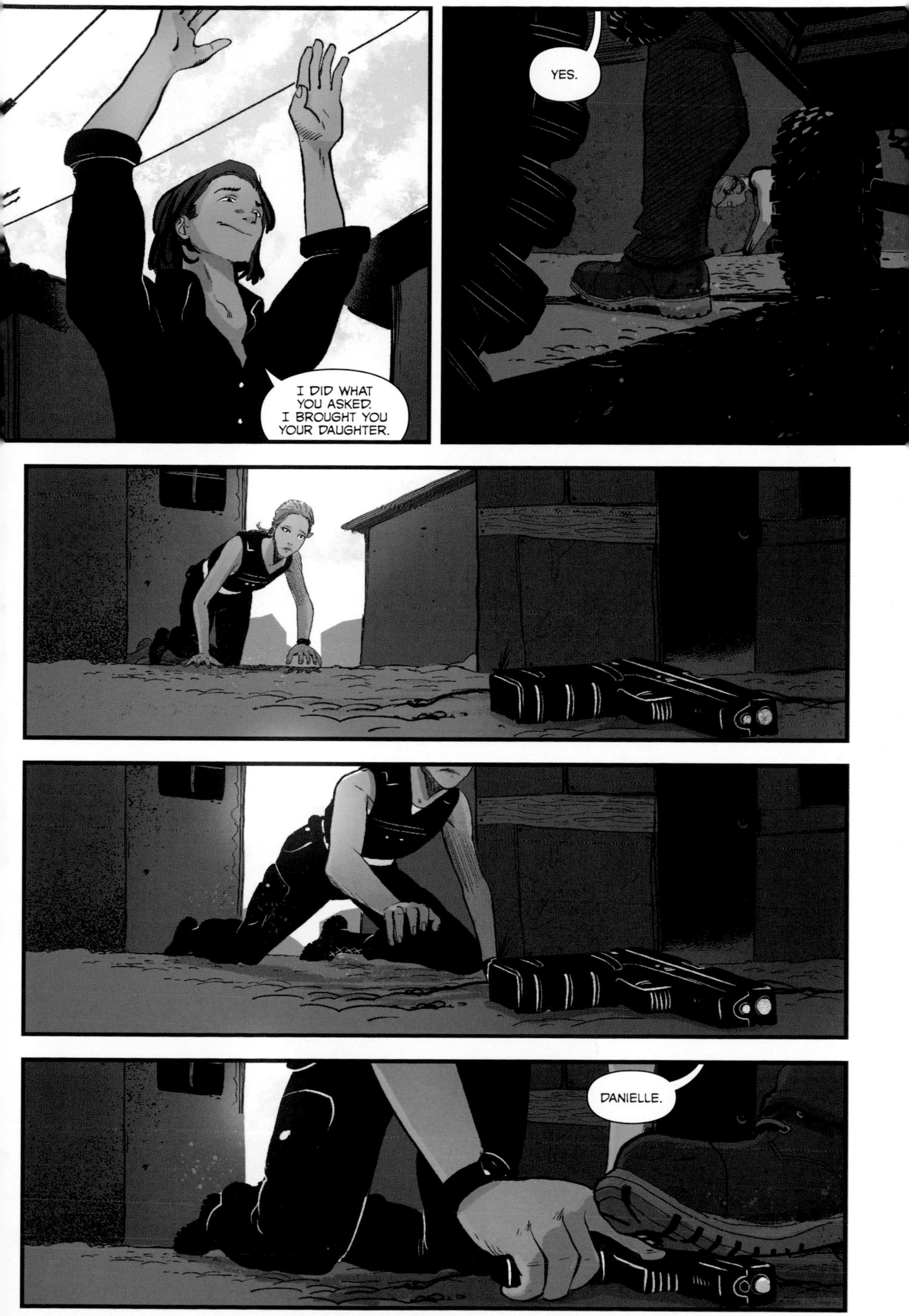
I DID WHAT YOU ASKED. I BROUGHT YOU YOUR DAUGHTER.
YES.
DANIELLE.

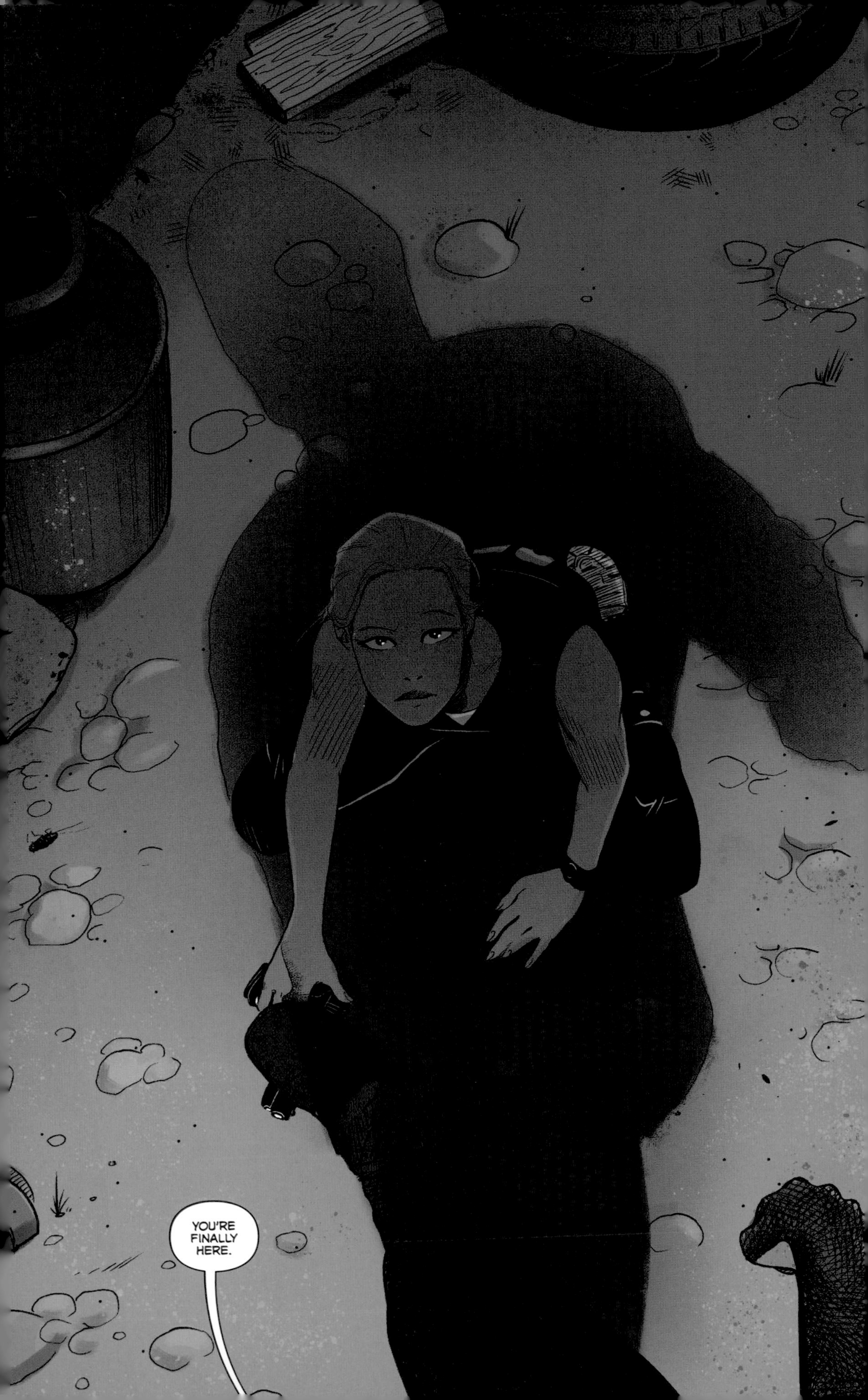
YOU'RE FINALLY HERE.

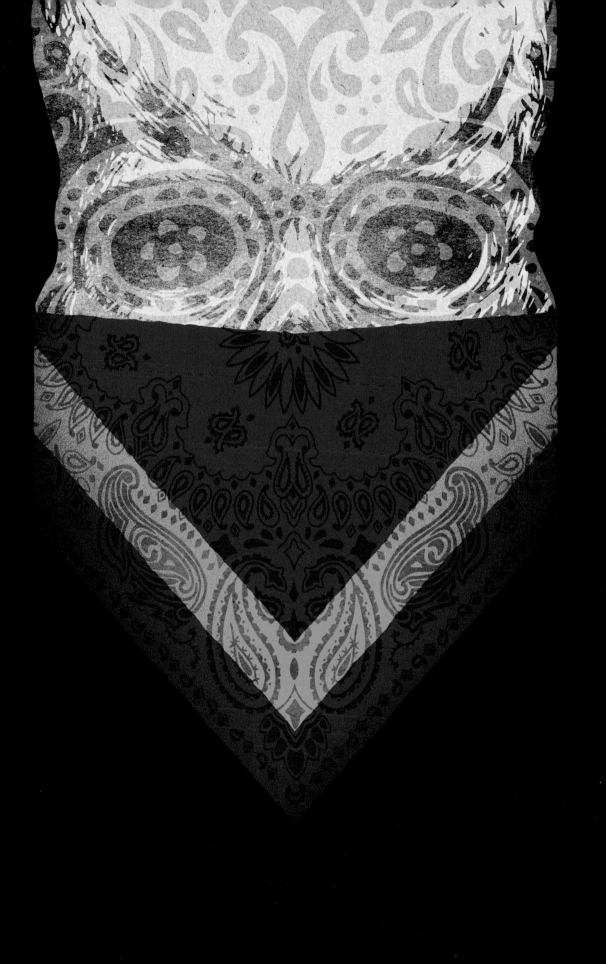

CHAPTER

THREE

CAPÍTULO TRES

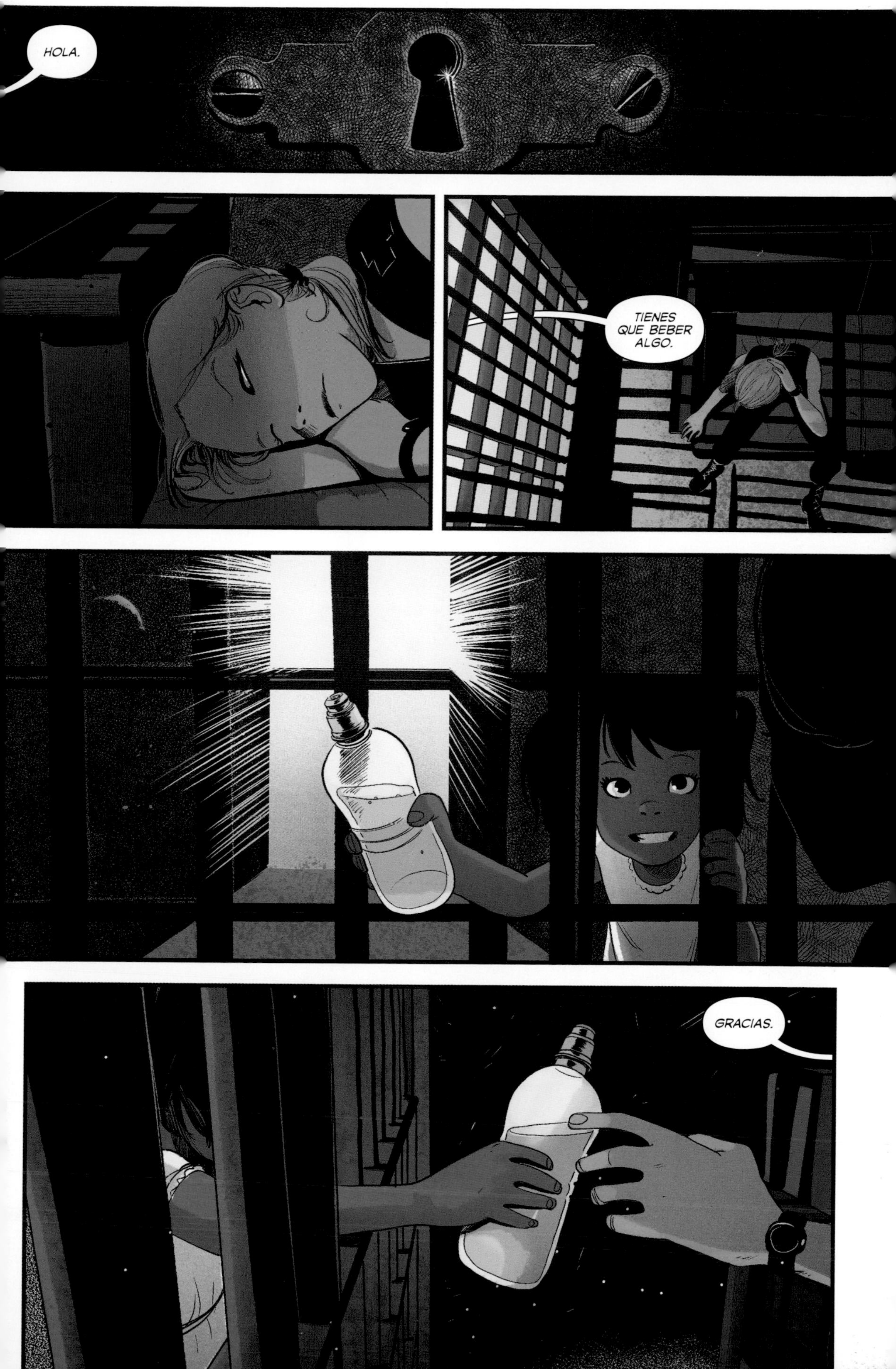
HOLA.
TIENES QUE BEBER ALGO.
GRACIAS.

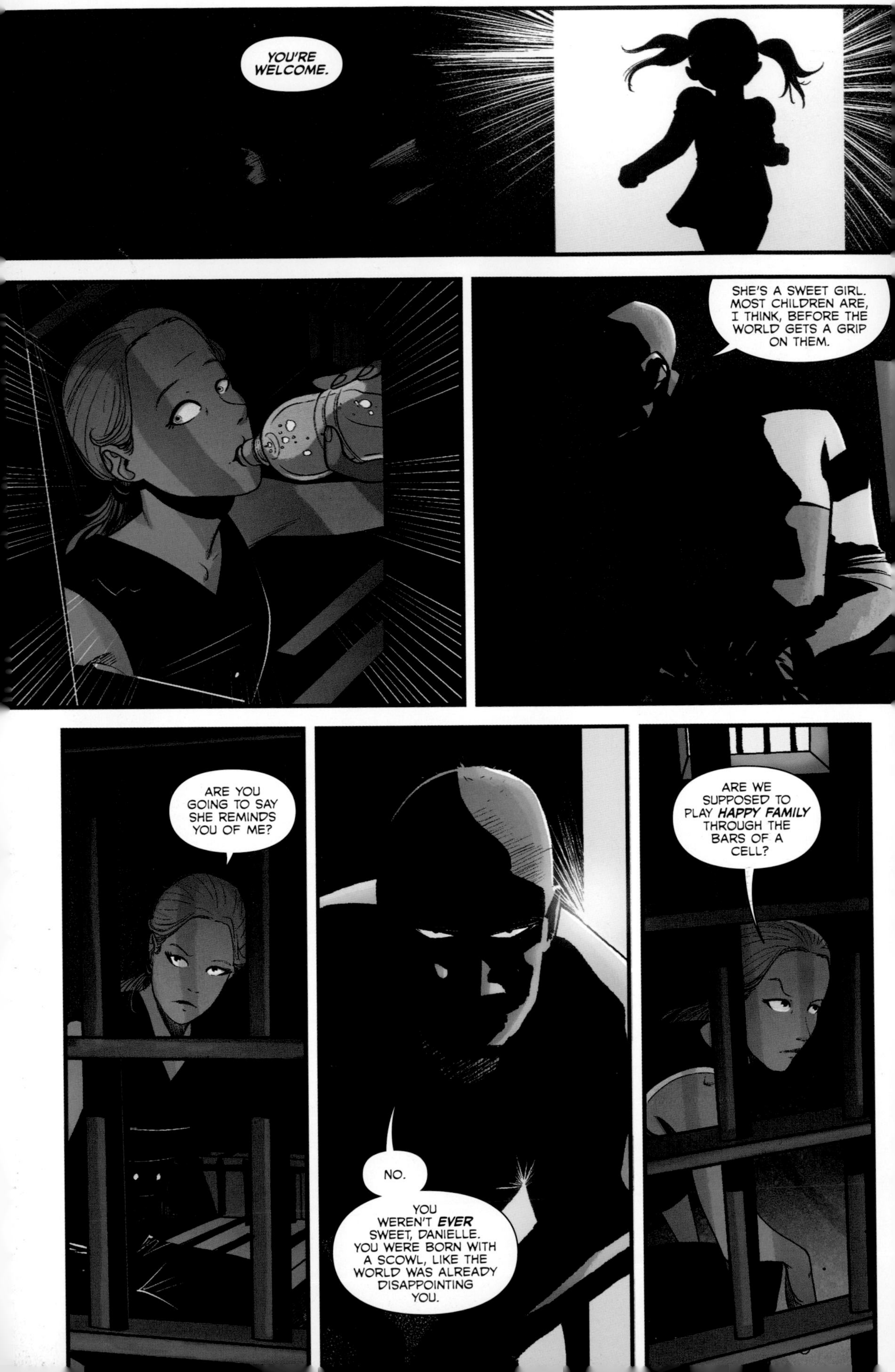
YOU'RE WELCOME.
SHE'S A SWEET GIRL. MOST CHILDREN ARE, I THINK, BEFORE THE WORLD GETS A GRIP ON THEM.
ARE YOU GOING TO SAY SHE REMINDS YOU OF ME?
NO.
YOU WEREN'T EVER SWEET, DANIELLE. YOU WERE BORN WITH A SCOWL, LIKE THE WORLD WAS ALREADY DISAPPOINTING YOU.
ARE WE SUPPOSED TO PLAY HAPPY FAMILY THROUGH THE BARS OF A CELL?

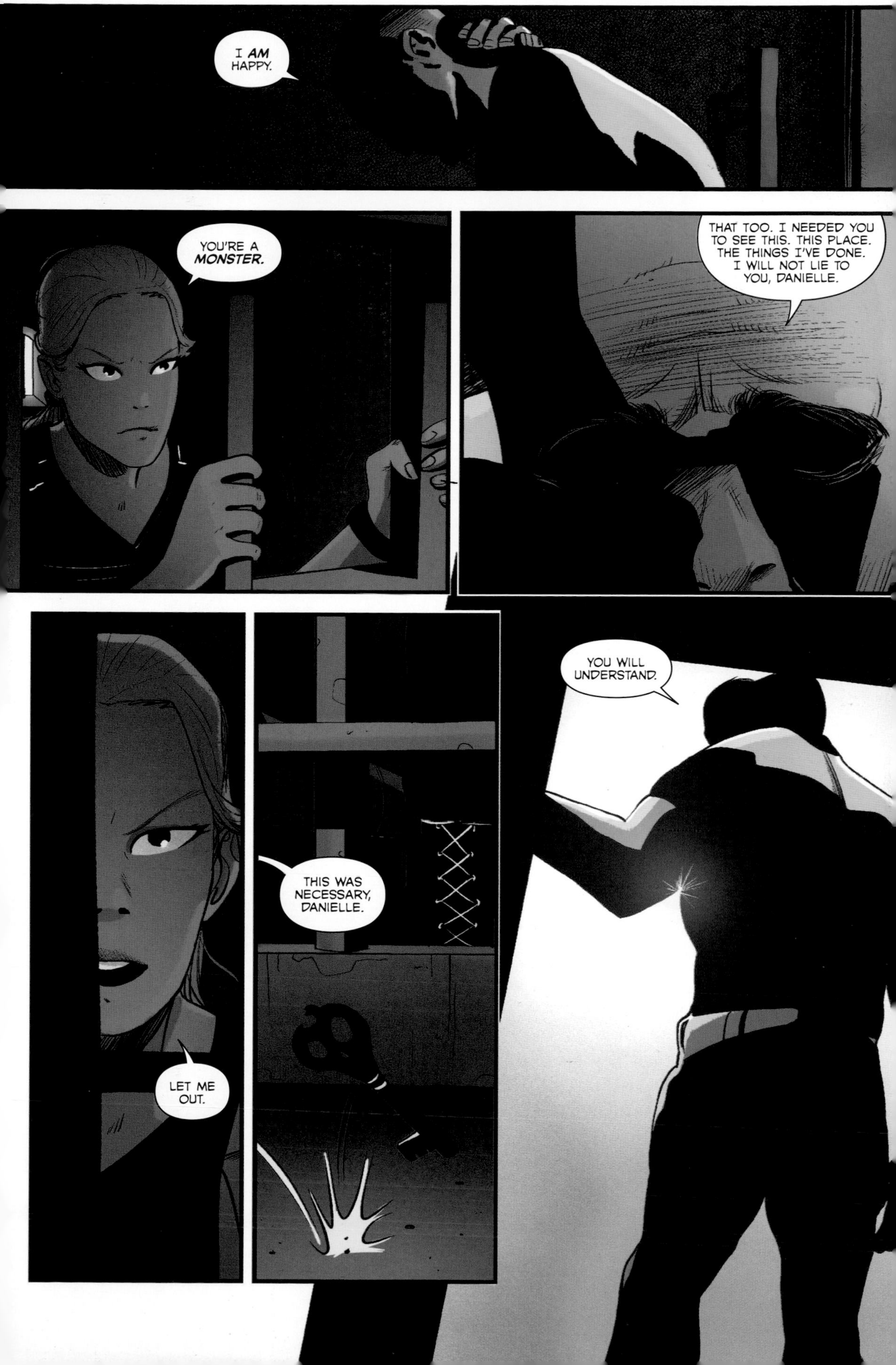
I AM HAPPY.
YOU'RE A MONSTER.
THAT TOO. I NEEDED YOU TO SEE THIS. THIS PLACE. THE THINGS I'VE DONE. I WILL NOT LIE TO YOU, DANIELLE.
LET ME OUT.
THIS WAS NECESSARY, DANIELLE.
YOU WILL UNDERSTAND.

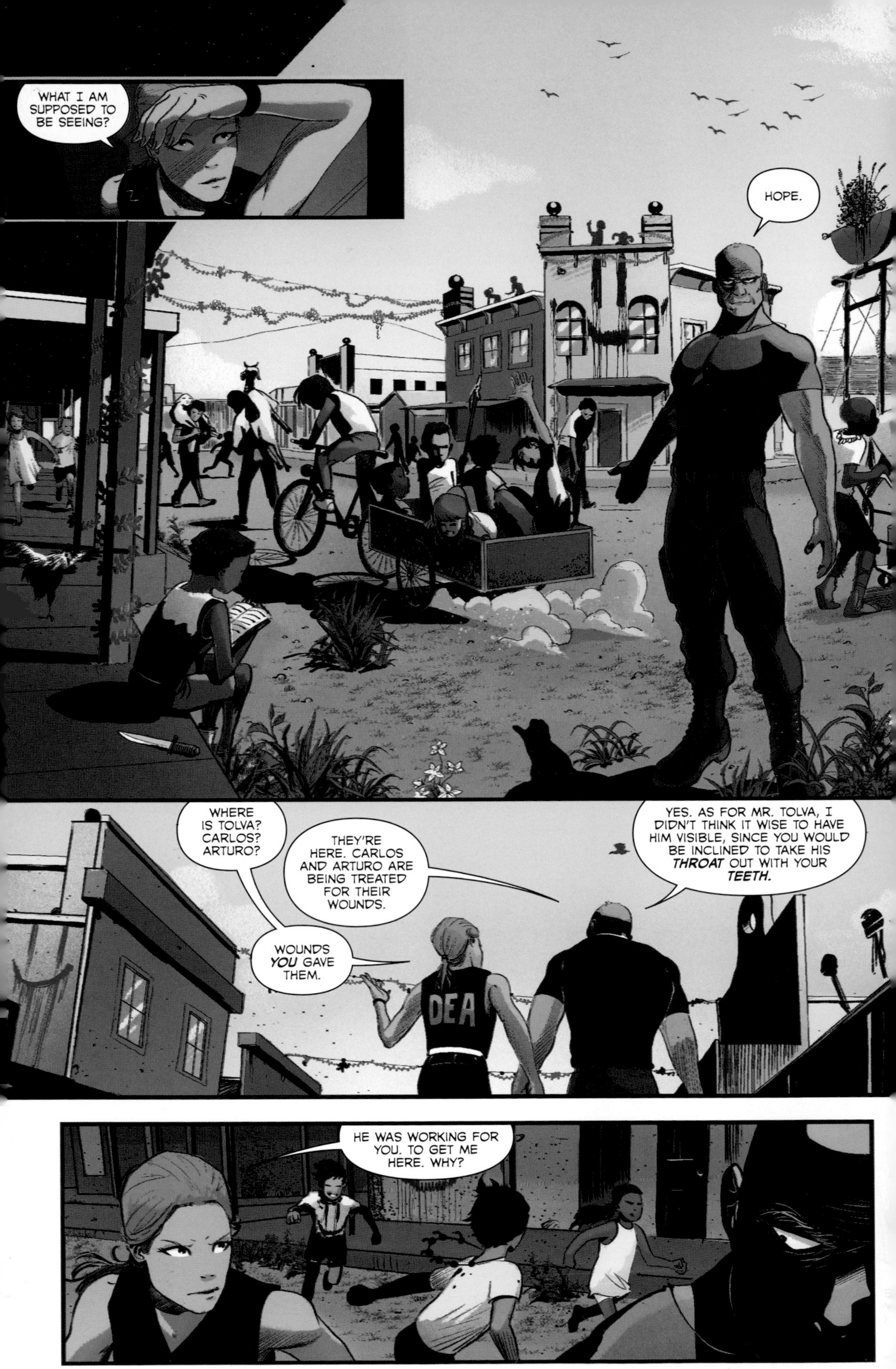
WHAT I AM SUPPOSED TO BE SEEING?
HOPE.
WHERE IS TOLVA? CARLOS? ARTURO?
THEY'RE HERE. CARLOS AND ARTURO ARE BEING TREATED FOR THEIR WOUNDS.
WOUNDS YOU GAVE THEM.
YES. AS FOR MR. TOLVA, I DIDN'T THINK IT WISE TO HAVE HIM VISIBLE, SINCE YOU WOULD BE INCLINED TO TAKE HIS THROAT OUT WITH YOUR TEETH.
DEA
HE WAS WORKING FOR YOU. TO GET ME HERE. WHY?

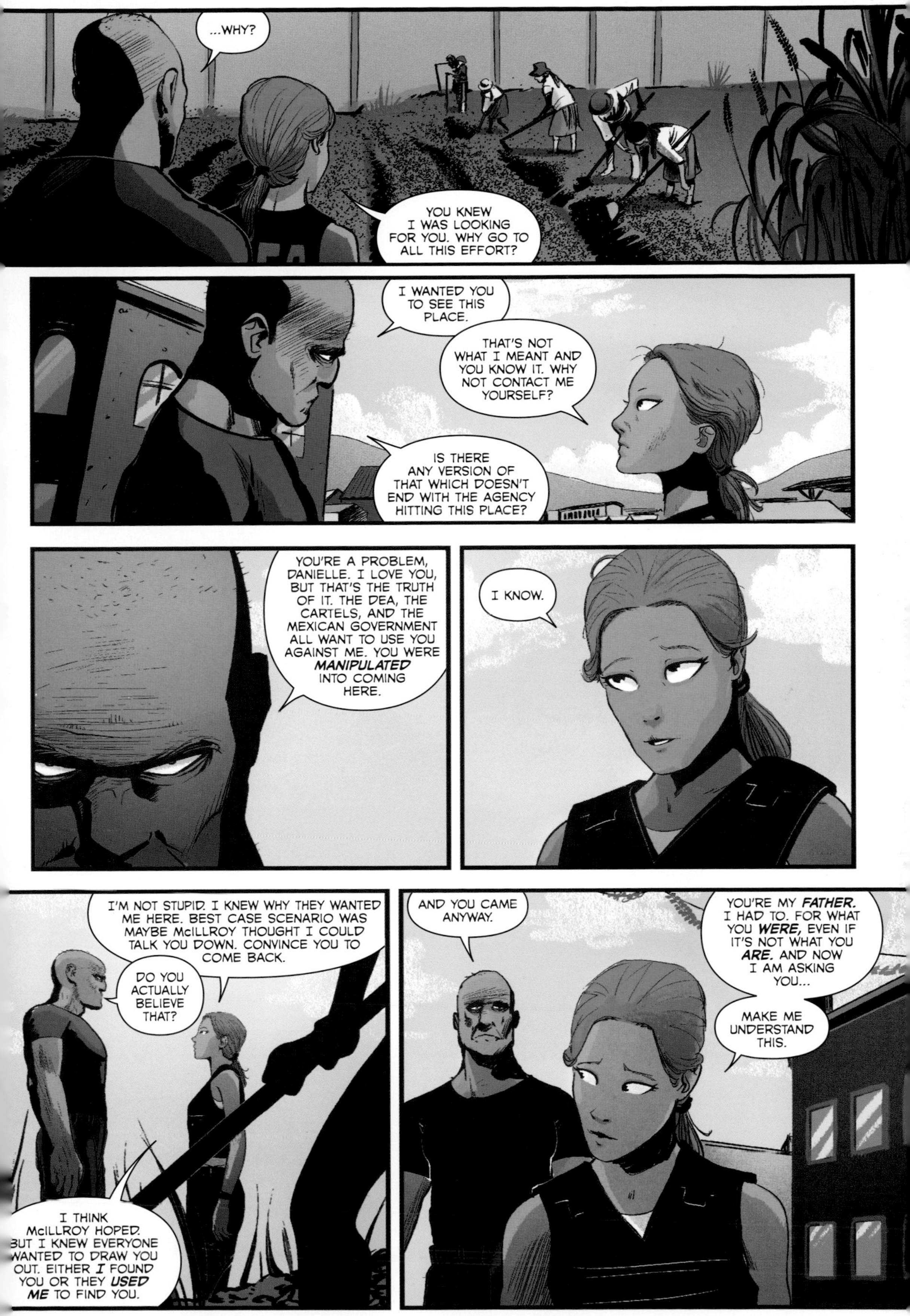
...WHY?
YOU KNEW I WAS LOOKING FOR YOU. WHY GO TO ALL THIS EFFORT?
I WANTED YOU TO SEE THIS PLACE.
THAT'S NOT WHAT I MEANT AND YOU KNOW IT. WHY NOT CONTACT ME YOURSELF?
IS THERE ANY VERSION OF THAT WHICH DOESN'T END WITH THE AGENCY HITTING THIS PLACE?
YOU'RE A PROBLEM, DANIELLE. I LOVE YOU, BUT THAT'S THE TRUTH OF IT. THE DEA, THE CARTELS, AND THE MEXICAN GOVERNMENT ALL WANT TO USE YOU AGAINST ME. YOU WERE ***MANIPULATED*** INTO COMING HERE.
I KNOW.
I'M NOT STUPID. I KNEW WHY THEY WANTED ME HERE. BEST CASE SCENARIO WAS MAYBE McILLROY THOUGHT I COULD TALK YOU DOWN. CONVINCE YOU TO COME BACK.
DO YOU ACTUALLY BELIEVE THAT?
I THINK McILLROY HOPED. BUT I KNEW EVERYONE WANTED TO DRAW YOU OUT. EITHER ***I*** FOUND YOU OR THEY ***USED ME*** TO FIND YOU.
AND YOU CAME ANYWAY.
YOU'RE MY ***FATHER.*** I HAD TO. FOR WHAT YOU ***WERE,*** EVEN IF IT'S NOT WHAT YOU ***ARE.*** AND NOW I AM ASKING YOU...
MAKE ME UNDERSTAND THIS.

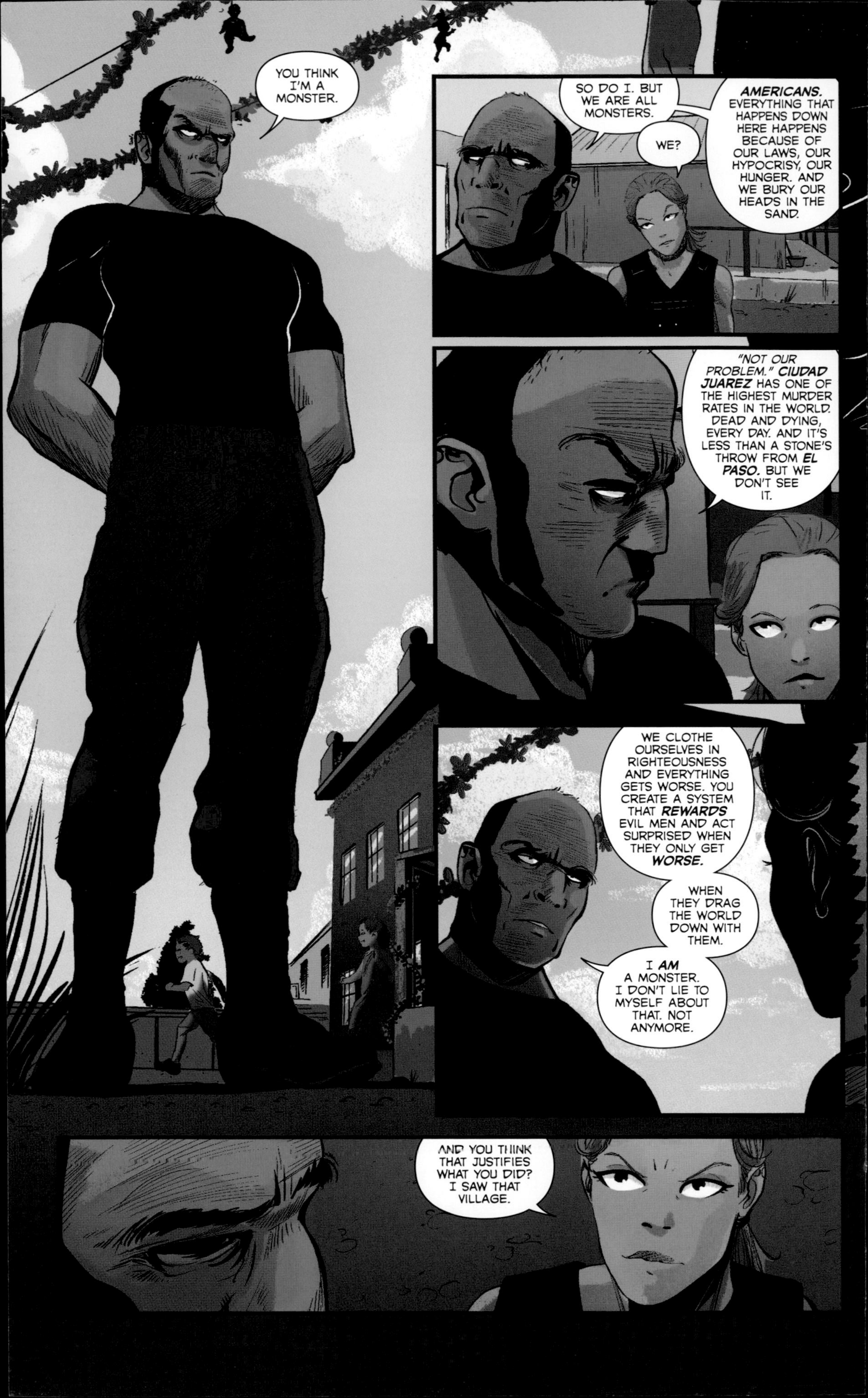
YOU THINK I'M A MONSTER.
SO DO I. BUT WE ARE ALL MONSTERS.
WE?
AMERICANS. EVERYTHING THAT HAPPENS DOWN HERE HAPPENS BECAUSE OF OUR LAWS, OUR HYPOCRISY, OUR HUNGER. AND WE BURY OUR HEADS IN THE SAND.
"NOT OUR PROBLEM." CIUDAD JUAREZ HAS ONE OF THE HIGHEST MURDER RATES IN THE WORLD. DEAD AND DYING, EVERY DAY. AND IT'S LESS THAN A STONE'S THROW FROM EL PASO. BUT WE DON'T SEE IT.
WE CLOTHE OURSELVES IN RIGHTEOUSNESS AND EVERYTHING GETS WORSE. YOU CREATE A SYSTEM THAT REWARDS EVIL MEN AND ACT SURPRISED WHEN THEY ONLY GET WORSE.
WHEN THEY DRAG THE WORLD DOWN WITH THEM.
I AM A MONSTER. I DON'T LIE TO MYSELF ABOUT THAT. NOT ANYMORE.
AND YOU THINK THAT JUSTIFIES WHAT YOU DID? I SAW THAT VILLAGE.

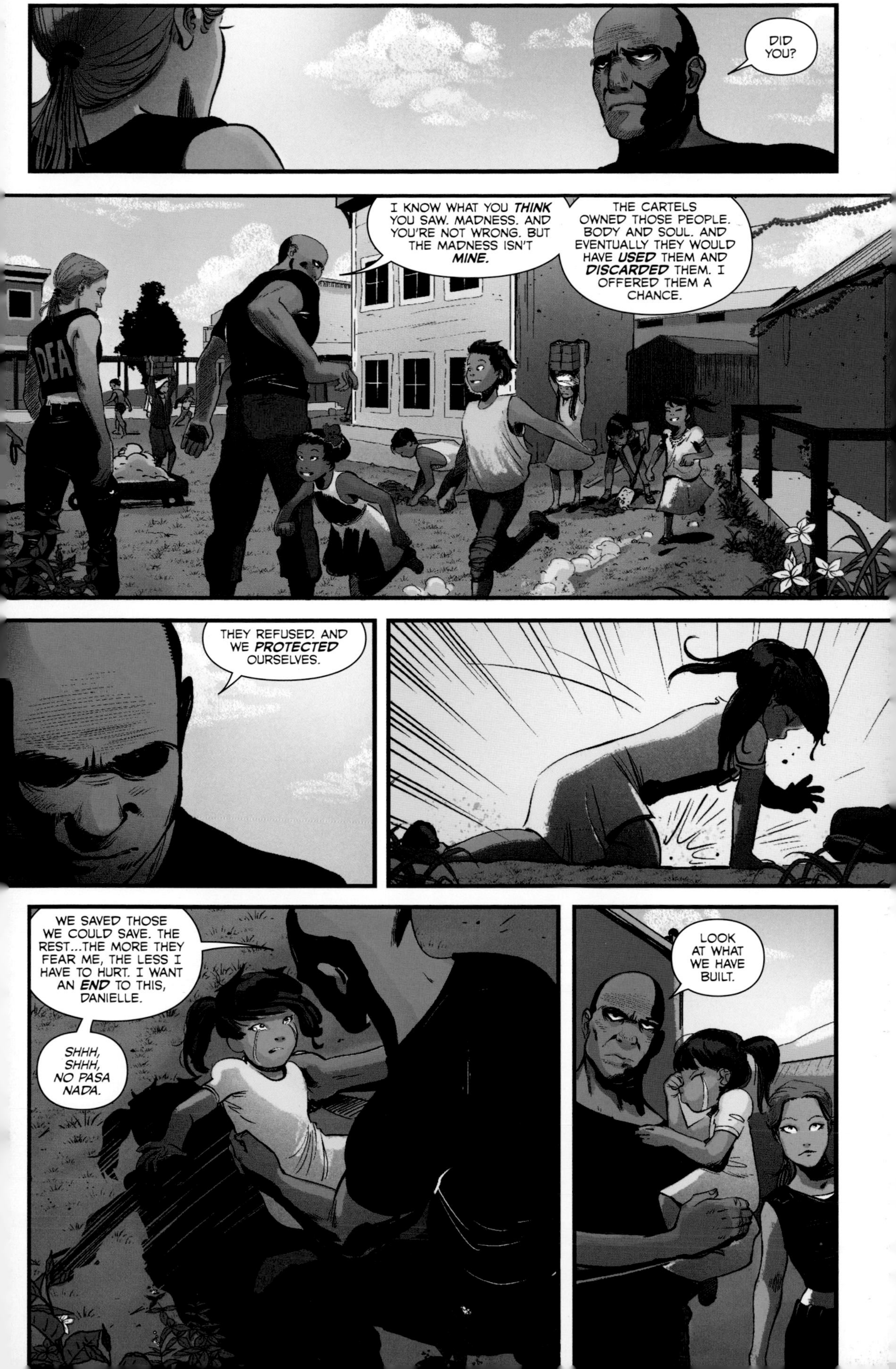
DID YOU?
I KNOW WHAT YOU THINK YOU SAW. MADNESS. AND YOU'RE NOT WRONG. BUT THE MADNESS ISN'T MINE.
THE CARTELS OWNED THOSE PEOPLE. BODY AND SOUL. AND EVENTUALLY THEY WOULD HAVE USED THEM AND DISCARDED THEM. I OFFERED THEM A CHANCE.
DEA
THEY REFUSED. AND WE PROTECTED OURSELVES.
WE SAVED THOSE WE COULD SAVE. THE REST...THE MORE THEY FEAR ME, THE LESS I HAVE TO HURT. I WANT AN END TO THIS, DANIELLE.
SHHH, SHHH, NO PASA NADA.
LOOK AT WHAT WE HAVE BUILT.

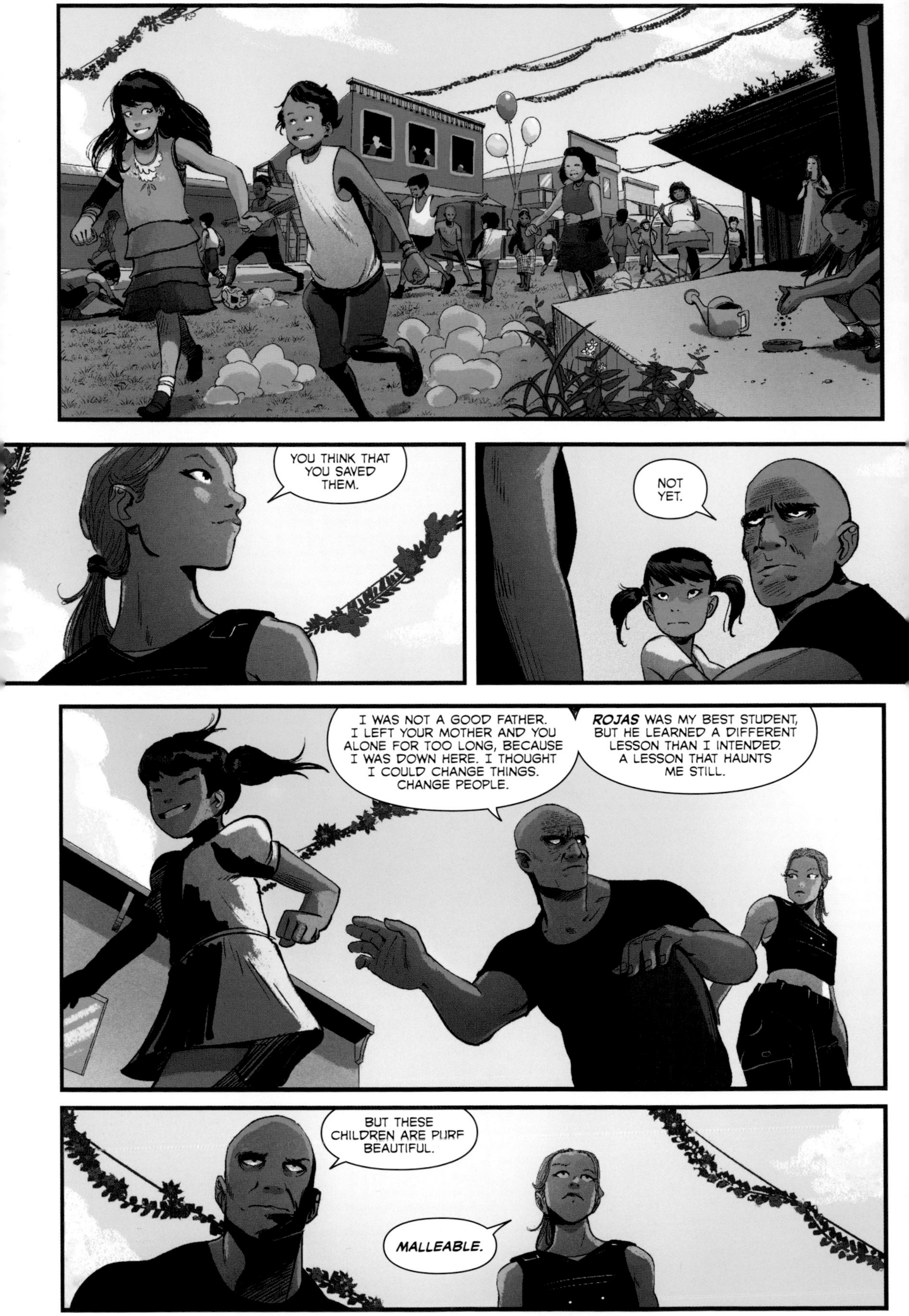
YOU THINK THAT YOU SAVED THEM.
NOT YET.
I WAS NOT A GOOD FATHER. I LEFT YOUR MOTHER AND YOU ALONE FOR TOO LONG, BECAUSE I WAS DOWN HERE. I THOUGHT I COULD CHANGE THINGS. CHANGE PEOPLE.
ROJAS WAS MY BEST STUDENT, BUT HE LEARNED A DIFFERENT LESSON THAN I INTENDED. A LESSON THAT HAUNTS ME STILL.
BUT THESE CHILDREN ARE PURE BEAUTIFUL.
MALLEABLE.

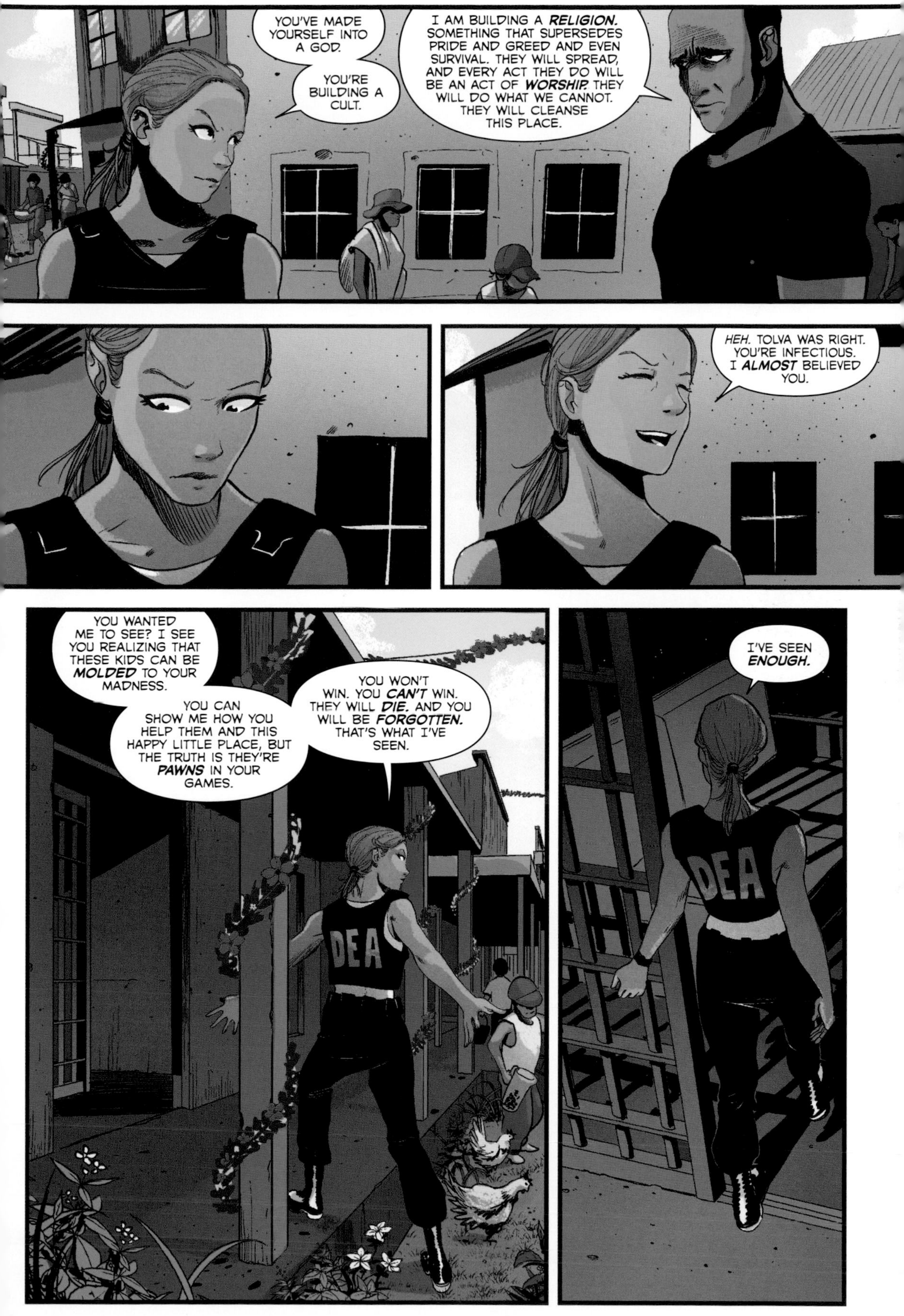
YOU'VE MADE YOURSELF INTO A GOD.
YOU'RE BUILDING A CULT.
I AM BUILDING A ***RELIGION.*** SOMETHING THAT SUPERSEDES PRIDE AND GREED AND EVEN SURVIVAL. THEY WILL SPREAD, AND EVERY ACT THEY DO WILL BE AN ACT OF ***WORSHIP.*** THEY WILL DO WHAT WE CANNOT. THEY WILL CLEANSE THIS PLACE.
HEH. TOLVA WAS RIGHT. YOU'RE INFECTIOUS. I ***ALMOST*** BELIEVED YOU.
YOU WANTED ME TO SEE? I SEE YOU REALIZING THAT THESE KIDS CAN BE ***MOLDED*** TO YOUR MADNESS.
YOU CAN SHOW ME HOW YOU HELP THEM AND THIS HAPPY LITTLE PLACE, BUT THE TRUTH IS THEY'RE ***PAWNS*** IN YOUR GAMES.
YOU WON'T WIN. YOU ***CAN'T*** WIN. THEY WILL ***DIE.*** AND YOU WILL BE ***FORGOTTEN.*** THAT'S WHAT I'VE SEEN.
DEA
I'VE SEEN ***ENOUGH.***
DEA

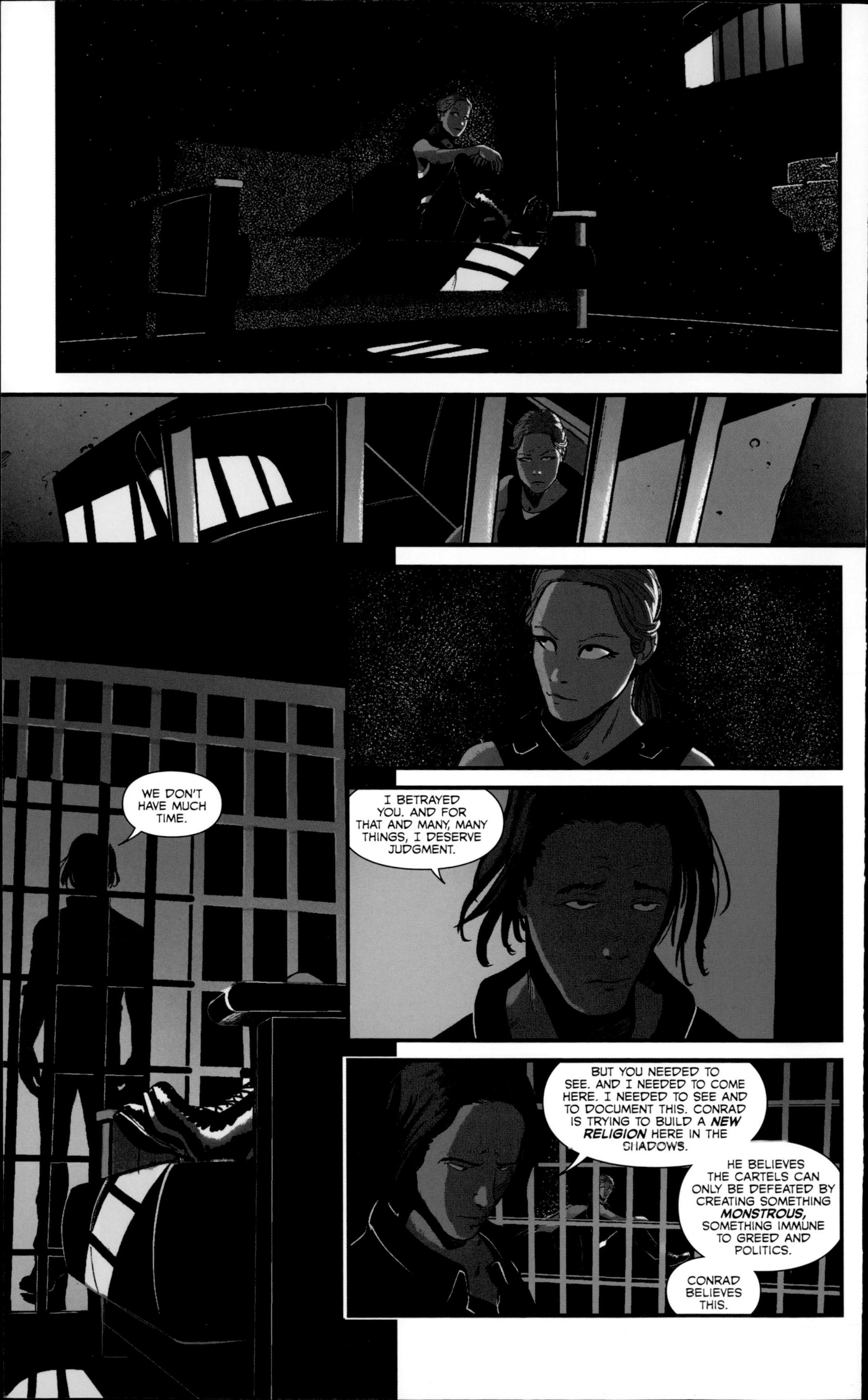

WE DON'T HAVE MUCH TIME.
I BETRAYED YOU. AND FOR THAT AND MANY, MANY THINGS, I DESERVE JUDGMENT.
BUT YOU NEEDED TO SEE. AND I NEEDED TO COME HERE. I NEEDED TO SEE AND TO DOCUMENT THIS. CONRAD IS TRYING TO BUILD A *NEW RELIGION* HERE IN THE SHADOWS.
HE BELIEVES THE CARTELS CAN ONLY BE DEFEATED BY CREATING SOMETHING *MONSTROUS,* SOMETHING IMMUNE TO GREED AND POLITICS.
CONRAD BELIEVES THIS.

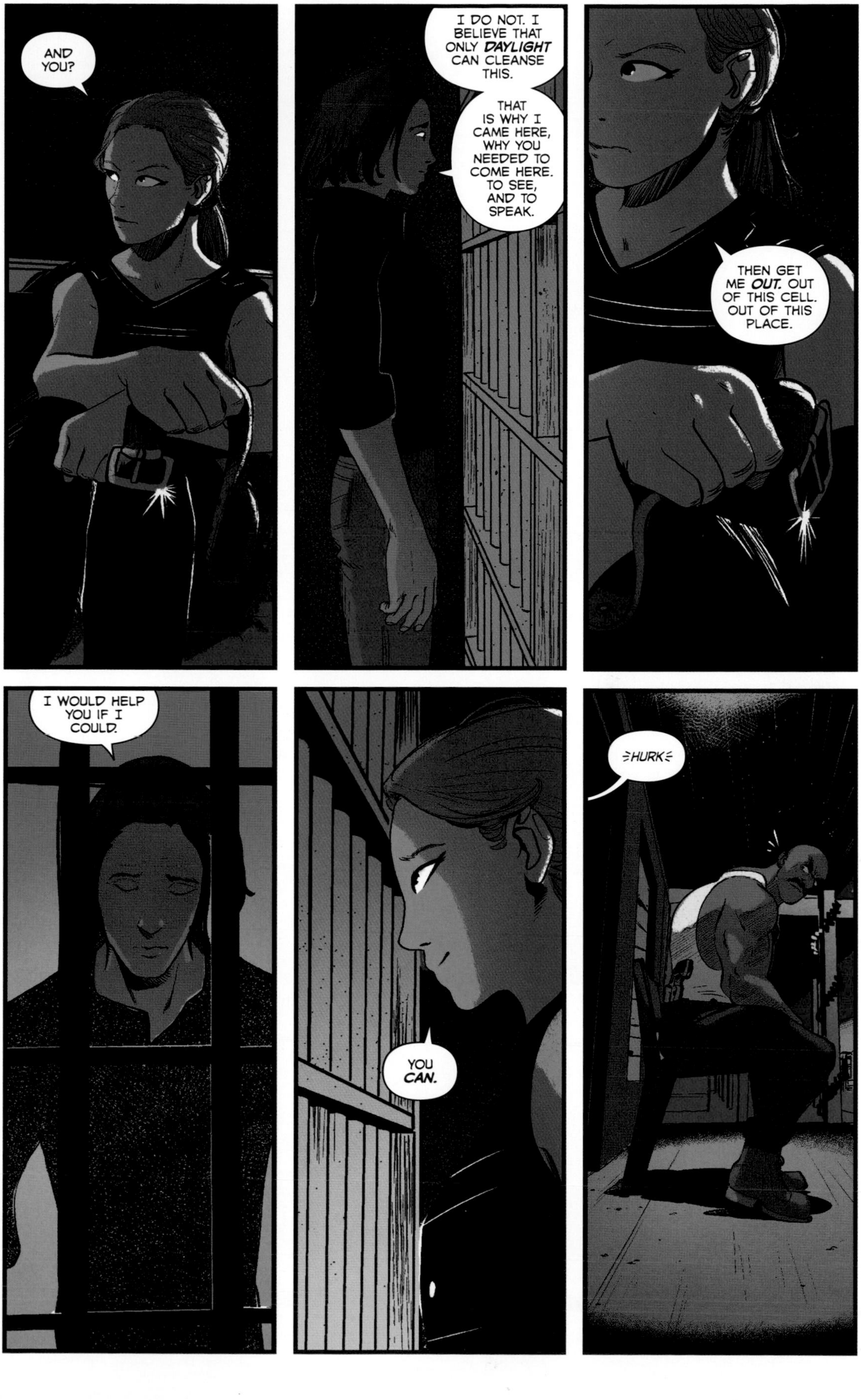
AND YOU?
I DO NOT. I BELIEVE THAT ONLY DAYLIGHT CAN CLEANSE THIS.
THAT IS WHY I CAME HERE, WHY YOU NEEDED TO COME HERE. TO SEE, AND TO SPEAK.
THEN GET ME OUT. OUT OF THIS CELL. OUT OF THIS PLACE.
I WOULD HELP YOU IF I COULD.
YOU CAN.
HURK

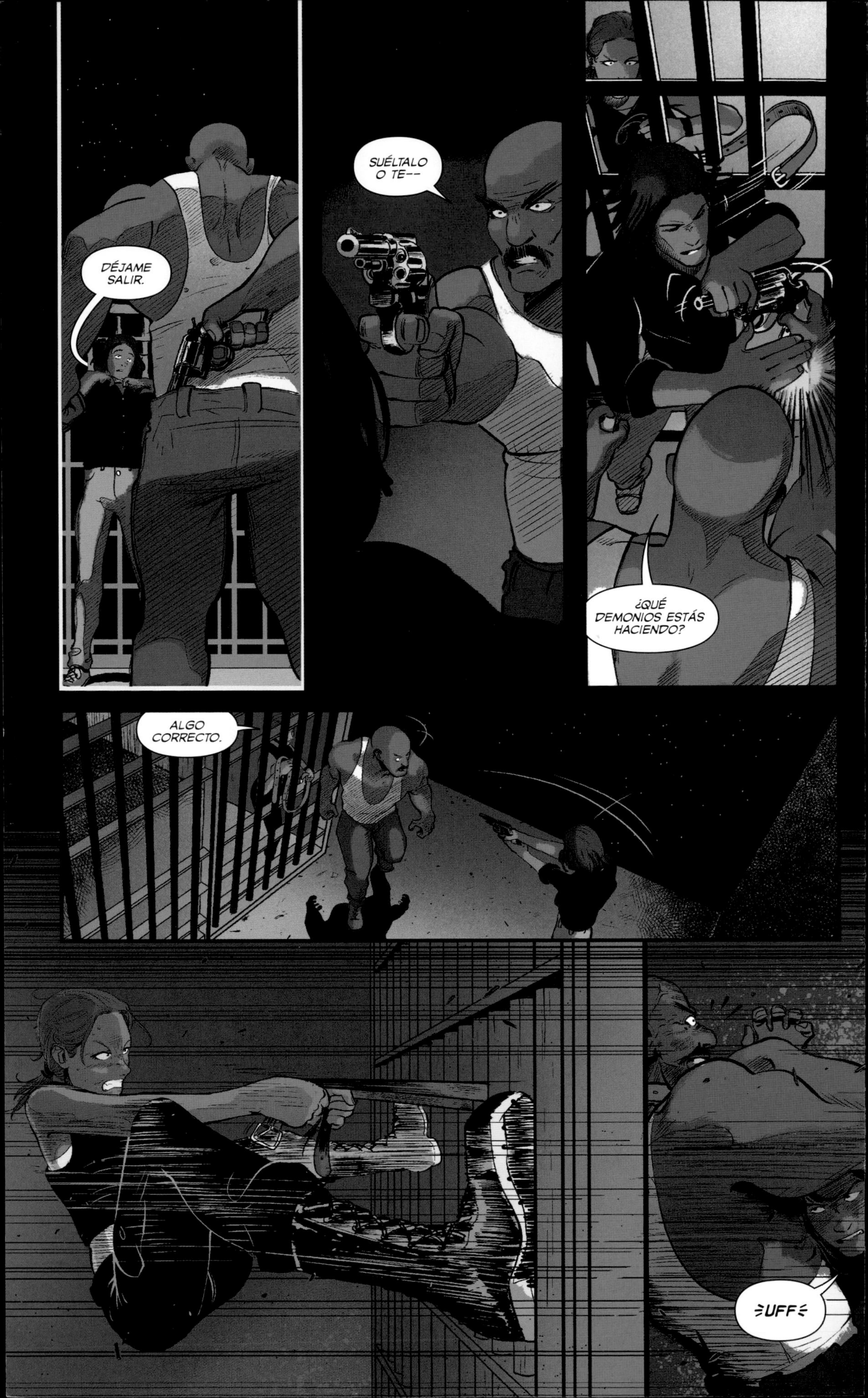
DÉJAME SALIR.
SUÉLTALO O TE--
¿QUÉ DEMONIOS ESTÁS HACIENDO?
ALGO CORRECTO.
UFF

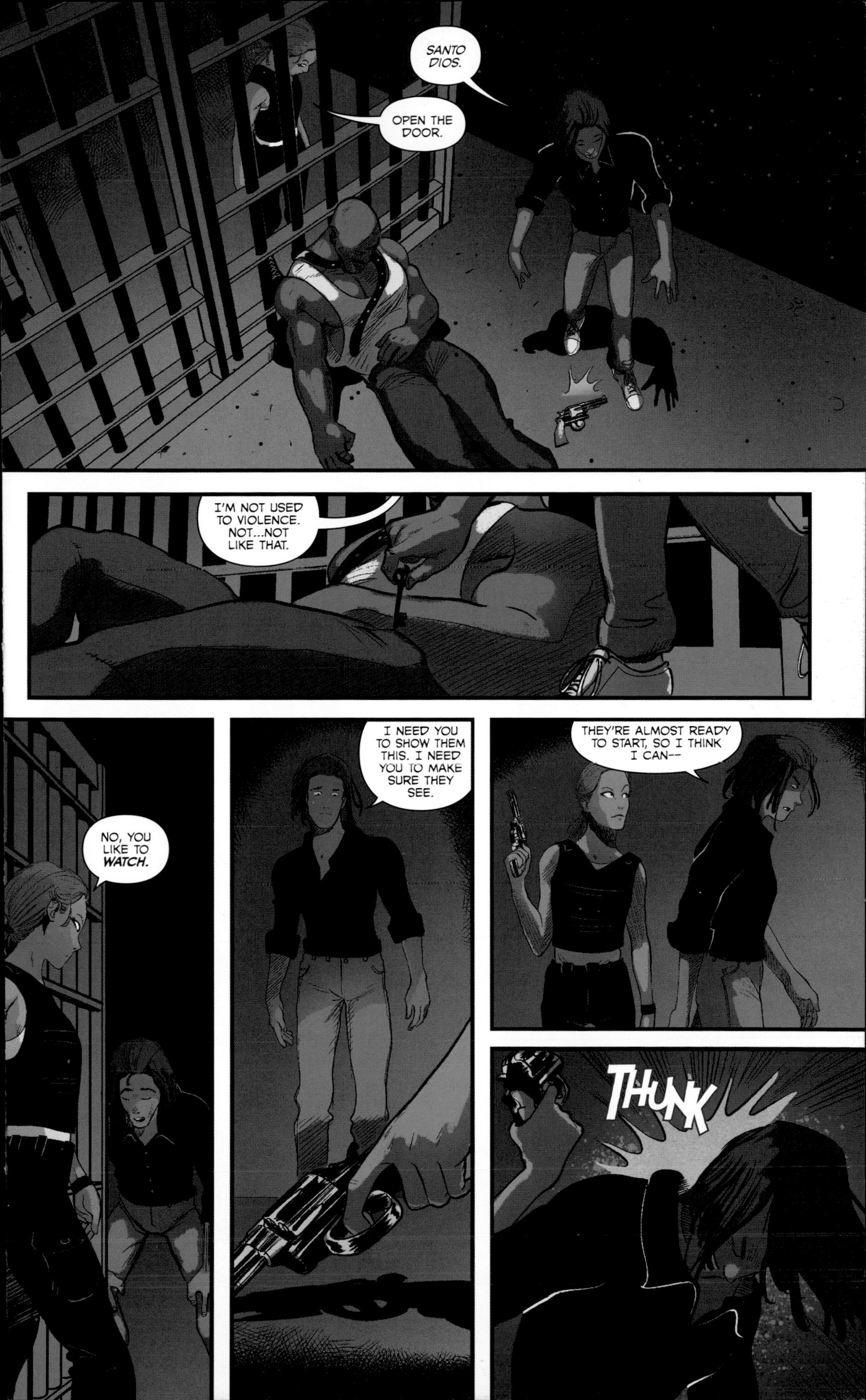
SANTO DIOS.
OPEN THE DOOR.
I'M NOT USED TO VIOLENCE. NOT...NOT LIKE THAT.
NO, YOU LIKE TO WATCH.
I NEED YOU TO SHOW THEM THIS. I NEED YOU TO MAKE SURE THEY SEE.
THEY'RE ALMOST READY TO START, SO I THINK I CAN--
THUNK

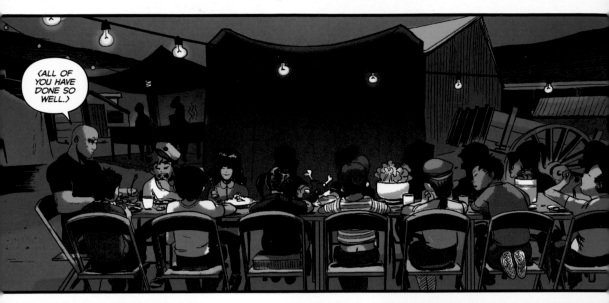

〈ALL OF YOU HAVE DONE SO WELL.〉

〈YOU HAVE WELCOMED ARTURO TO US.〉

〈AND NOW IT'S TIME.〉

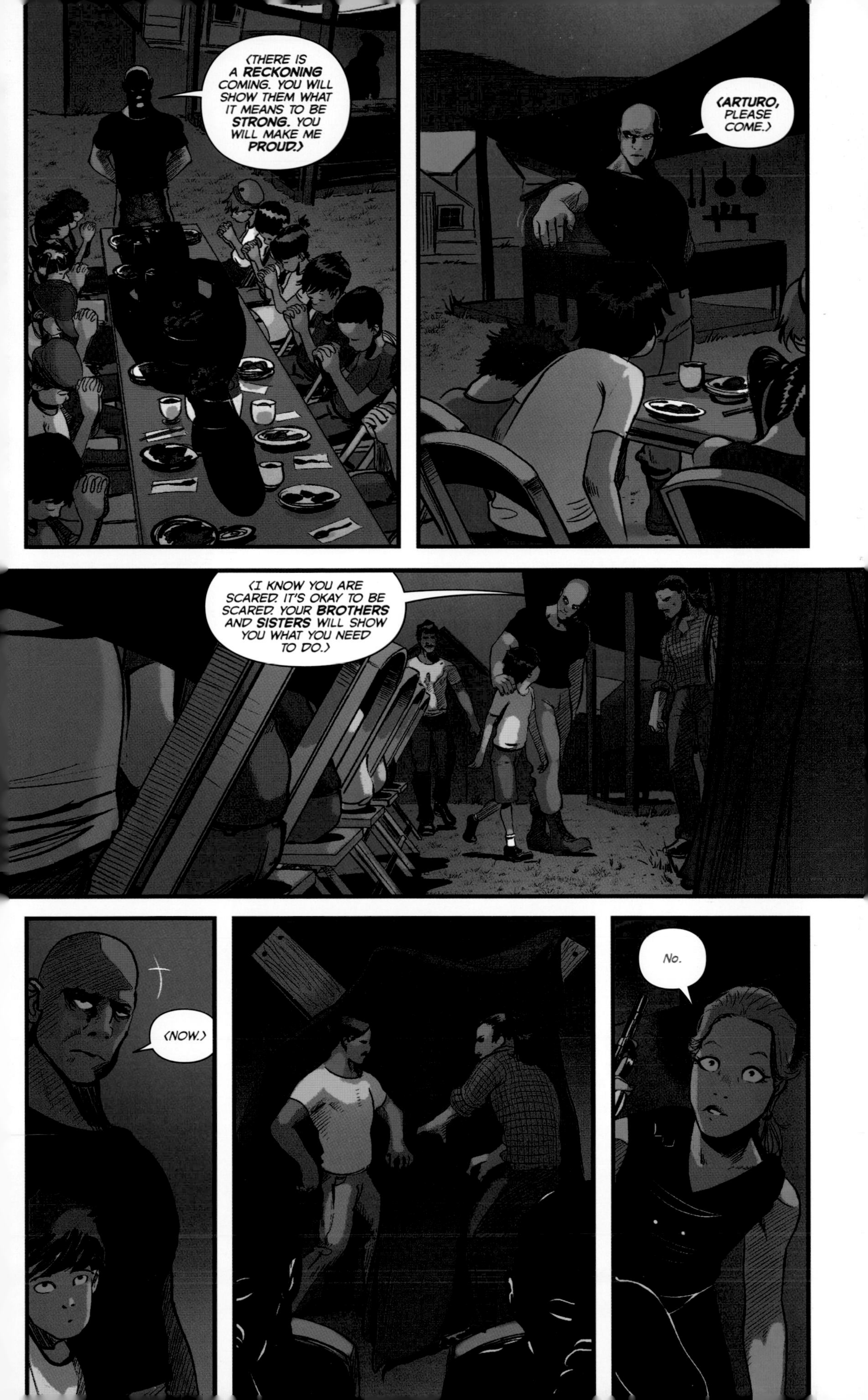
‹THERE IS A RECKONING COMING. YOU WILL SHOW THEM WHAT IT MEANS TO BE STRONG. YOU WILL MAKE ME PROUD.›
‹ARTURO, PLEASE COME.›
‹I KNOW YOU ARE SCARED. IT'S OKAY TO BE SCARED. YOUR BROTHERS AND SISTERS WILL SHOW YOU WHAT YOU NEED TO DO.›
‹NOW.›
No.

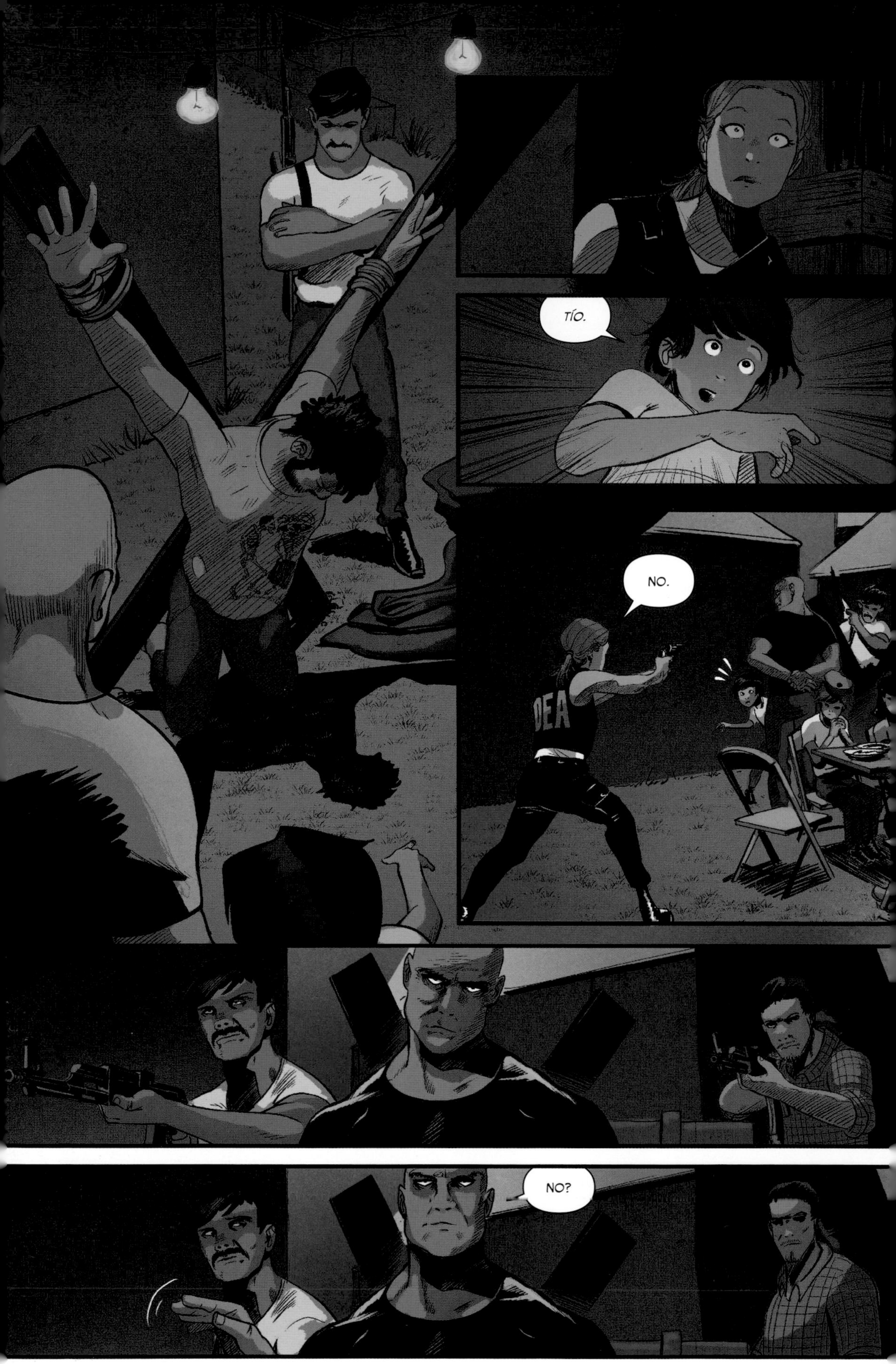
TÍO.
NO.
NO?

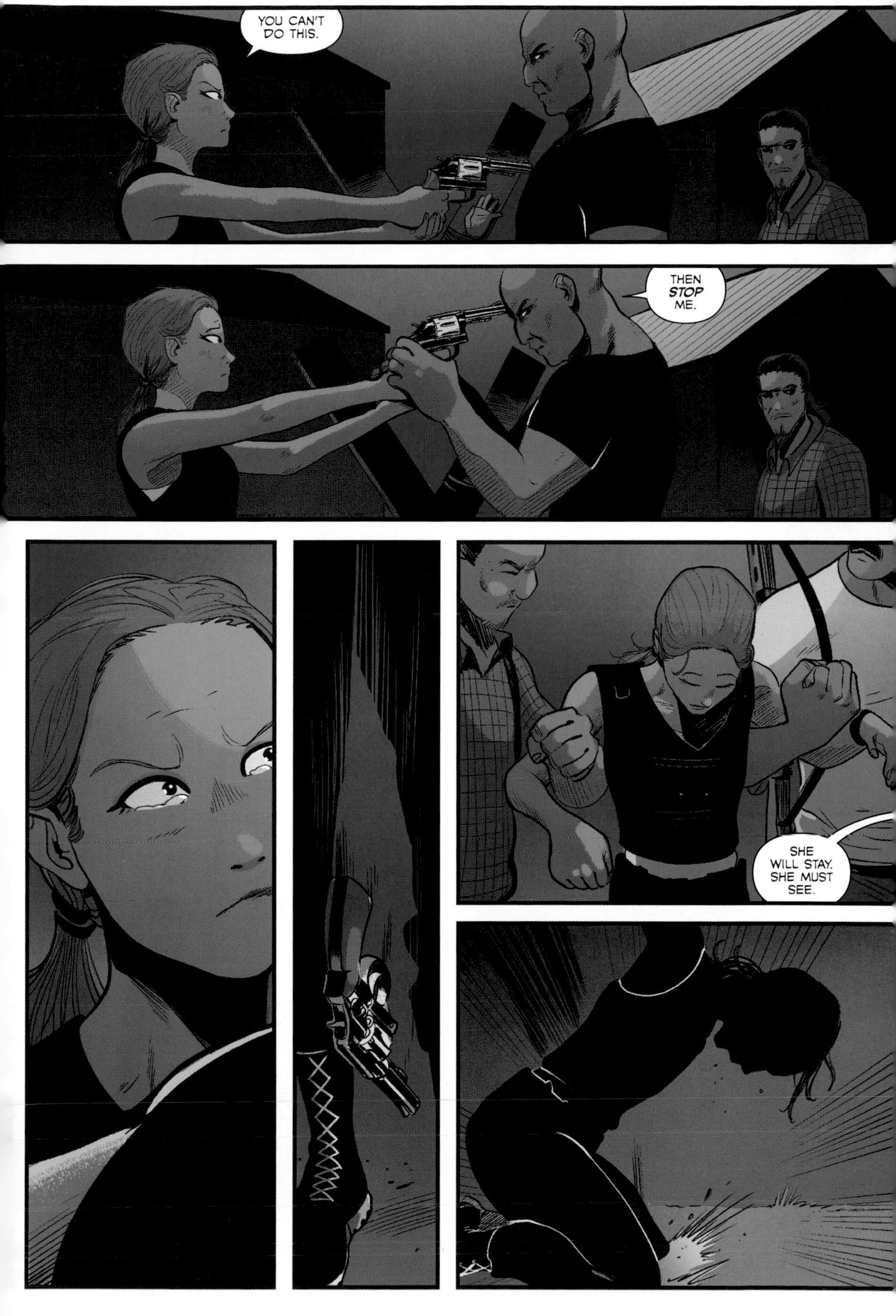
YOU CAN'T DO THIS.
THEN *STOP* ME.
SHE WILL STAY. SHE MUST SEE.

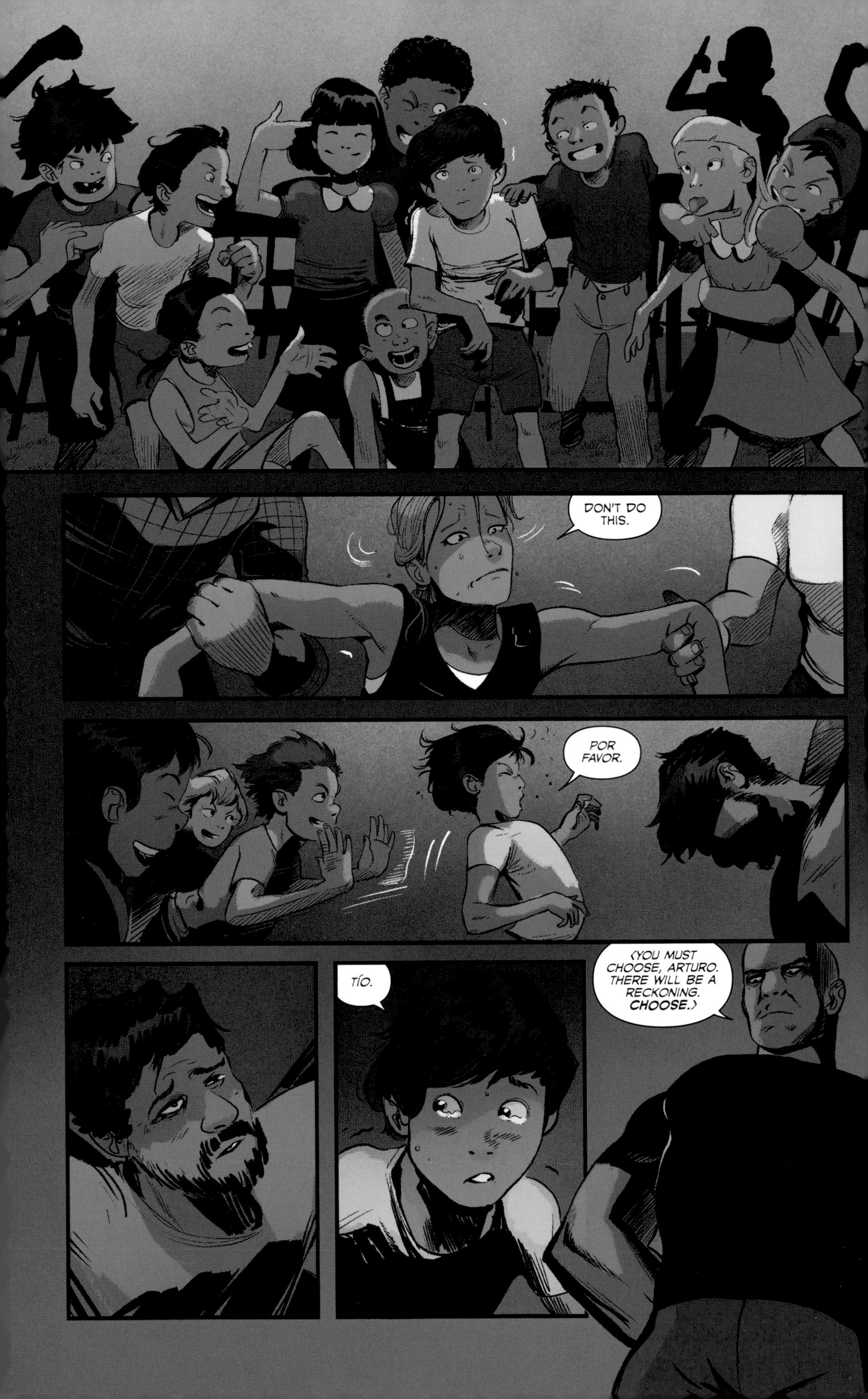
DON'T DO THIS.
POR FAVOR.
TÍO.
<YOU MUST CHOOSE, ARTURO. THERE WILL BE A RECKONING. **CHOOSE.**>

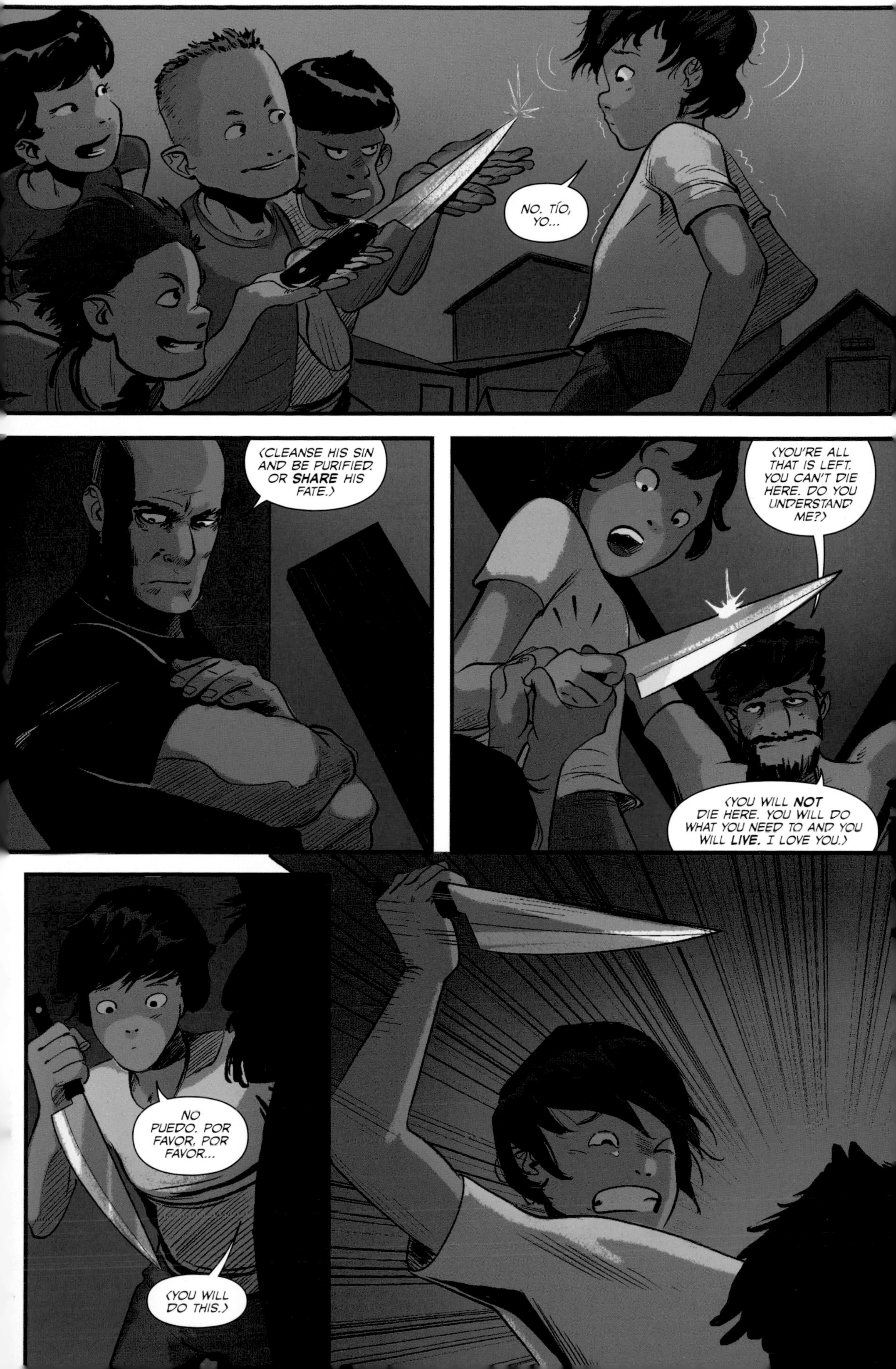
NO. TÍO, YO...
<CLEANSE HIS SIN AND BE PURIFIED. OR **SHARE** HIS FATE.>
<YOU'RE ALL THAT IS LEFT. YOU CAN'T DIE HERE. DO YOU UNDERSTAND ME?>
<YOU WILL **NOT** DIE HERE. YOU WILL DO WHAT YOU NEED TO AND YOU WILL **LIVE.** I LOVE YOU.>
NO PUEDO. POR FAVOR, POR FAVOR...
<YOU WILL DO THIS.>

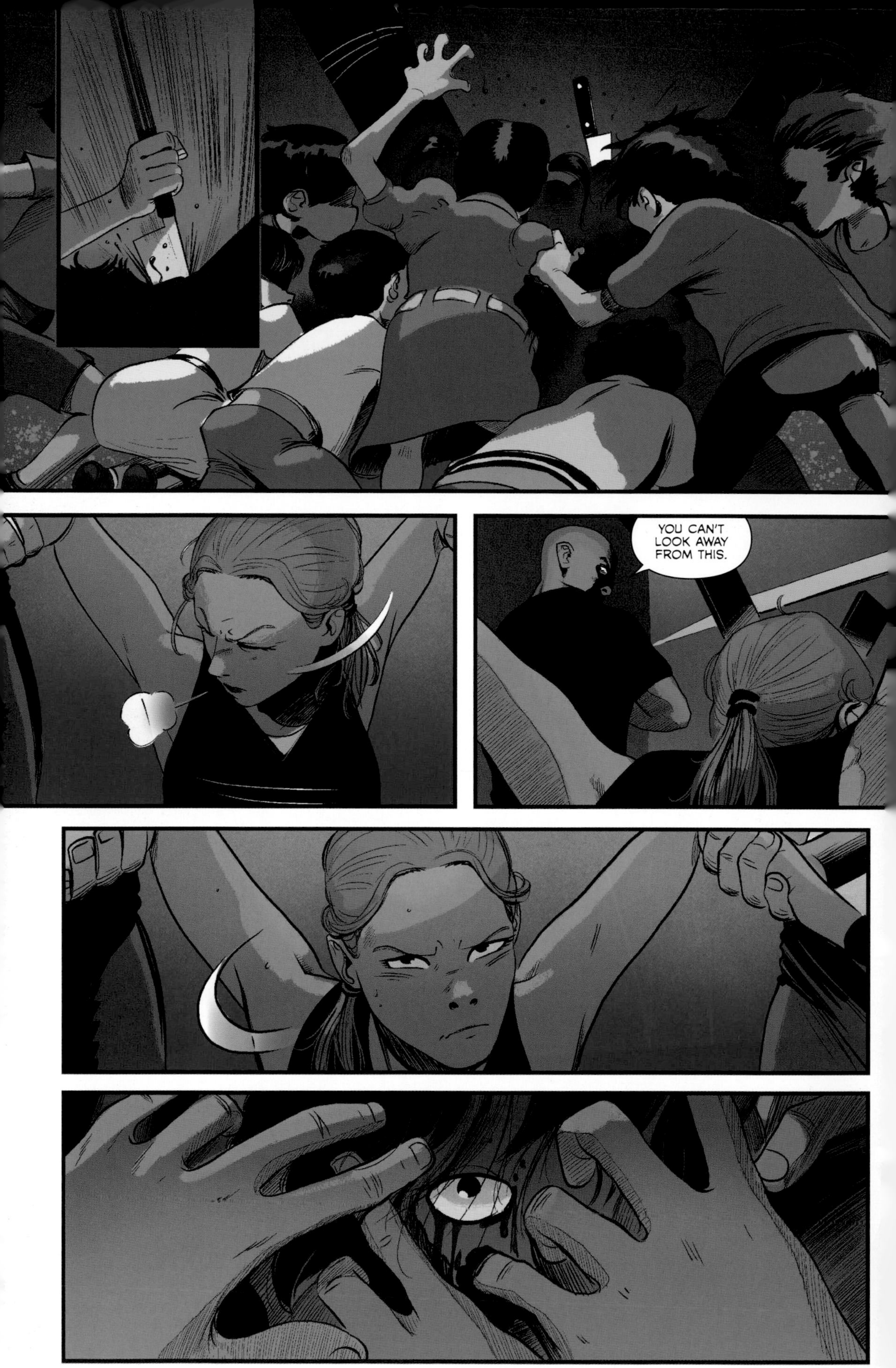
YOU CAN'T LOOK AWAY FROM THIS.

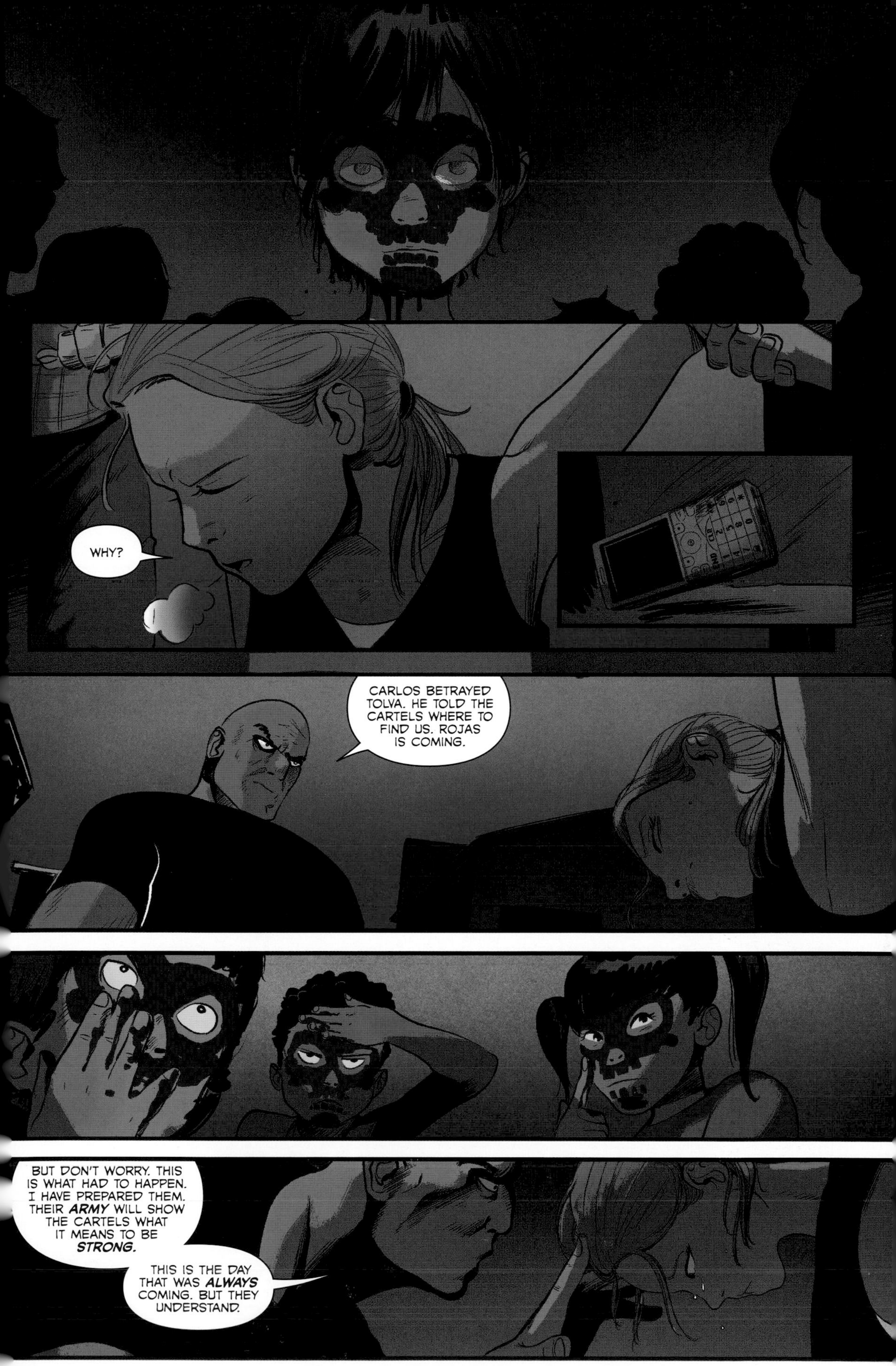
WHY?
CARLOS BETRAYED TOLVA. HE TOLD THE CARTELS WHERE TO FIND US. ROJAS IS COMING.
BUT DON'T WORRY. THIS IS WHAT HAD TO HAPPEN. I HAVE PREPARED THEM. THEIR ARMY WILL SHOW THE CARTELS WHAT IT MEANS TO BE STRONG.
THIS IS THE DAY THAT WAS ALWAYS COMING. BUT THEY UNDERSTAND.

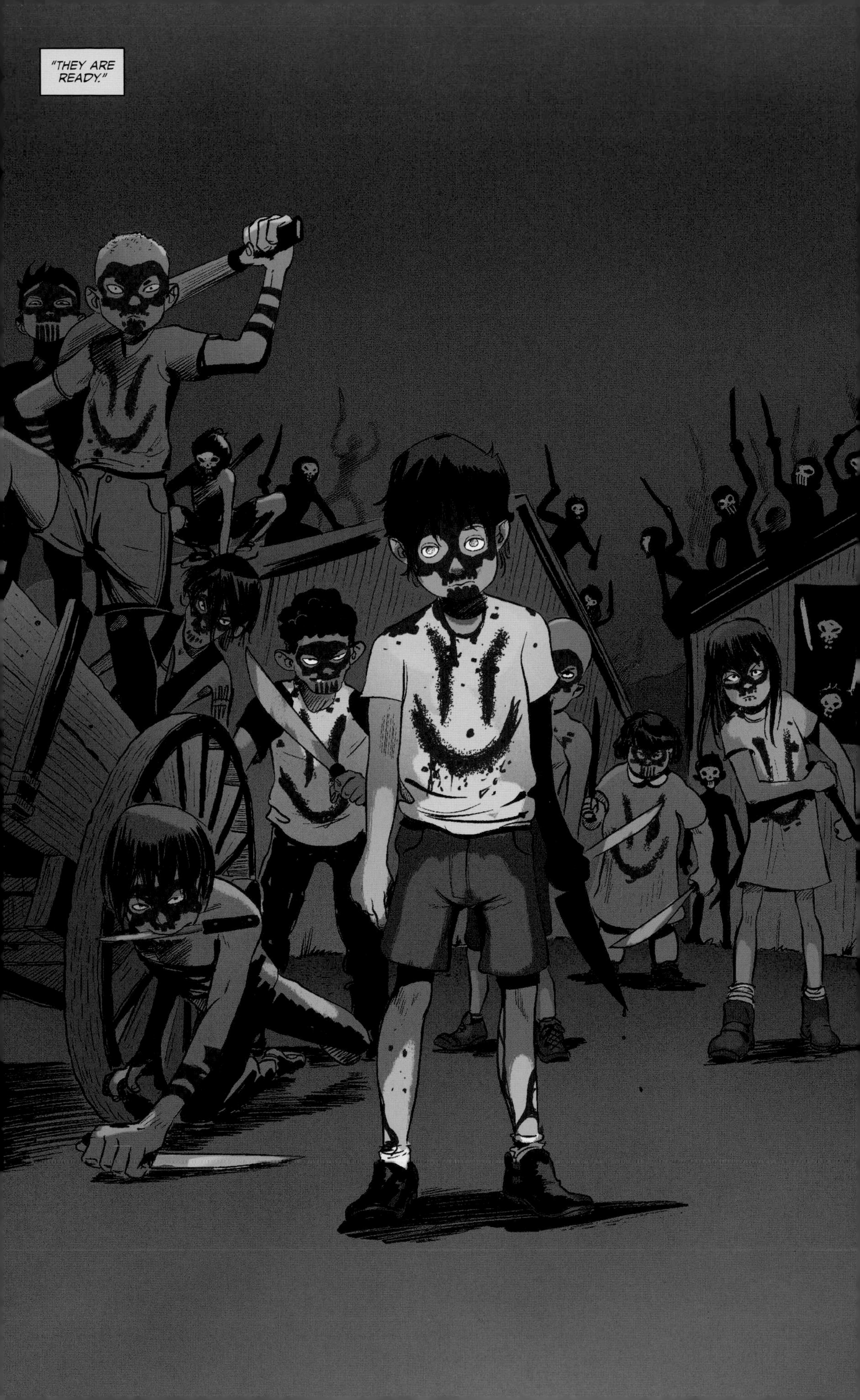
"THEY ARE READY."

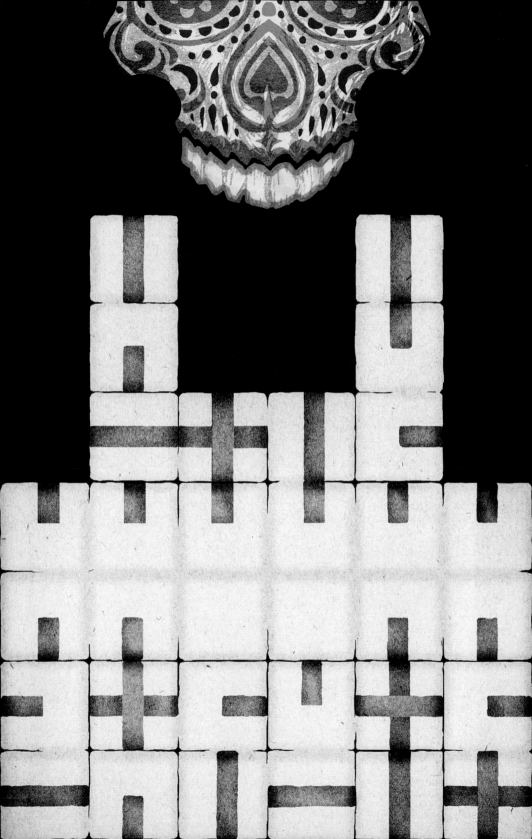

CHAPTER
FOUR
CAPÍTULO CUATRO

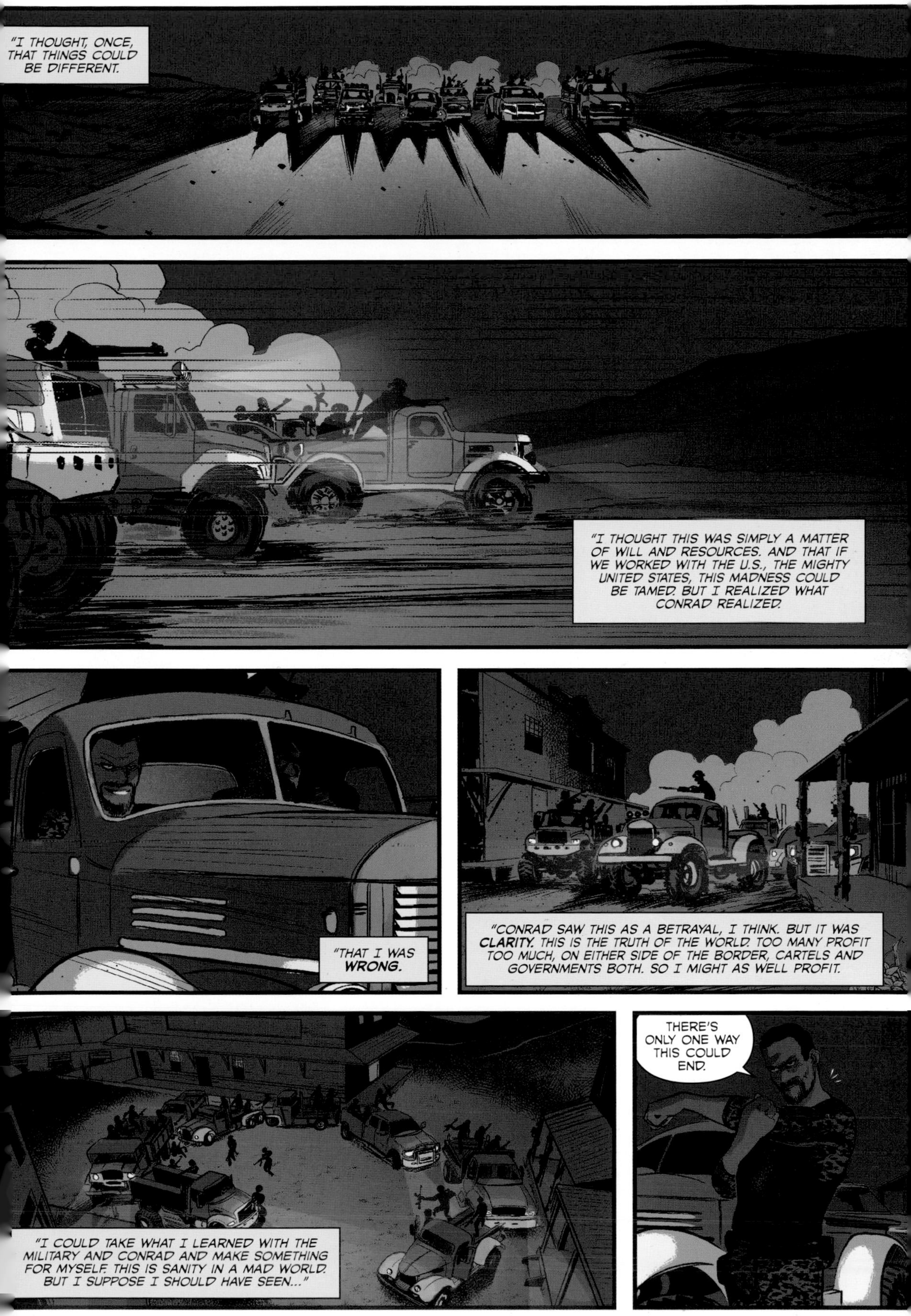
"I THOUGHT, ONCE, THAT THINGS COULD BE DIFFERENT.
"I THOUGHT THIS WAS SIMPLY A MATTER OF WILL AND RESOURCES. AND THAT IF WE WORKED WITH THE U.S., THE MIGHTY UNITED STATES, THIS MADNESS COULD BE TAMED. BUT I REALIZED WHAT CONRAD REALIZED.
"THAT I WAS **WRONG.**
"CONRAD SAW THIS AS A BETRAYAL, I THINK. BUT IT WAS **CLARITY.** THIS IS THE TRUTH OF THE WORLD. TOO MANY PROFIT TOO MUCH, ON EITHER SIDE OF THE BORDER, CARTELS AND GOVERNMENTS BOTH. SO I MIGHT AS WELL PROFIT.
"I COULD TAKE WHAT I LEARNED WITH THE MILITARY AND CONRAD AND MAKE SOMETHING FOR MYSELF. THIS IS SANITY IN A MAD WORLD. BUT I SUPPOSE I SHOULD HAVE SEEN..."
THERE'S ONLY ONE WAY THIS COULD END.

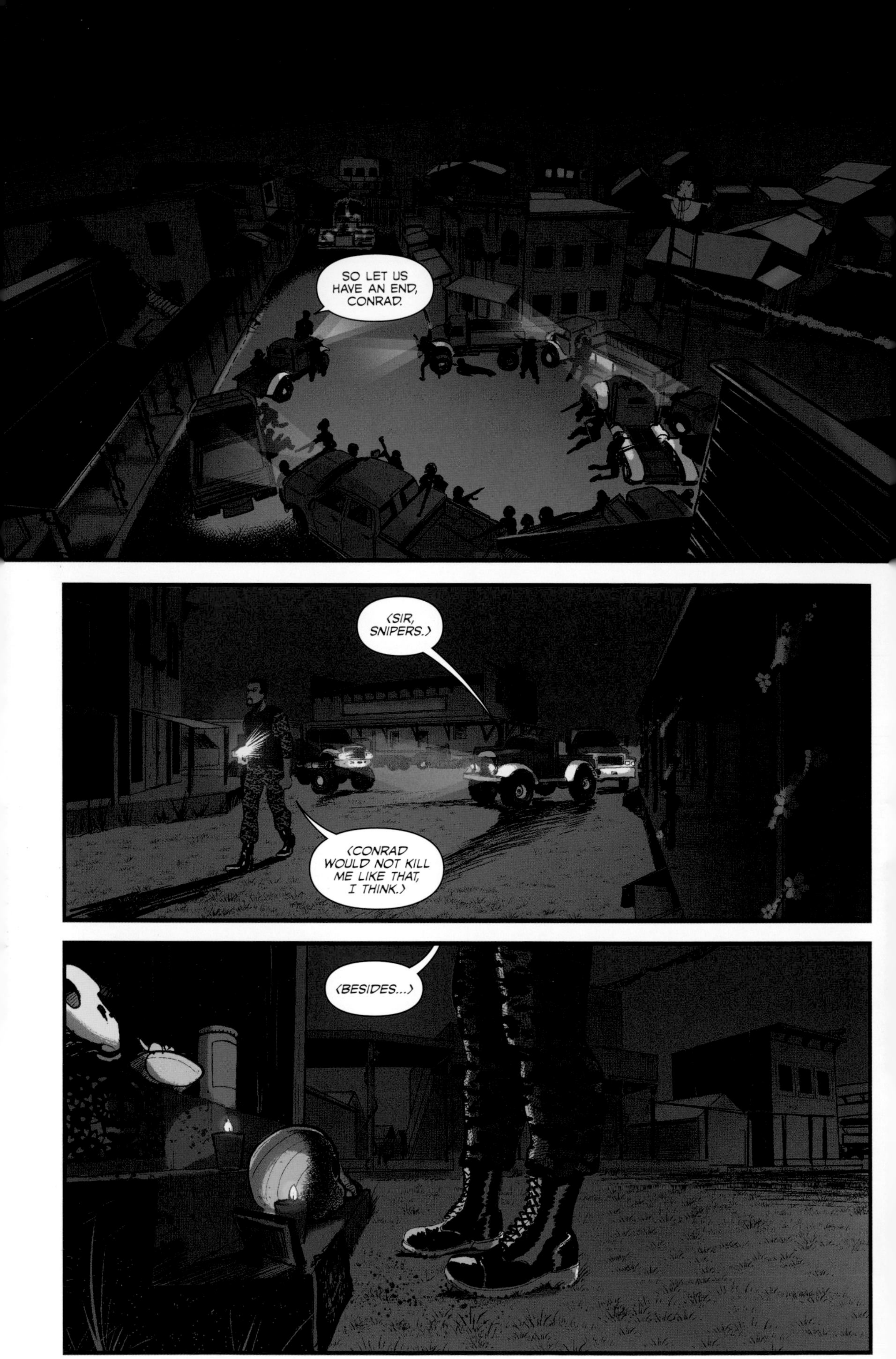
SO LET US HAVE AN END, CONRAD.
‹SIR, SNIPERS.›
‹CONRAD WOULD NOT KILL ME LIKE THAT, I THINK.›
‹BESIDES...›

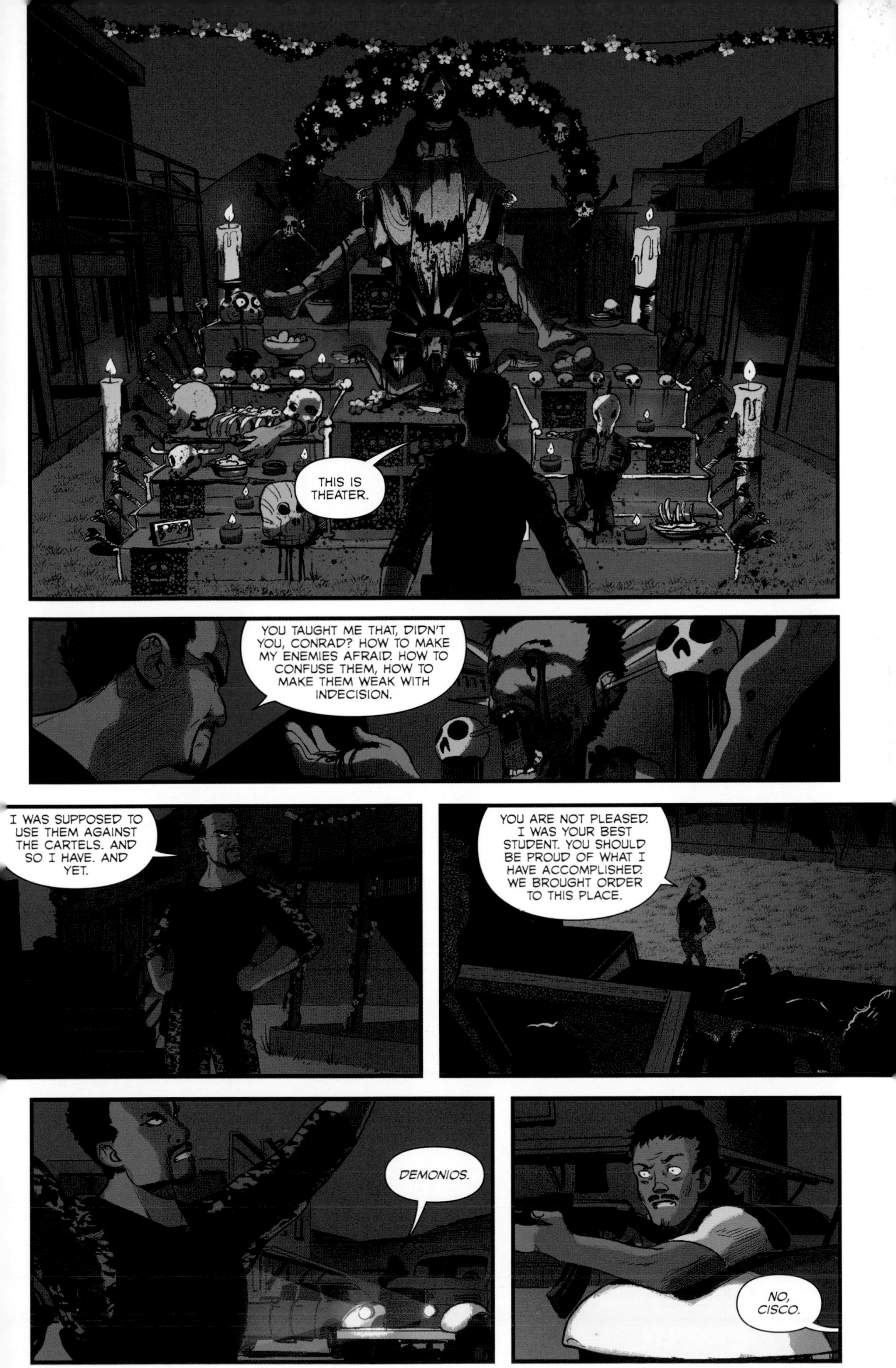
THIS IS THEATER.
YOU TAUGHT ME THAT, DIDN'T YOU, CONRAD? HOW TO MAKE MY ENEMIES AFRAID. HOW TO CONFUSE THEM, HOW TO MAKE THEM WEAK WITH INDECISION.
I WAS SUPPOSED TO USE THEM AGAINST THE CARTELS. AND SO I HAVE. AND YET.
YOU ARE NOT PLEASED. I WAS YOUR BEST STUDENT. YOU SHOULD BE PROUD OF WHAT I HAVE ACCOMPLISHED. WE BROUGHT ORDER TO THIS PLACE.
DEMONIOS.
NO, CISCO.

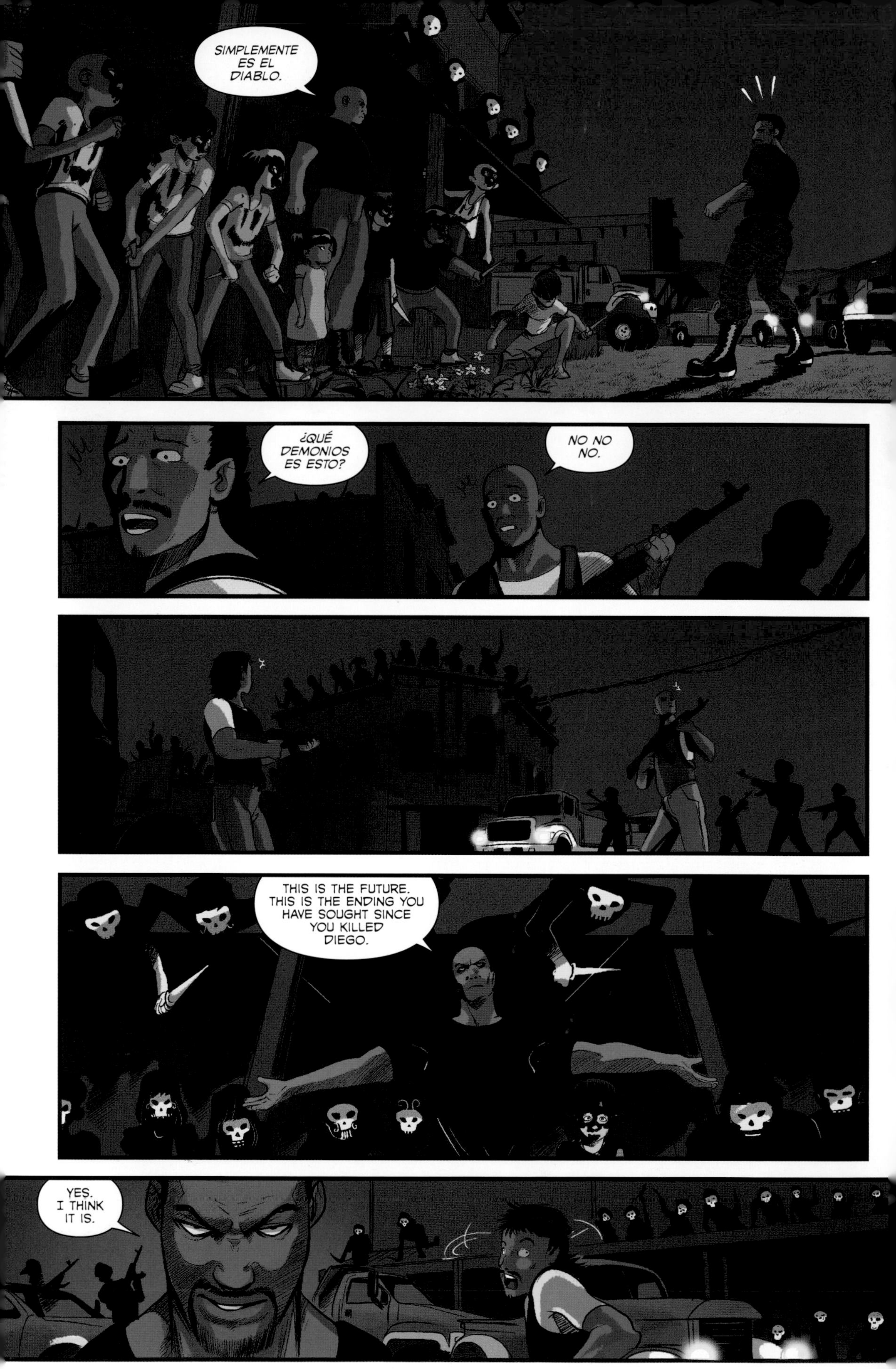
SIMPLEMENTE ES EL DIABLO.
¿QUÉ DEMONIOS ES ESTO?
NO NO NO.
THIS IS THE FUTURE. THIS IS THE ENDING YOU HAVE SOUGHT SINCE YOU KILLED DIEGO.
YES. I THINK IT IS.

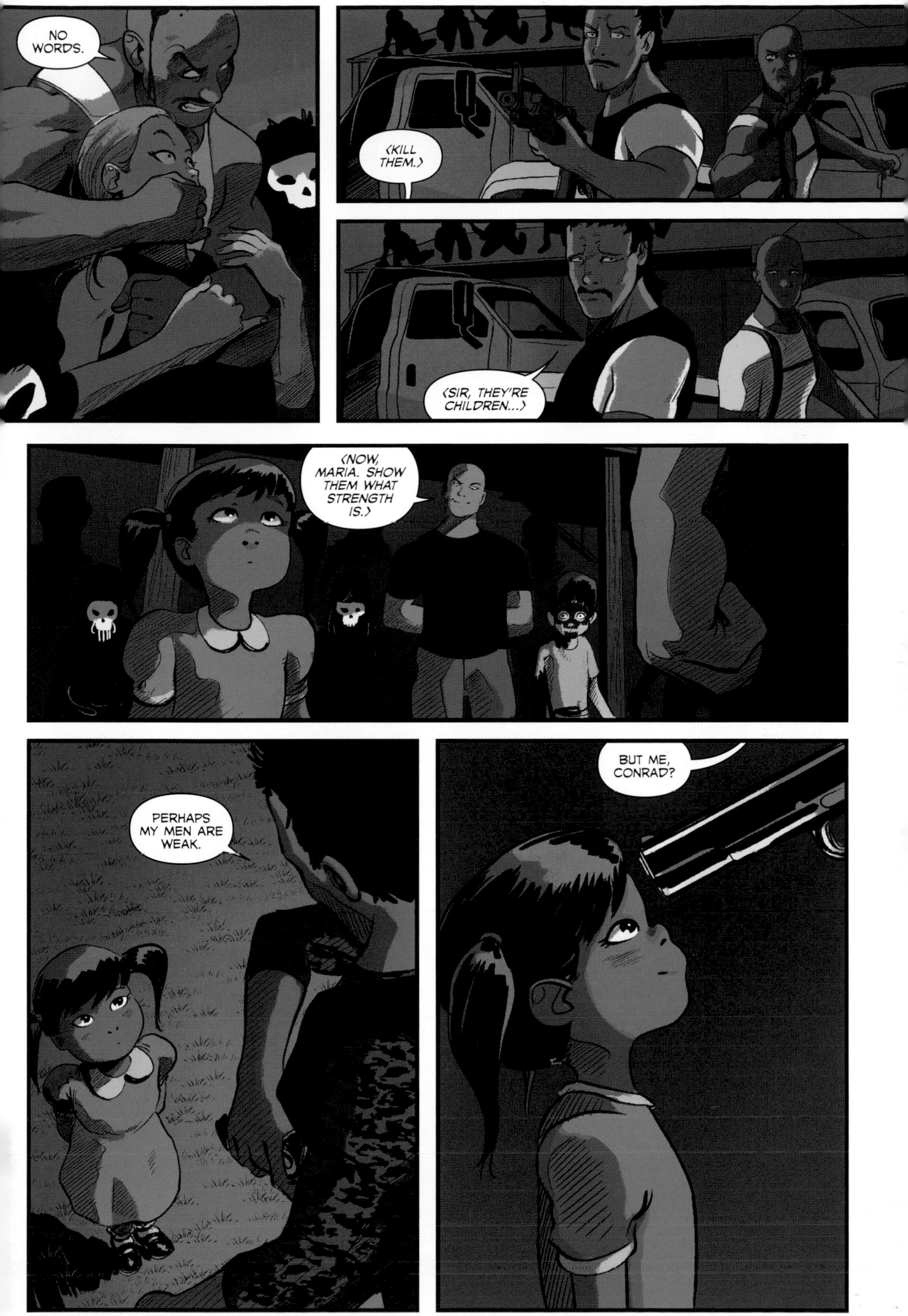
NO WORDS.
‹KILL THEM.›
‹SIR, THEY'RE CHILDREN...›
‹NOW, MARIA. SHOW THEM WHAT STRENGTH IS.›
PERHAPS MY MEN ARE WEAK.
BUT ME, CONRAD?

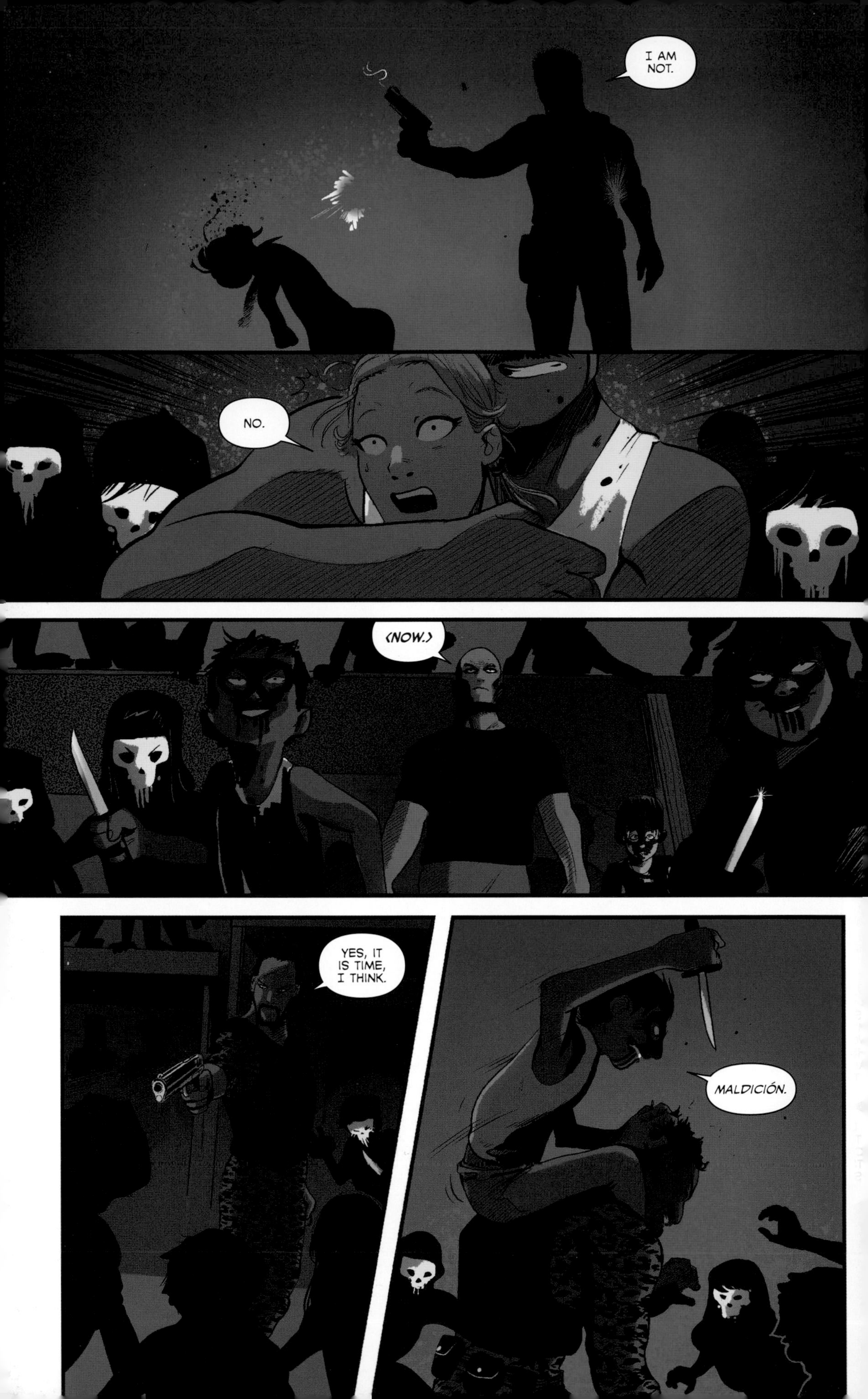
I AM NOT.
NO.
‹NOW.›
YES, IT IS TIME, I THINK.
MALDICIÓN.

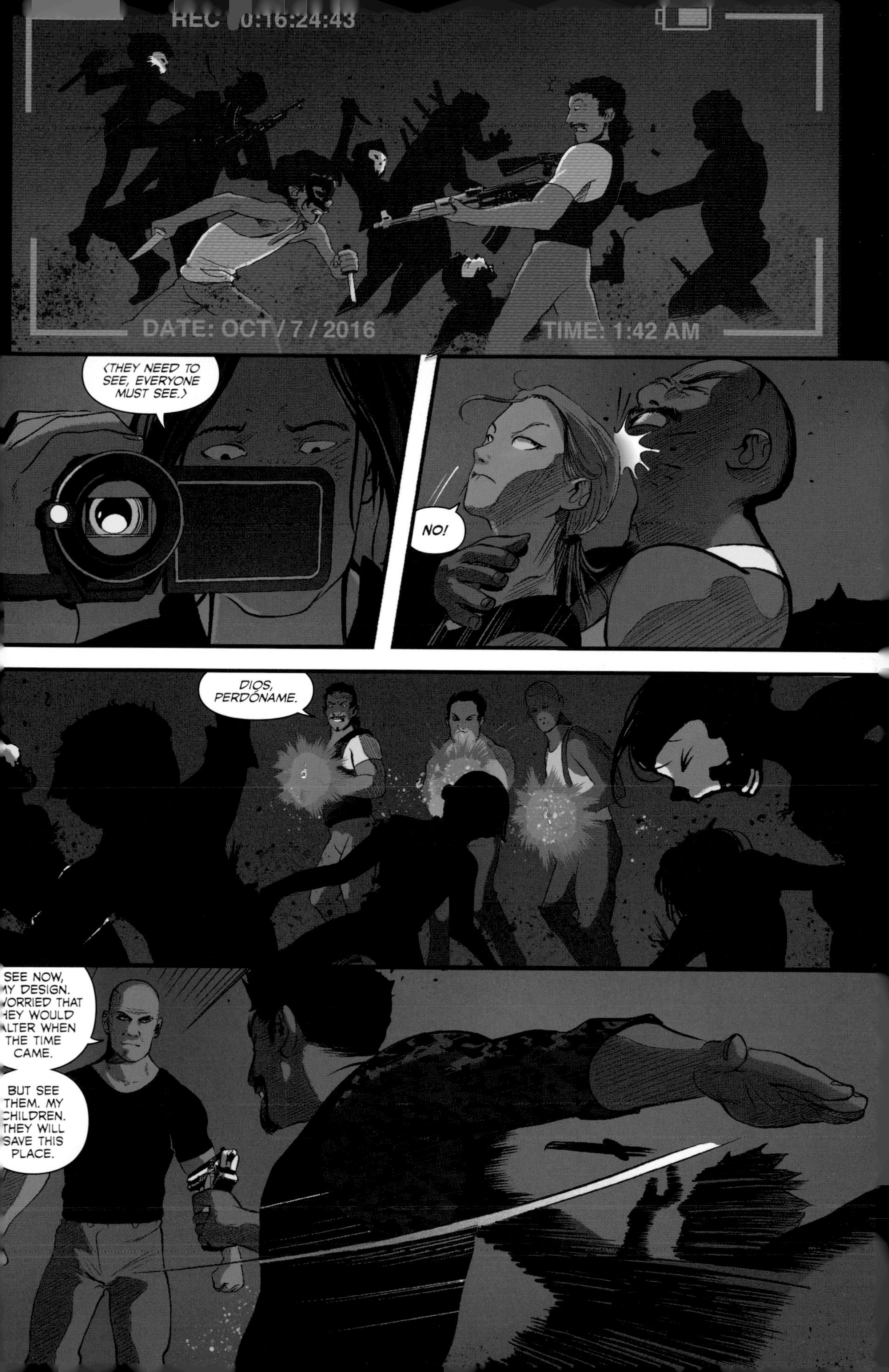

REC 0:16:24:43
DATE: OCT / 7 / 2016
TIME: 1:42 AM
‹THEY NEED TO SEE, EVERYONE MUST SEE.›
NO!
DIOS, PERDÓNAME.
SEE NOW, MY DESIGN. ORRIED THAT HEY WOULD LTER WHEN THE TIME CAME.
BUT SEE THEM. MY HILDREN. THEY WILL SAVE THIS PLACE.

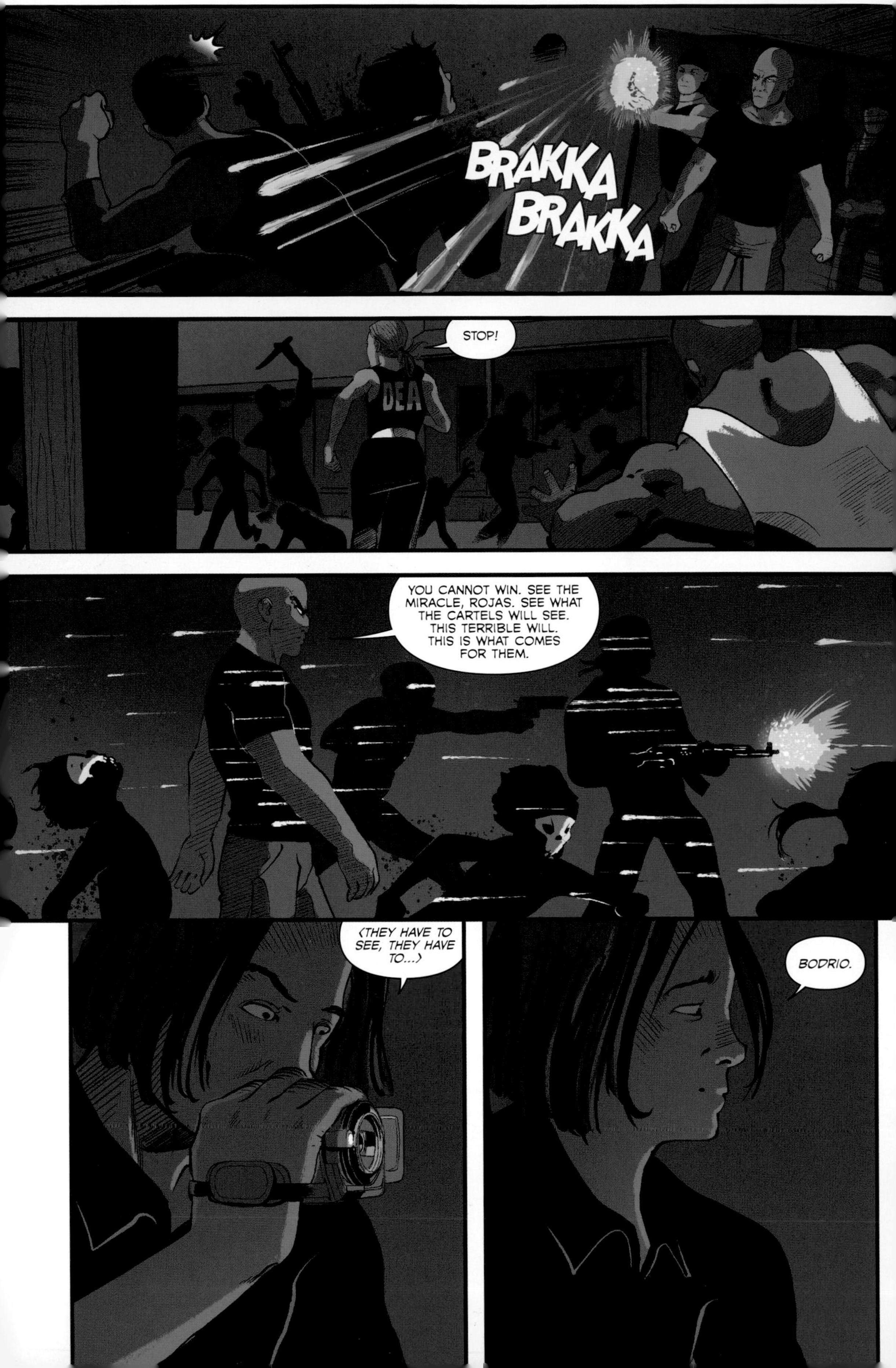
BRAKKA BRAKKA
STOP!
YOU CANNOT WIN. SEE THE MIRACLE, ROJAS. SEE WHAT THE CARTELS WILL SEE. THIS TERRIBLE WILL. THIS IS WHAT COMES FOR THEM.
‹THEY HAVE TO SEE, THEY HAVE TO...›
BODRIO.

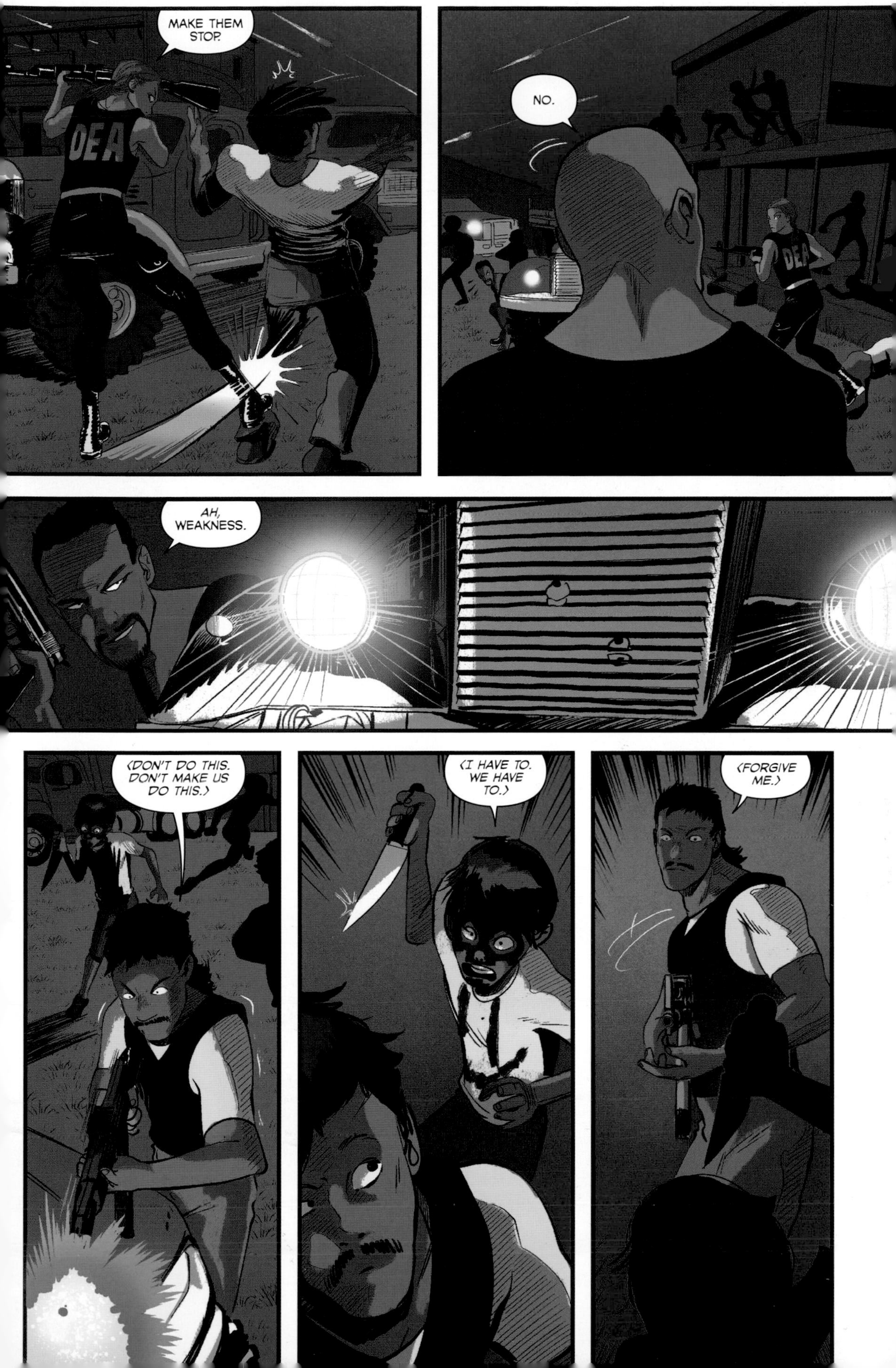
MAKE THEM STOP.
NO.
AH, WEAKNESS.
‹DON'T DO THIS. DON'T MAKE US DO THIS.›
‹I HAVE TO. WE HAVE TO.›
‹FORGIVE ME.›

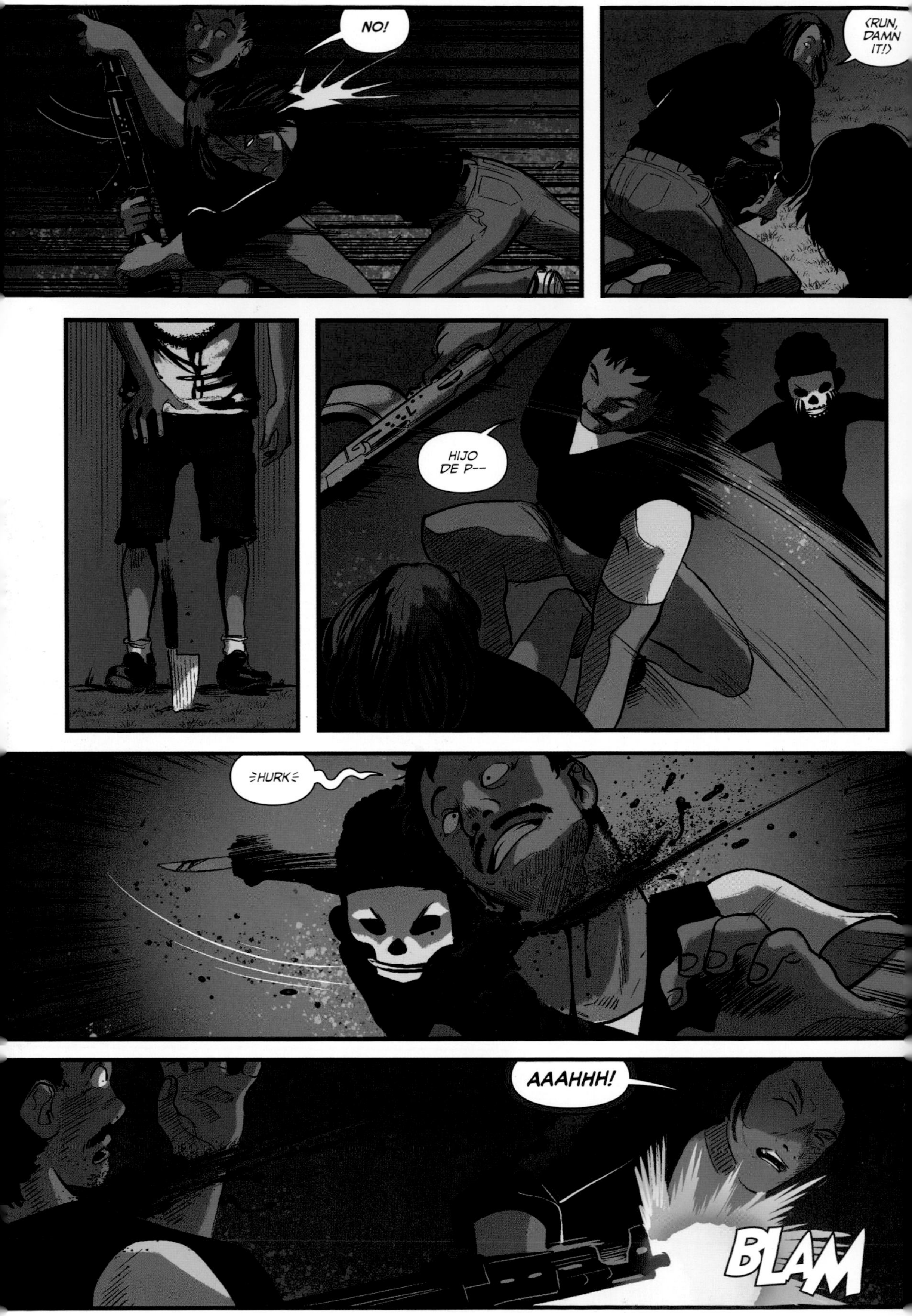
NO!
‹RUN, DAMN IT!›
HIJO DE P--
HURK
AAAHHH!
BLAM

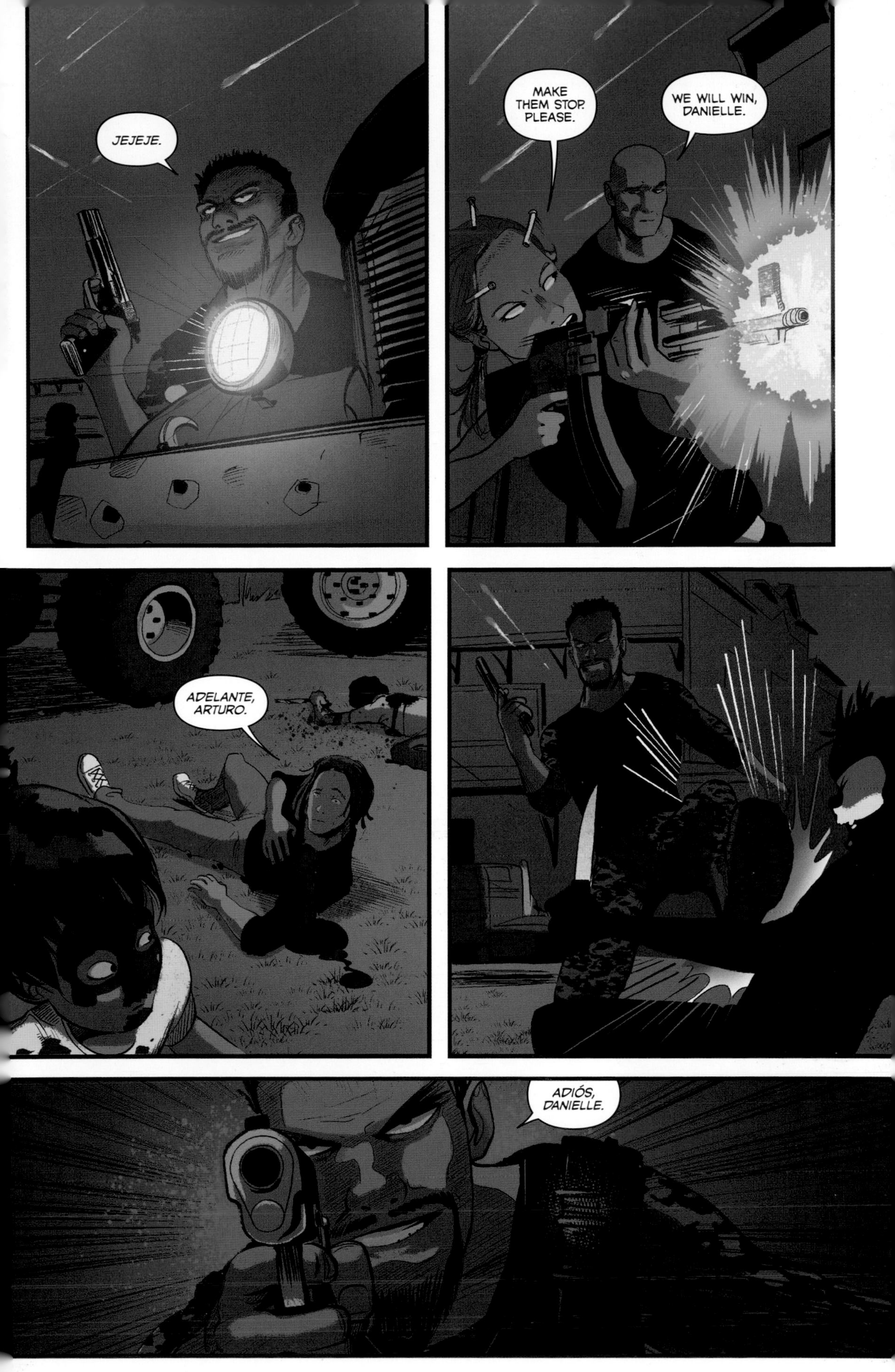
JEJEJE.
MAKE THEM STOP. PLEASE.
WE WILL WIN, DANIELLE.
ADELANTE, ARTURO.
ADIÓS, DANIELLE.

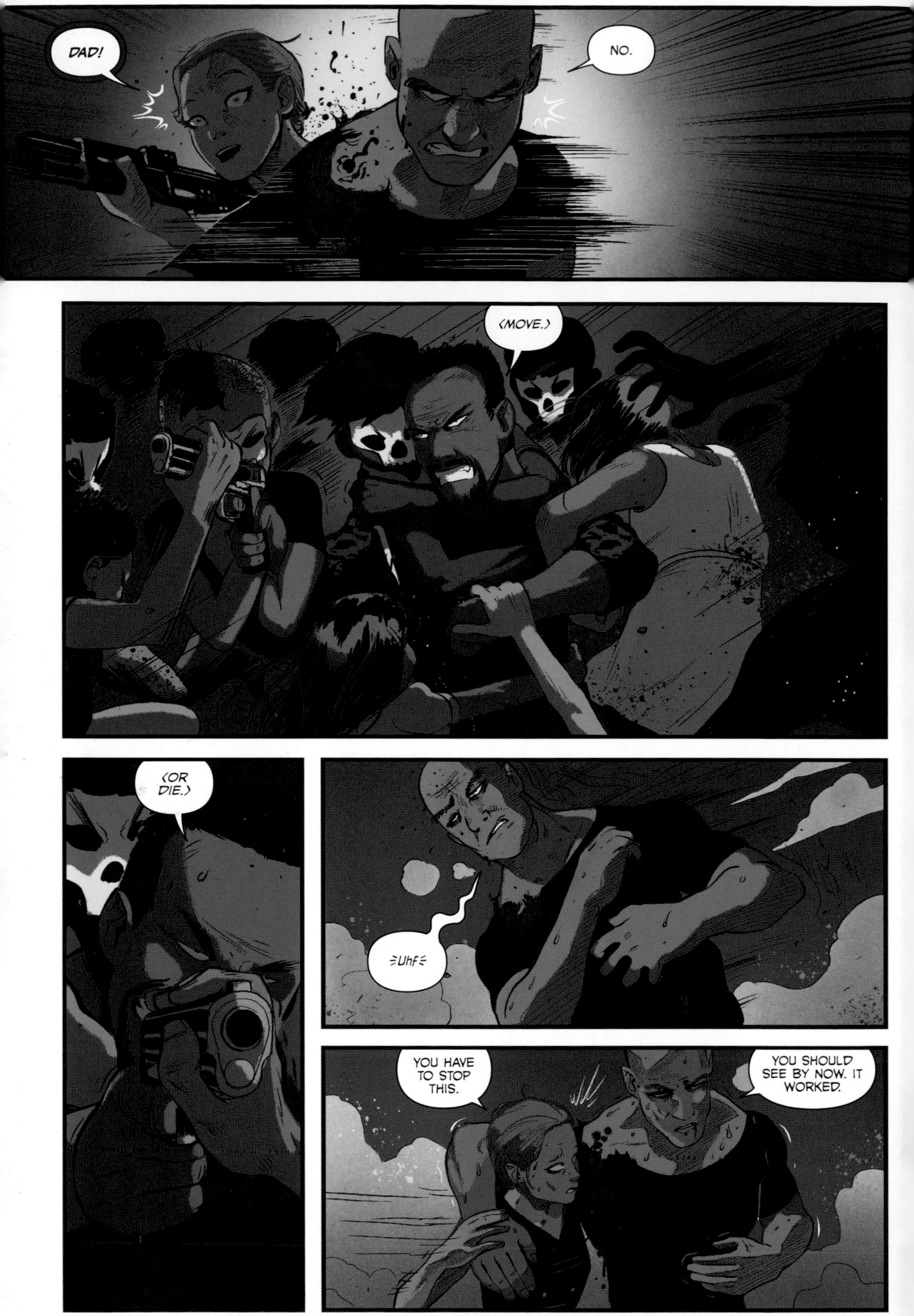
DAD!
NO.
(MOVE.)
(OR DIE.)
Uhf
YOU HAVE TO STOP THIS.
YOU SHOULD SEE BY NOW. IT WORKED.

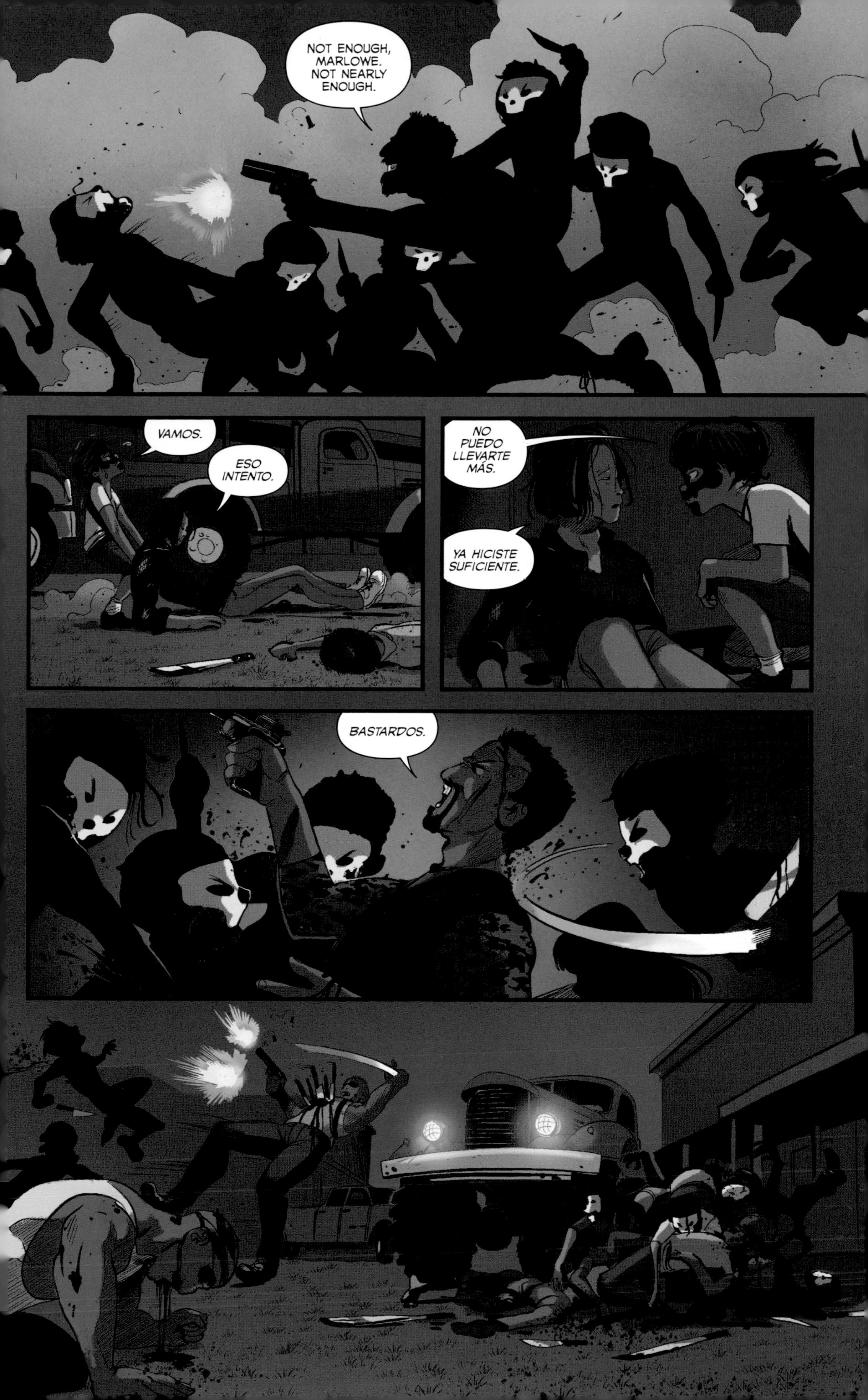
NOT ENOUGH, MARLOWE. NOT NEARLY ENOUGH.
VAMOS.
ESO INTENTO.
NO PUEDO LLEVARTE MÁS.
YA HICISTE SUFICIENTE.
BASTARDOS.

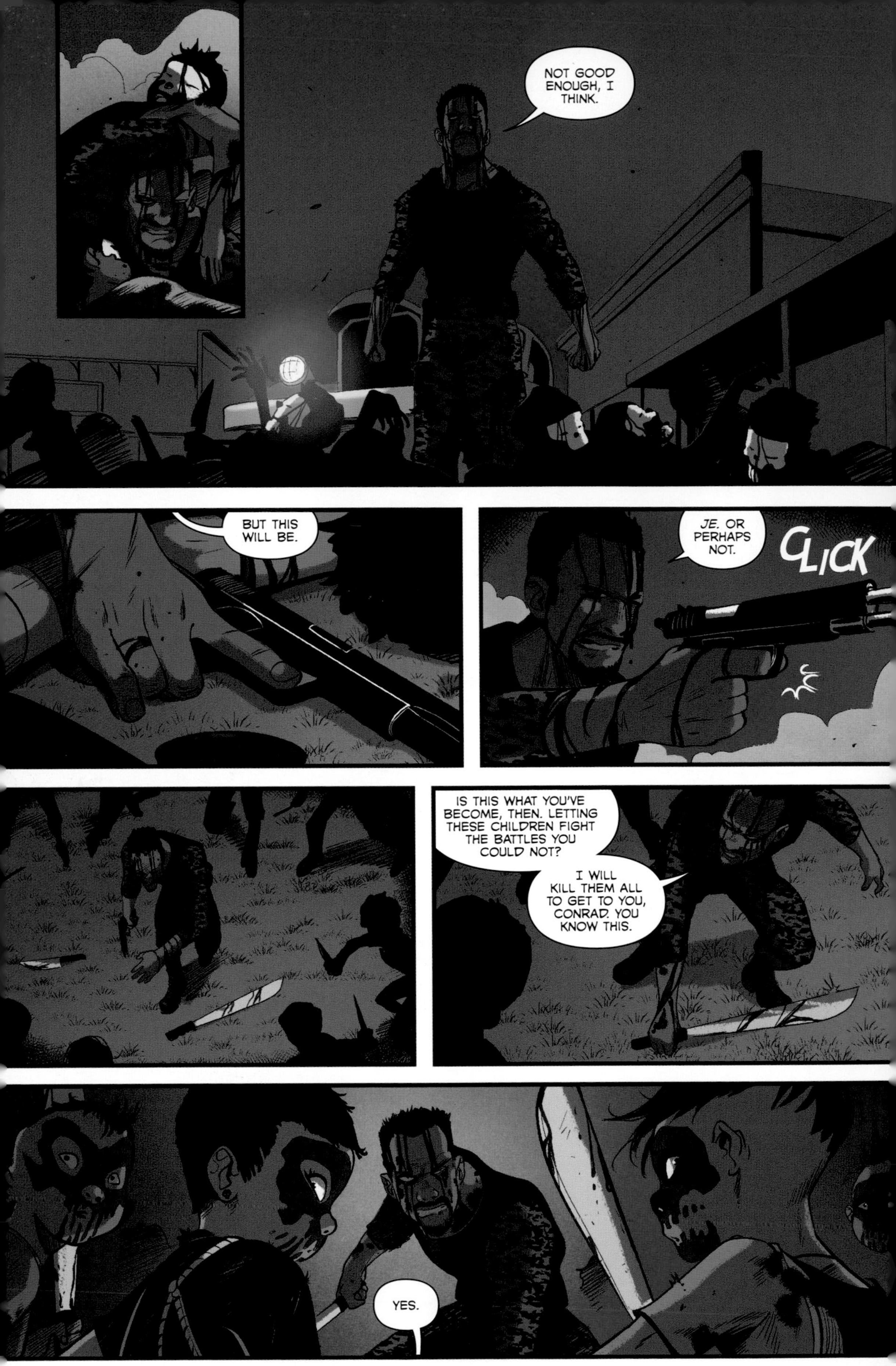
NOT GOOD ENOUGH, I THINK.
BUT THIS WILL BE.
JE. OR PERHAPS NOT.
CLICK
IS THIS WHAT YOU'VE BECOME, THEN. LETTING THESE CHILDREN FIGHT THE BATTLES YOU COULD NOT?
I WILL KILL THEM ALL TO GET TO YOU, CONRAD. YOU KNOW THIS.
YES.

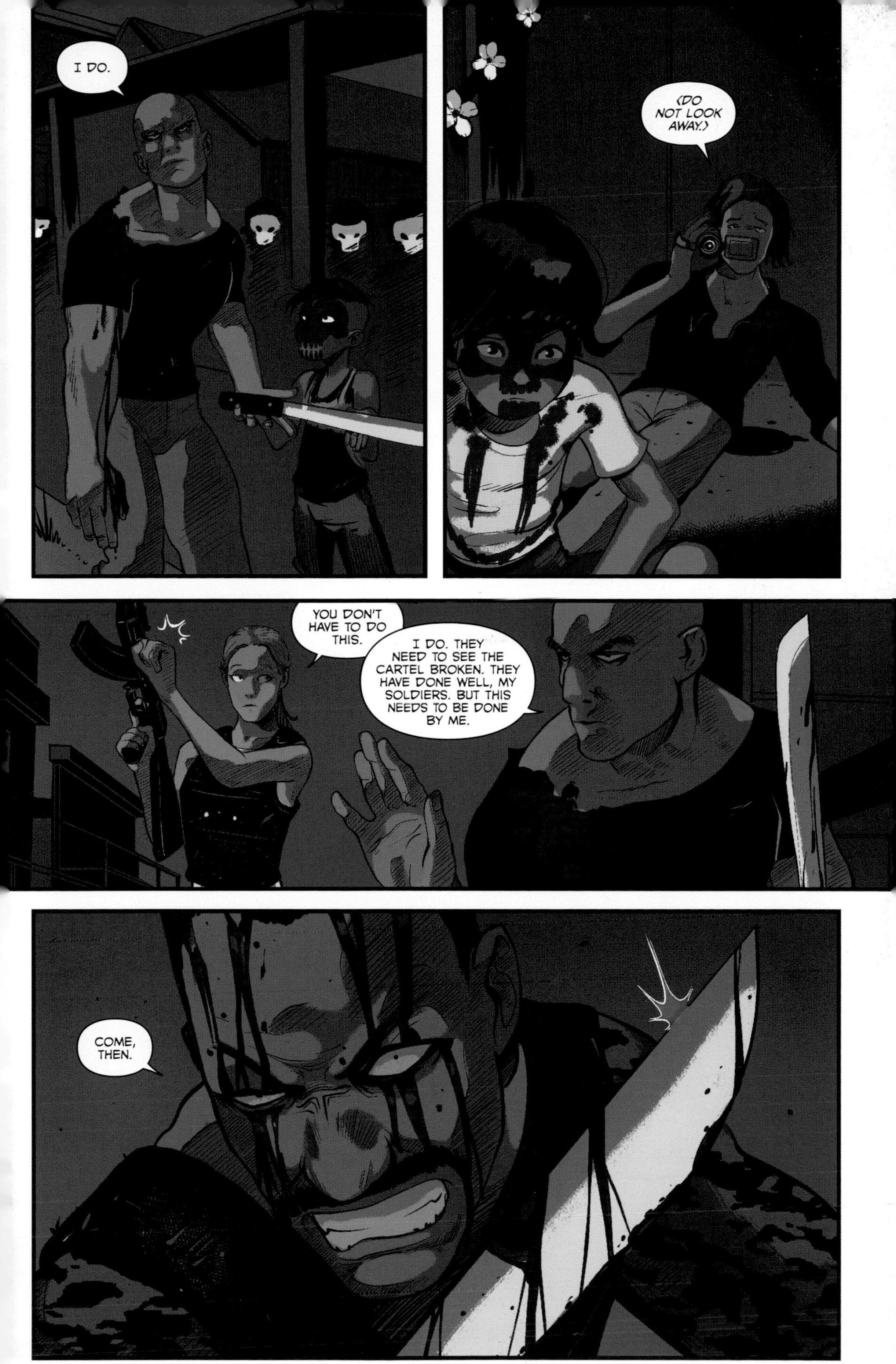
I DO.
(DO NOT LOOK AWAY.)
YOU DON'T HAVE TO DO THIS.
I DO. THEY NEED TO SEE THE CARTEL BROKEN. THEY HAVE DONE WELL, MY SOLDIERS. BUT THIS NEEDS TO BE DONE BY ME.
COME, THEN.

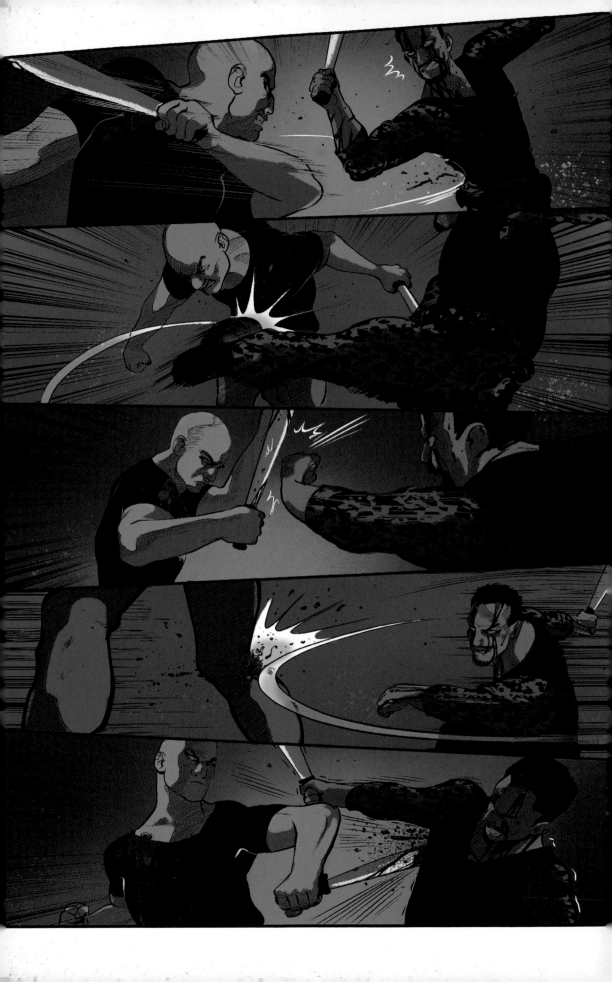

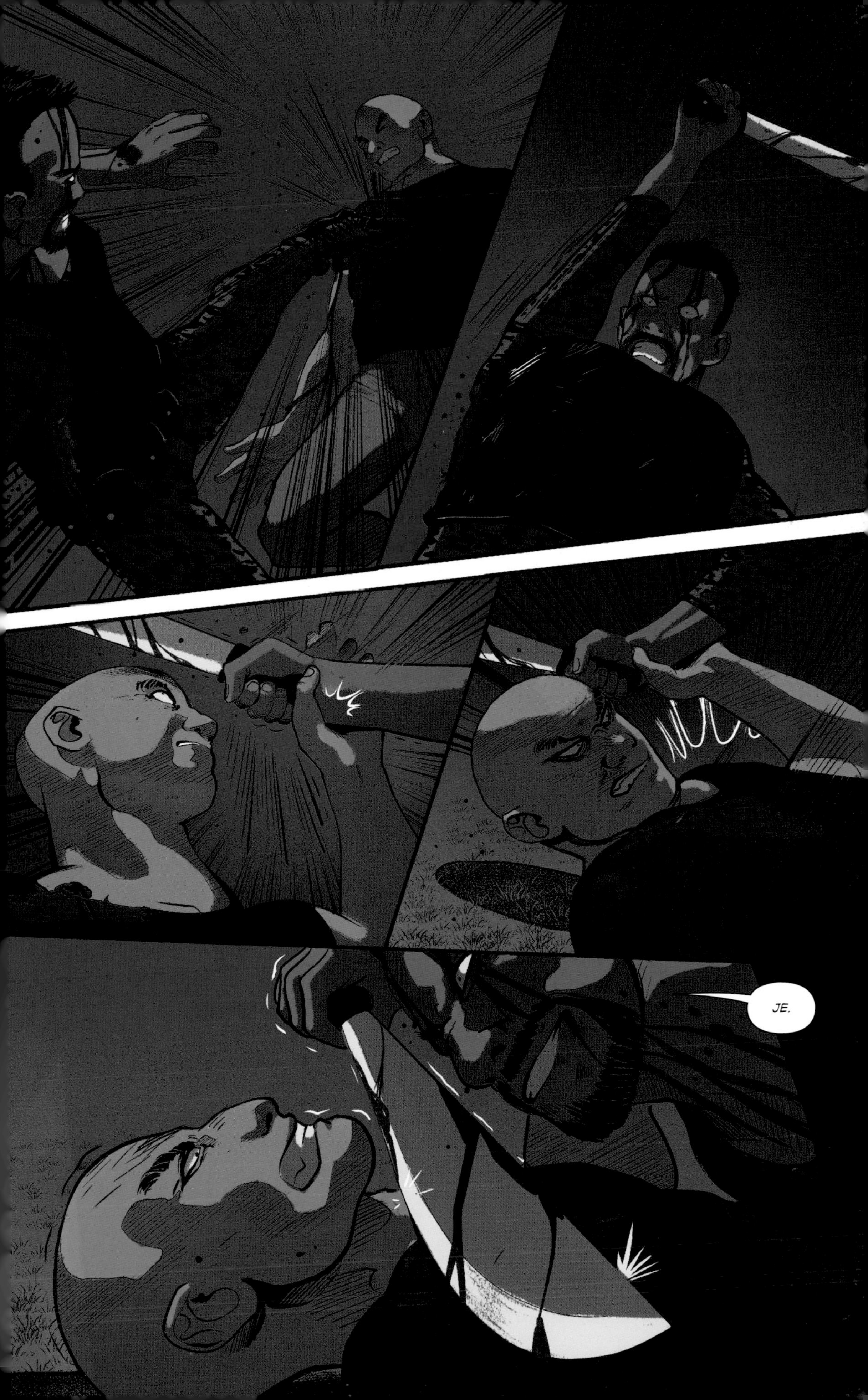
JE.

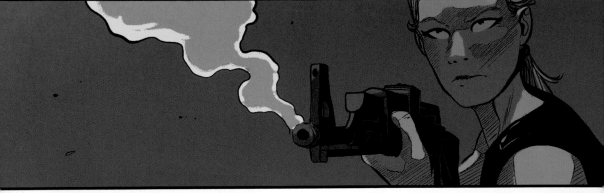

YOU SHOULD NOT HAVE DONE THAT.

HE WOULD HAVE KILLED YOU. YOU NEED TO BE BROUGHT TO JUSTICE, OR WHATEVER PASSES FOR IT.

THEN YOU SHOULD. THIS DOESN'T STOP WITH ME. IF I LIVE OR IF I DIE, THIS CONTINUES. CHOOSE.

BANG

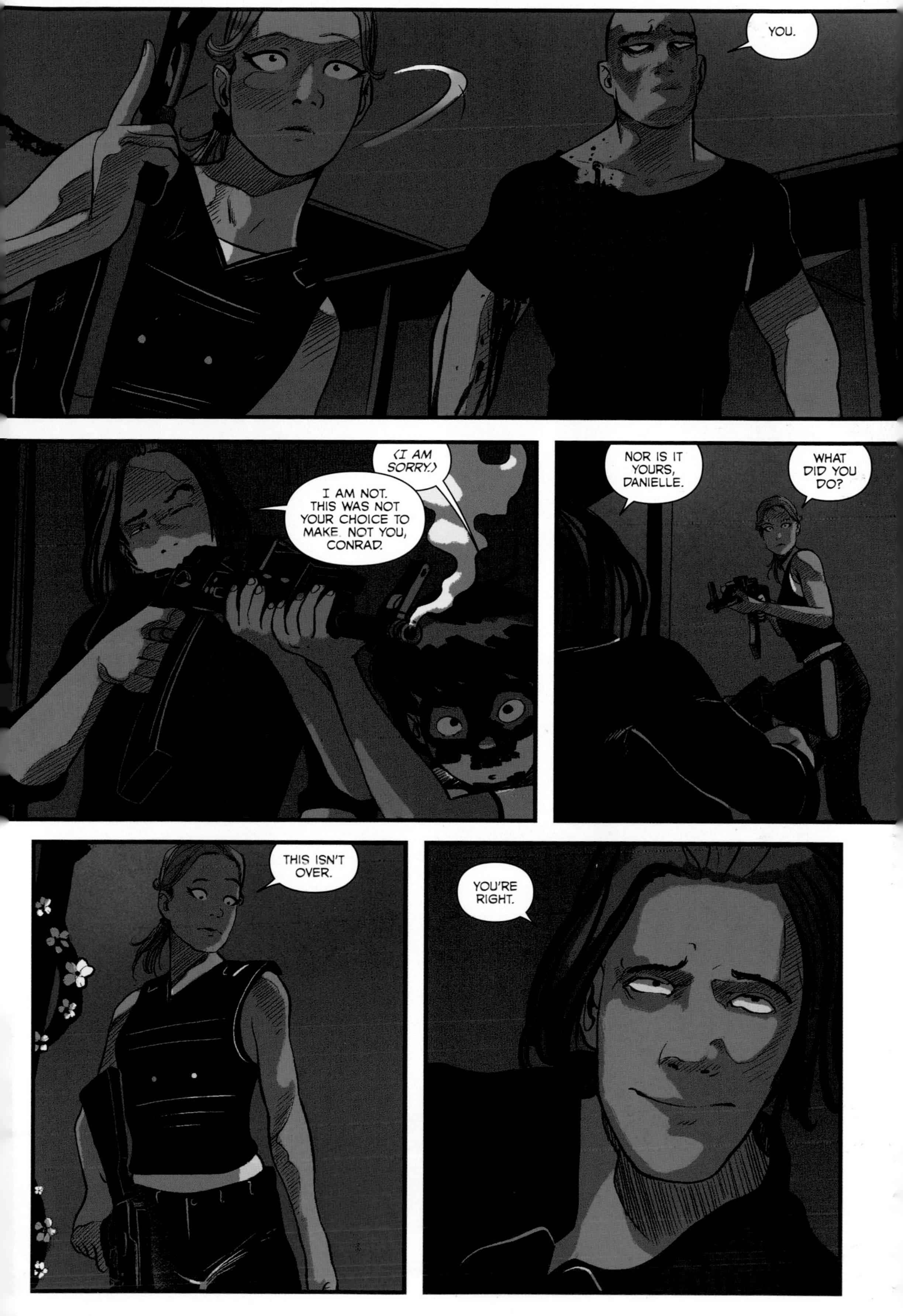
YOU.
<I AM SORRY.>
I AM NOT. THIS WAS NOT YOUR CHOICE TO MAKE. NOT YOU, CONRAD.
WHAT DID YOU DO?
NOR IS IT YOURS, DANIELLE.
THIS ISN'T OVER.
YOU'RE RIGHT.

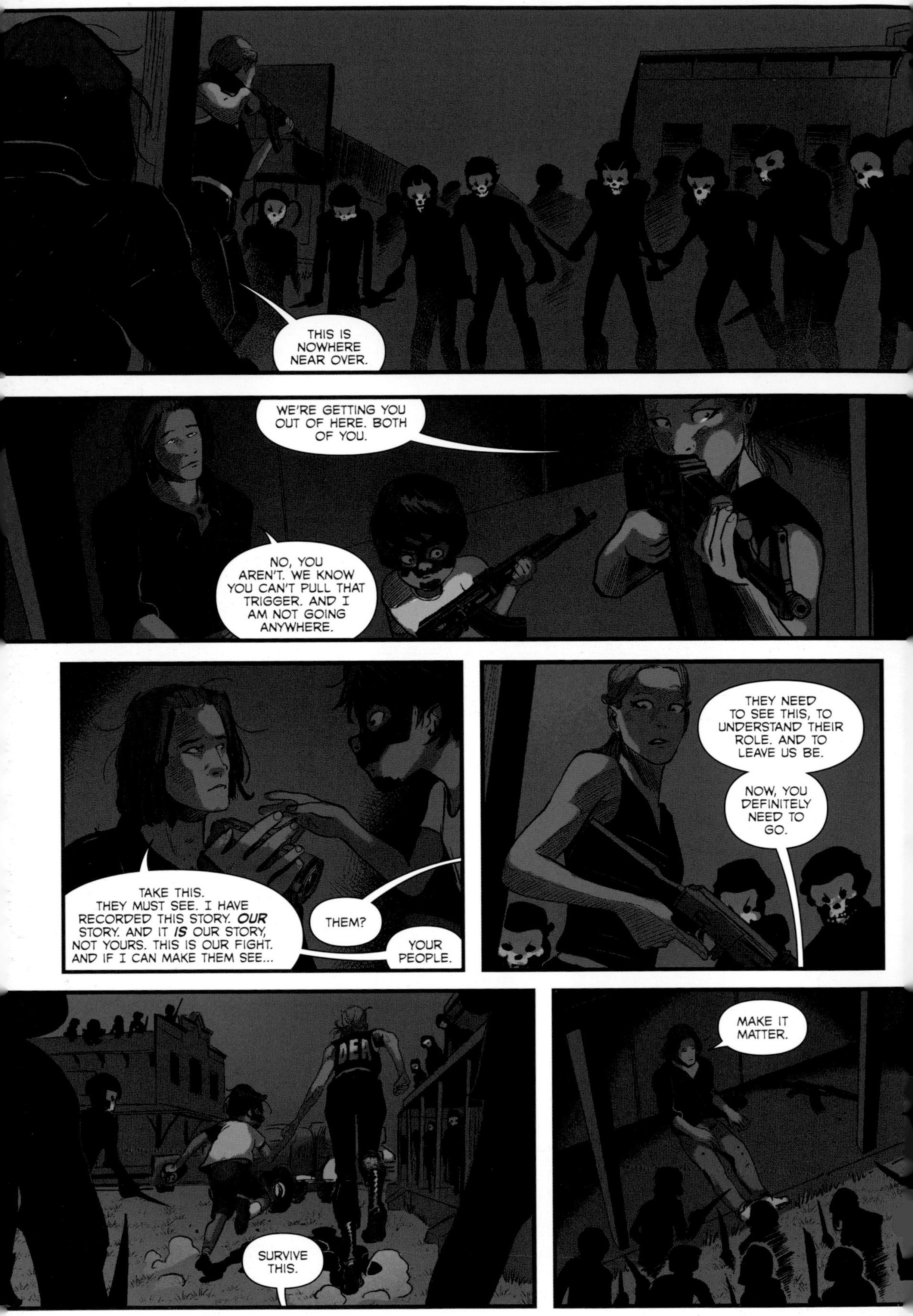
THIS IS NOWHERE NEAR OVER.
WE'RE GETTING YOU OUT OF HERE. BOTH OF YOU.
NO, YOU AREN'T. WE KNOW YOU CAN'T PULL THAT TRIGGER. AND I AM NOT GOING ANYWHERE.
TAKE THIS. THEY MUST SEE. I HAVE RECORDED THIS STORY. *OUR* STORY. AND IT *IS* OUR STORY, NOT YOURS. THIS IS OUR FIGHT. AND IF I CAN MAKE THEM SEE...
THEM?
YOUR PEOPLE.
THEY NEED TO SEE THIS, TO UNDERSTAND THEIR ROLE. AND TO LEAVE US BE.
NOW, YOU DEFINITELY NEED TO GO.
SURVIVE THIS.
MAKE IT MATTER.

MY NAME IS ESTEBAN TOLVA. AND I HATE TO BE CLICHÉD, BUT I AM ALMOST CERTAINLY DEAD.

00:01:01

ANOTHER VICTIM, ULTIMATELY, OF THE CARTELS. LIKE MANY OTHERS. AND A **VICTIM** OF OTHERS.

00:04:36

OF THE AMERICAN BELIEF THAT EVERYTHING IS A PROBLEM TO BE SOLVED. THAT WE NEED YOUR HELP.

00:07:35

AND WE DESCENDED DEEPER INTO MADNESS. THIS IS NOT AN ANOMALY. THIS IS INEVITABILITY.

00:09:52

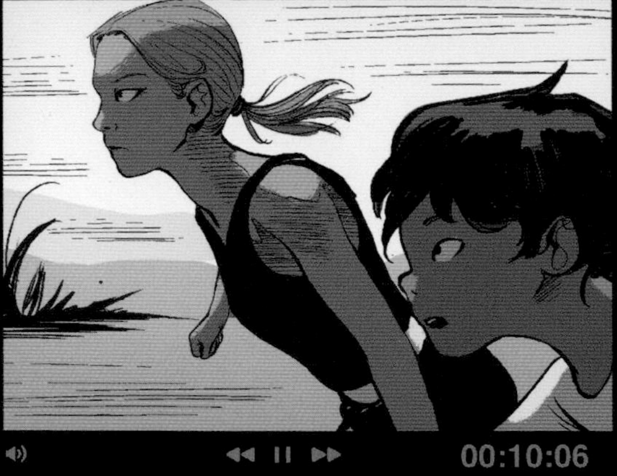
00:10:06

OURS TO SOLVE.
OURS TO REPAIR.

AMERICANS CAN HELP. REFORM YOUR
LAWS. END A FRUITLESS WAR.

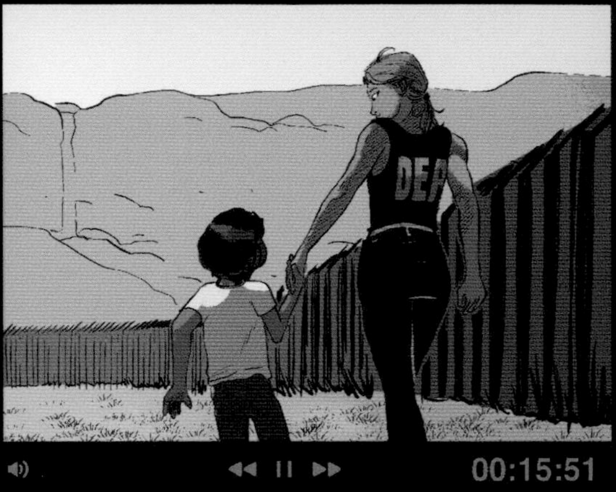
00:15:51

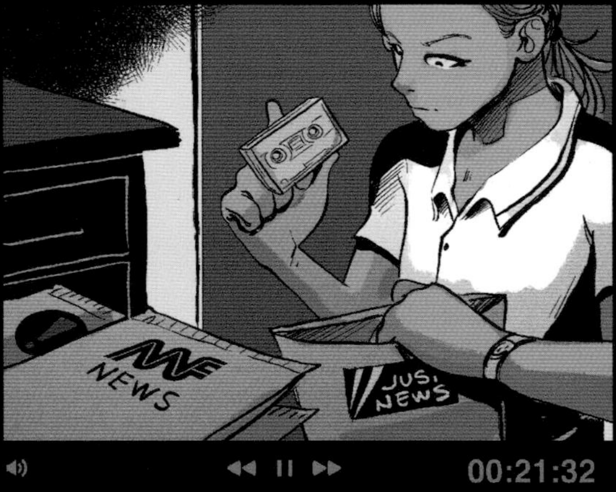
NEWS
NEWS
00:21:32

WE CAN REBUILD.
WE CAN BE BETTER.

BUT THIS IS NOT
YOUR FIGHT. IT
CAN'T BE.

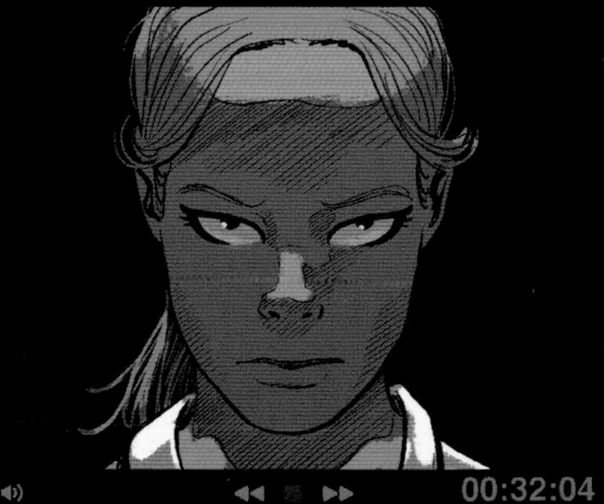
00:32:04

AFTERWORD

There is no better way to overcome a bad experience than through art. I was not sure about working on this title because of the subject matter. After going through a bad experience in my home country with two members of my family, I did not wish to work on a title with weapons or cartel themes. But why run from this? So I decided to accept the project after Editor Eric Harburn told me more about it. In addition to working to finish the miniseries, I also gave myself the task of transforming a bad experience into an artistic collaboration. So I thought of this transformation almost all the time while I was working.

The story, even if fiction, is not far from reality, but confronting this bad experience with an artistic profile helped me transform it. Sometimes I stop and think, *"Creating is fantastic."* And all this leads me to a resolution: *"The power is inside the creator, not on the outside."* As creators, we can transform realities, ours, yours, everyone's. And it is precisely the magic of this. Although we draw comics, it is not for me a refuge but a way of expressing myself, and I think that helped me a lot. Because if it were a shelter, I would be in my world without thinking about others. So I try to take great care of that, because if the comic is anything, it's a dialogue between the author, the work, and the reader. An incredible act.

I already had an interest in working with Justin years ago, but conditions were not there to make it happen. So this was another reason I accepted this project. I realized that all the conditions were there for this to happen.

Sombra was a project that helped me face that bad experience, not to forget it, but to lighten its load. It helped me artistically improve my way of working and working as a team. Working with Eric Harburn and Cameron Chittock as my editors was very enriching. For they contributed a lot to the development of this title.

I close this project with an excellent experience: I finish it with more professional and personal realizations. And although the story itself had its significant challenges, I concluded it satisfied and happy.

And in the end, I could see that collaboration can transform a bad experience into something great.

Thank you very much for helping me on this.

RAÚL TREVIÑO
Monterrey, Nuevo León - Mexico

EPÍLOGO

No hay mejor forma de vencer una mala experiencia que mediante el arte. No estaba seguro de trabajar en este título por la temática. Después de pasar por una mala experiencia en mi país natal con dos miembros de mi familia, no tenía ganas de trabajar en un título con armas o temáticas de cárteles. Pero, ¿por qué huir de esto? Así que decidí aceptar el proyecto después de que Eric Harburn me habló más de él. Además de comprometerme a concluir esta mini serie de cuatro números, me di a la tarea de transformar una mala experiencia, en una colaboración artística. Así que pensaba casi todo el tiempo en esta transformación.

La historia, aún siendo ficción, no está muy lejos de la realidad, pero enfrentar esta mala experiencia con un perfil artístico me ayudó a transformarla. Algunas veces me detenía y pensaba, *"crear es fantástico"*. Y todo esto me condujo a una resolución: *"El poder está en el interior del creador, no en el exterior."* Como creadores podemos transformar realidades, la nuestra, la tuya, la de todos. Y es precisamente lo mágico de esto. Aunque dibujar cómics, no es para mí un refugio sino una forma de expresarme, y creo que eso me ayudó en demasía. Porque si fuese un refugio, estaría en mi mundo sin pensar en los demás. Así que cuido mucho eso, pues si algo tiene el cómic es el diálogo que se genera entre el autor, la obra y el lector. Un acto maravilloso.

Ya había tenido el interés de trabajar con Justin hace años, pero no se habían dado las condiciones. Así que este fue otro de los motivos por los cuales acepté el proyecto. Me di cuenta que todas la condiciones estaban ahí para que esto sucediera.

Sombra fue un proyecto que me ayudó a afrontar esa mala experiencia, no a olvidarla, pero a aligerar su carga. Me ayudó artísticamente a mejorar mi forma de trabajar y a trabajar en equipo. Trabajar con Eric Harburn y Cameron Chittock como mis editores fue muy enriquecedor. Pues contribuyeron mucho en el desarrollo de este título.

Cierro este proyecto con una muy buena experiencia, lo termino con más realizaciones profesionales y personales. Y aunque la historia en sí tuvo sus grandes retos, pues sentía que mi dibujo no encajaba en la historia, lo concluí contento y satisfecho.

Y al final pude comprobar que una colaboración, puede transformar un mala experiencia en algo grandioso.

Muchas gracias por ayudarme en esto.

RAÚL TREVIÑO
Monterrey, Nuevo León - México

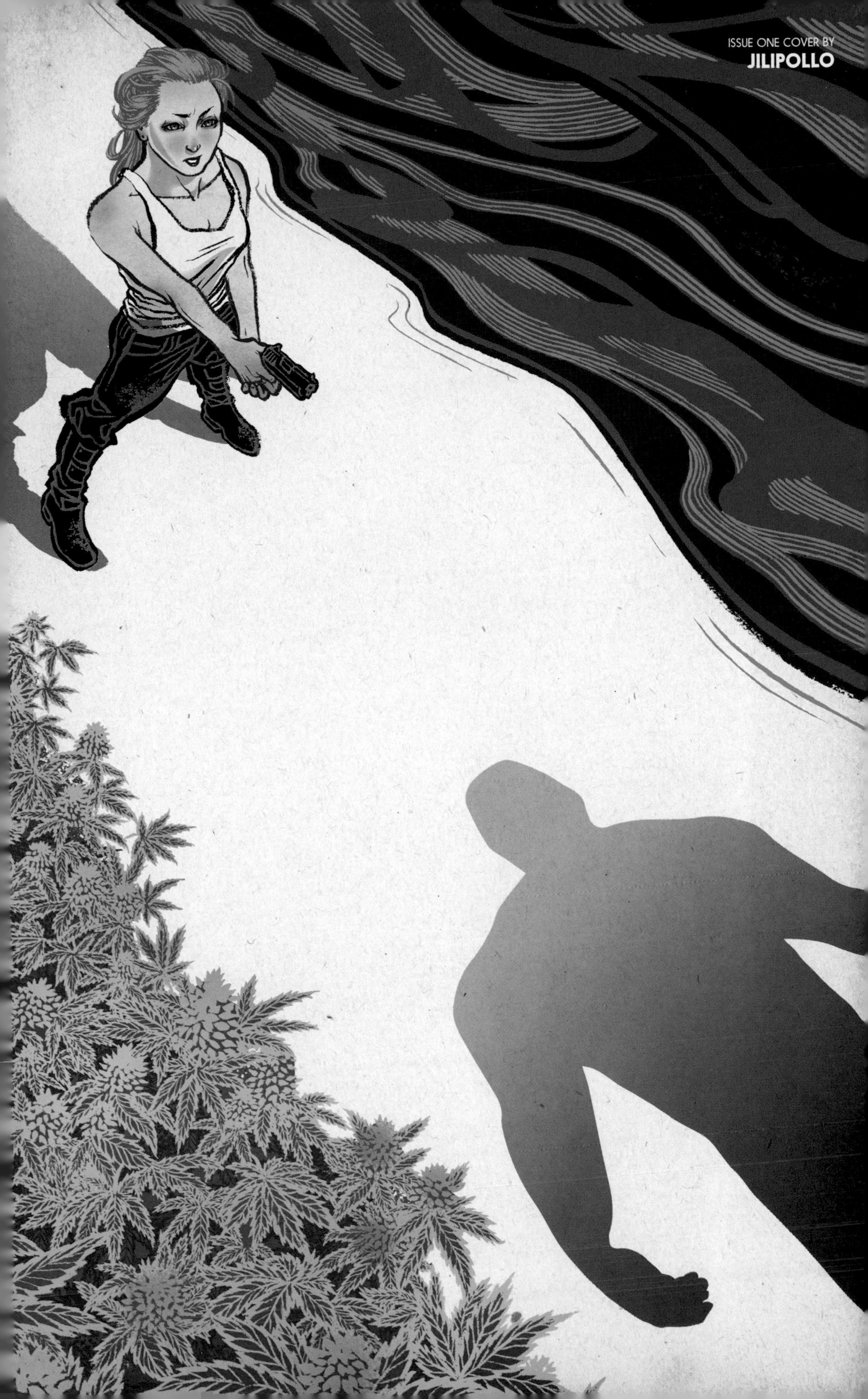

ISSUE ONE COVER BY
JILIPOLLO

ISSUE ONE UNLOCKED RETAILER VARIANT COVER BY
CHRIS BRUNNER
WITH COLORS BY **RICO RENZI**

ISSUE ONE SPANISH LANGUAGE EDITION COVER BY
RAÚL TREVIÑO

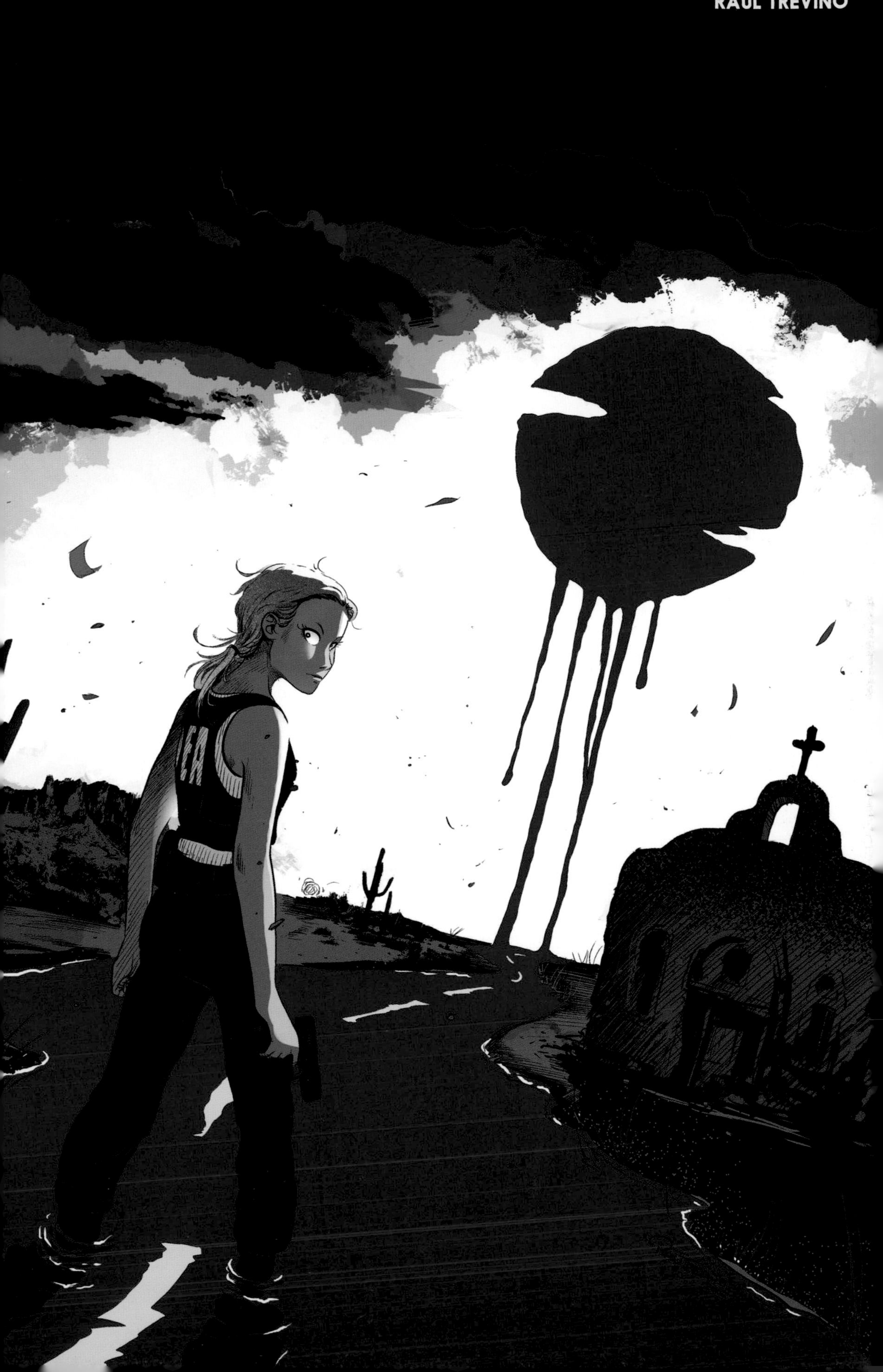

ISSUE TWO COVER BY
JILIPOLLO

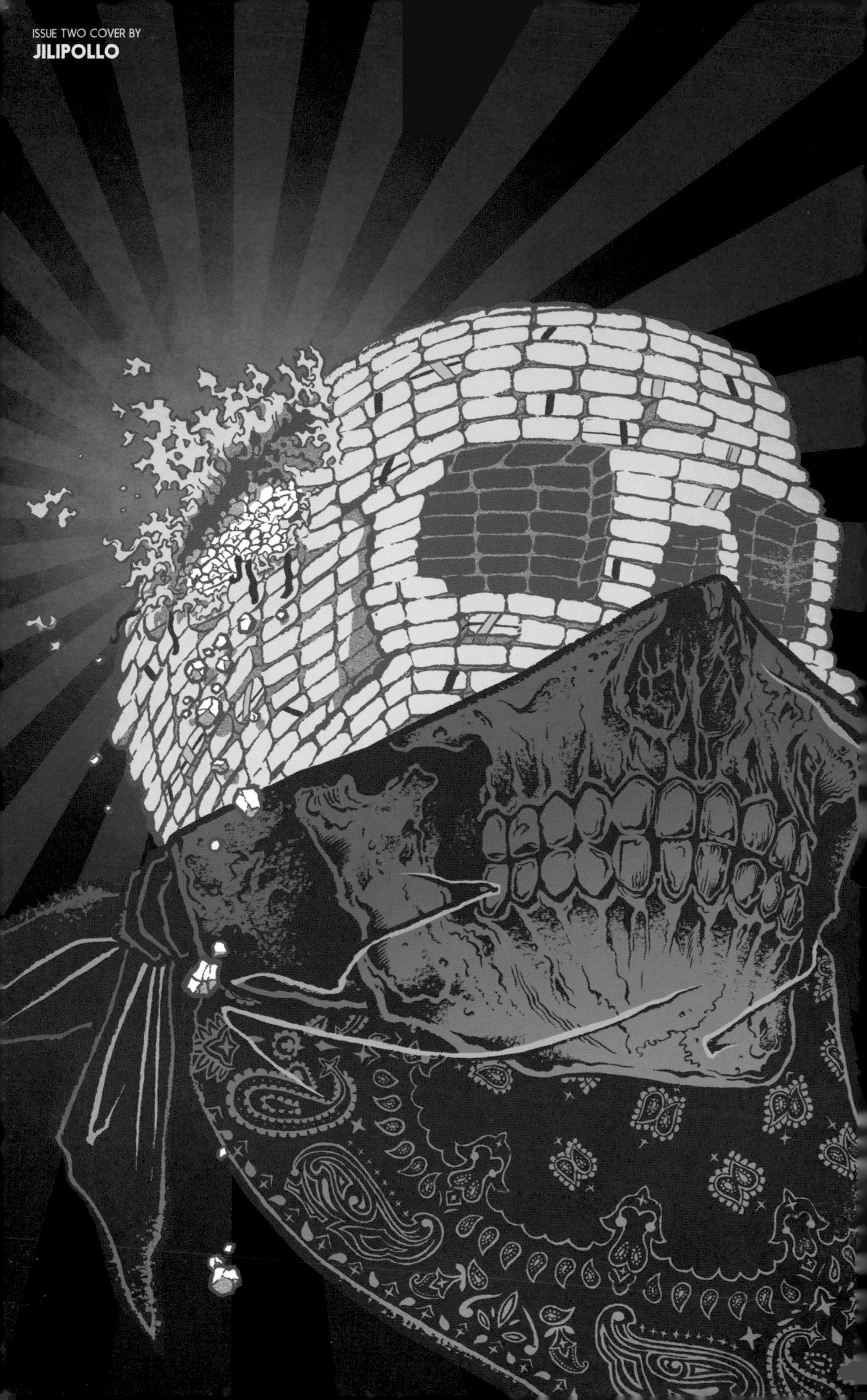

ISSUE THREE COVER BY
JILIPOLLO

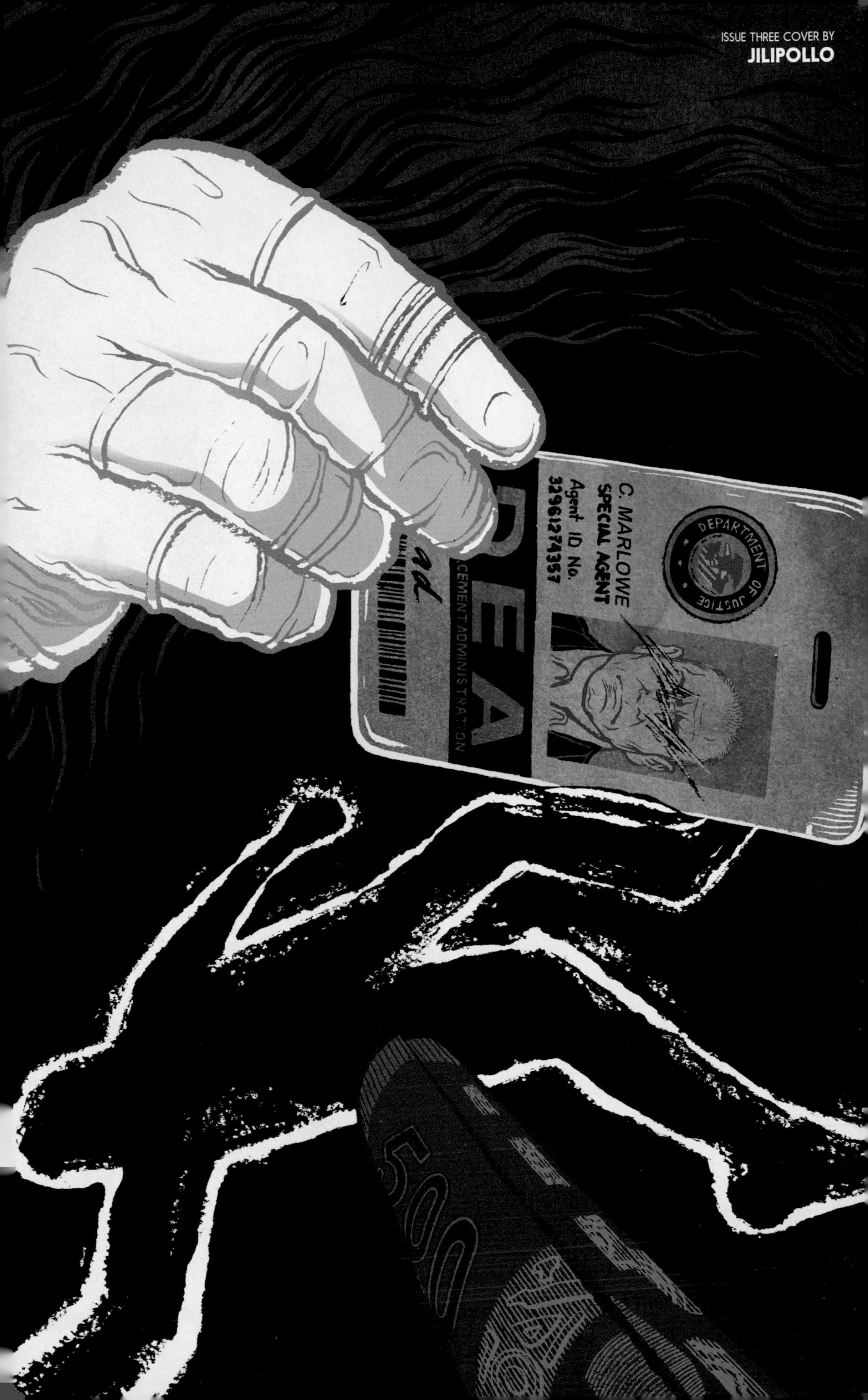

DEPARTMENT OF JUSTICE
C. MARLOWE
SPECIAL AGENT
Agent ID No.
DEA

ISSUE FOUR COVER BY
JILIPOLLO

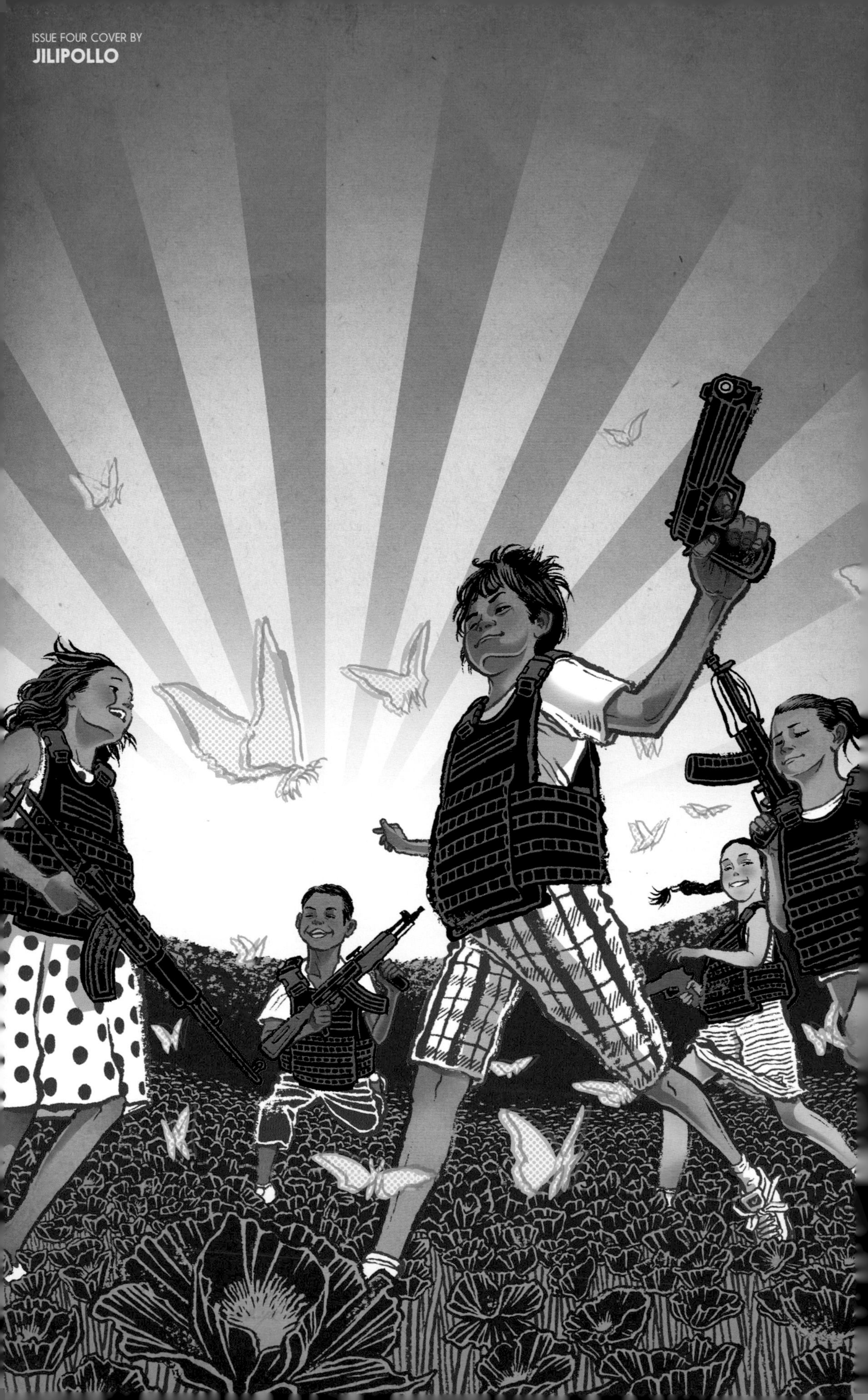

DESIGNING SOMBRA
WITH RAÚL TREVIÑO

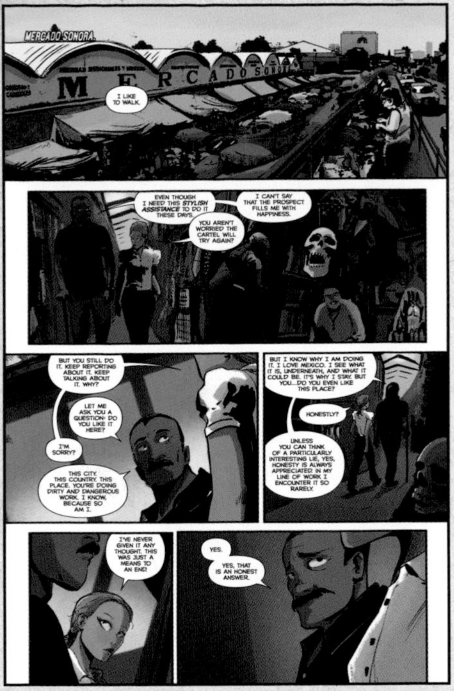
MERCADO SONORA.
MERCADO SONORA
I LIKE TO WALK.
EVEN THOUGH I NEED THIS STYLISH ASSISTANCE TO DO IT THESE DAYS.
I CAN'T SAY THAT THE PROSPECT FILLS ME WITH HAPPINESS.
YOU AREN'T WORRIED THE CARTEL WILL TRY AGAIN?
BUT YOU STILL DO IT. KEEP REPORTING ABOUT IT. KEEP TALKING ABOUT IT. WHY?
LET ME ASK YOU A QUESTION: DO YOU LIKE IT HERE?
I'M SORRY?
THIS CITY. THIS COUNTRY. THIS PLACE. YOU'RE DOING DIRTY AND DANGEROUS WORK. I KNOW, BECAUSE SO AM I.
BUT I KNOW WHY I AM DOING IT. I LOVE MEXICO. I SEE WHAT IT IS, UNDERNEATH, AND WHAT IT COULD BE. IT'S WHY I STAY. BUT YOU...DO YOU EVEN LIKE THIS PLACE?
HONESTLY?
UNLESS YOU CAN THINK OF A PARTICULARLY INTERESTING LIE, YES, HONESTY IS ALWAYS APPRECIATED. IN MY LINE OF WORK I ENCOUNTER IT SO RARELY.
I'VE NEVER GIVEN IT ANY THOUGHT. THIS WAS JUST A MEANS TO AN END.
YES.
YES, THAT IS AN HONEST ANSWER.

In addition to the drug conflict and Mexican culture, drawing locations is one of the aspects that made me understand why Justin wanted a Mexican artist for *Sombra*. On Issue #1 Page 15, I gave Justin a couple of options for a scene taking place in a market. And one of them was the "Sonora Market" in Mexico City ("Mercado Sonora" if you dare to Google it). And it was the perfect place, since this one is related to witches and sorcery. When I got his reply, he said: "It's cool as hell looking."

Another suggestion that I gave to this story was the altar on Issue #4 Page 3. My intention was to mix the traditional Day of the Dead altar with Conrad's ideology to inflict fear. It was a fun approach that enriched the fiction with real Mexican cultural elements.

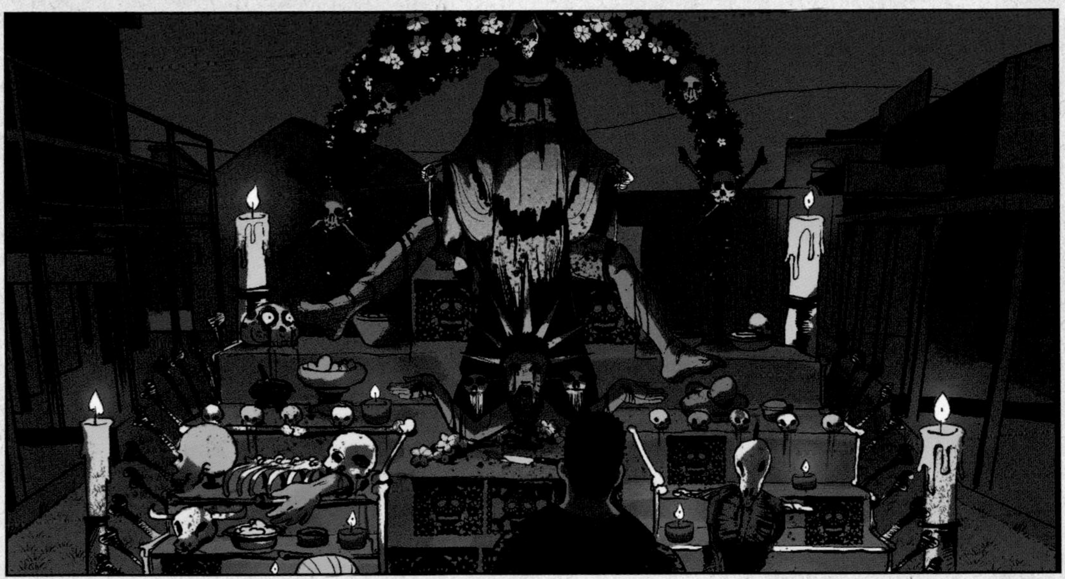

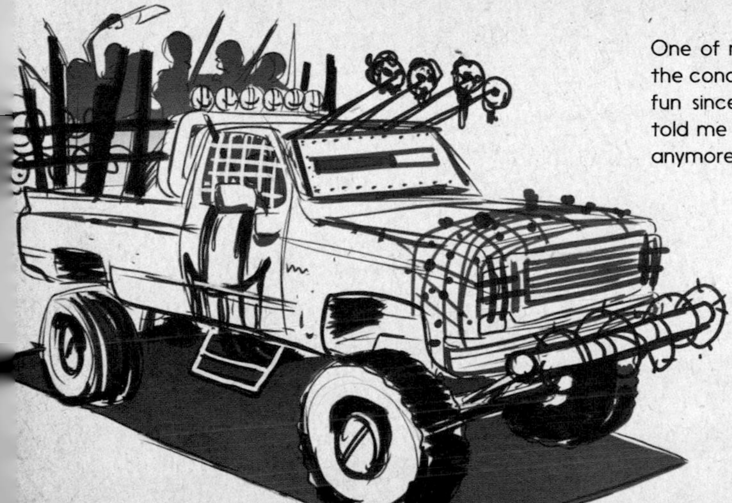

One of my favorite parts of doing this book was the concept art, and designing Conrad's truck was fun since I like the Mad Max universe. But Justin told me that the truck was not going to appear anymore in Issue #4, so what a bummer!